PARTNERS, NOT RIVALS

Partners, Not Rivals

Privatization and the Public Good

MARTHA MINOW

Beacon Press

BOSTON

Beacon Press
25 Beacon Street
Boston, Massachusetts 02108-2892
www.beacon.org

Beacon Press books
are published under the auspices of
the Unitarian Universalist Association of Congregations.

06 05 04 03 02   8 7 6 5 4 3 2 1

This book is printed on acid-free paper that meets the uncoated paper
ANSI/NISO specifications for permanence as revised in 1992.

Text design by Elizabeth Elsas

Composition by Wilsted & Taylor Publishing Services

Library of Congress Cataloging-in-Publication Data
Minow, Martha.
      Partners, not rivals : privatization and the public good / Martha Minow.
         p.   cm.
Includes bibliographical references.
      ISBN 0-8070-4336-2 (hardcover : alk. paper)
      1. Privatization—United States. 2. Public contracts—United States.
3. Social service—Contracting out—United States. 4. Medical care—
Contracting out—United States. 5. Public welfare—Contracting out—
United States. 6. Educational vouchers—United States. 7. United States—
Social policy—1993- I. Title.
      HD3861.U6 M56 2002
      338.973'05—dc21

                                                        2002002907

IN MEMORY OF ROBERT COVER

CONTENTS

CHAPTER I

Choice or Commonality

Proposals for school choice moved from the margins to the mainstream over the past twenty-five years. I am torn about the idea. Should public dollars fund vouchers, freeing parents to select a public or a private school, a secular or a religious school, a neighborhood or a distant school? Should the public system still operate apart from private and religious options but generate choices among public schools? Should public dollars finance new entrepreneurs to start charter schools?

On the one hand, I think we should explore every possible strategy for improving schooling for all children. Private choice harnesses commitments to individual freedom, competition, and pluralism. On the other hand, I do not want to abandon the vision of common, integrated schooling, eroding borders between religion and government and undermining the schools and teachers who already have too hard a time teaching and reaching their students.

But a funny thing happened while I was looking around for another hand or a more conclusive argument about school choice. I started to notice striking parallels in other fields, blurring lines between public and private, religious and secular, profit and nonprofit. One example is welfare reform. The Personal Responsibility and Work Opportunity Reconciliation Act of 1996—otherwise known as welfare reform—introduced "charitable choice," a provision allowing states to direct their share of federal dollars to religious organizations, including houses of worship. Under charitable choice, states can contract with religious organizations to deliver welfare benefits; states also can give individual vouchers that can be redeemed for benefits at private, including religious, entities. The statute also allows states to contract with for-profit companies to administer their welfare programs—just as communities have built relationships with for-profit companies to manage their schools.

Similar, though not identical, issues arise in medicine and law. Increasing privatization of public hospitals accompanies intensifying competition among for-profit hospitals, public entities, and nonprofits, including religiously affiliated hospitals. The one growth sector for nonprofit hospitals is religious—chiefly Catholic—entities. With cost-containment pressures surrounding health care delivery, this is a period of reorganization in the way medicine is practiced, in-home care is delivered, and nursing home care is managed. Yet there are few public toeholds for getting into the decisions creating and reflecting these trends—even though they will seriously affect access to and quality of care.

In the legal realm, for-profit prisons, including some held by publicly traded companies, may startle some people. But these are simply part of a larger pattern, which makes room not only for profit-making forms but also for religious organizations to provide prison programs, halfway houses, mediation and negotiation services, and guidance for individual lawyers and judges. Legal services, for the most part, are provided by private attorneys who seek profits, but publicly funded legal services for the poor increasingly work through contracts and competitive bids with private attorneys. Governmental restrictions on what publicly funded legal services can do, curbs on the power of the bar to secure pro bono services, changes in rules affecting attorneys' fees and class actions, and competitive pressures in the private bar sharply shape access to legal services for those who cannot afford them. But these effects are buried in a welter of specific decisions. There is scant public debate about whether these arrangements jeopardize public commitments to equality, due process, and democracy.

Foster care, adoption, and substance abuse programs work through private and public providers, combining private and public dollars. Religious, secular nonprofit, and for-profit players operate in each of these fields, and governments contract with them. Should policies against discrimination on the basis of race, religion, gender, sexual orientation apply to the private providers? Are there viable options for people who are not comfortable with a particular religious provider? These questions can be raised about schools and welfare as well.

Looking across fields, I started to realize that a sea change is at work, something larger than the school-choice debate. Private and market-style mechanisms are increasingly employed to provide what government had taken as duties. Religious groups join secular nonprofit and for-profit providers of services paid for or sought by government. Decision makers in education, health care, social services, and law constantly cross the boundaries between public and private, religious and secular, profit and nonprofit. A spirit of experimenting to meet human needs and redress inequalities animates this moment. What remains troubling is the danger that the accumulation of specific decisions to privatize and to shift relationships between government and religion may end up altering our lives in ways we never have a chance to influence. Levels of social solidarity; patterns of inequality; relationships among religious, racial, and other groups; quality and intensity of political engagement; liberties of individuals; and the character of the larger society are all affected by the growing use of market mechanisms and the increasing presence of religious actors. Does more choice undermine commonality? Does it instead cement the commonality that allows diverse people to live together?

Sorting out views about school choice and related changes in welfare, health care, and law requires working through how society as a whole can address these competing goals:

1. Responding to basic human needs and redressing inequalities in access to such responses;
2. Promoting freedom for individuals and for groups to express their visions of the good life;
3. Nurturing a vibrant but not toxic or self-destructive plural-

ism, acknowledging the value of religious groups and other
private associations for individual freedom and mutual aid;

4. Promoting democratic participation by individuals and
   groups in self-government and holding people in positions
   of authority accountable and responsive;

5. Respecting and supporting professional expertise but also
   eliciting volunteer service and grassroots action;

6. Promoting the accountability of those who provide care,
   especially to people who are unable to monitor care or
   advocate for themselves.

More succinctly, how can the United States redress inequalities
and promote economic and political freedom? Society—organized through governments, private organizations, as well as individuals—should be able to promote the kinds of freedoms exemplified by markets and individual rights while also sustaining
mutual obligation and concern for others in the family, neighborhood, religion, civic association, town, state, nation, and world.
The smaller of these groups, especially, promote a shared sense of
mutual vulnerability and mutual responsibility; each also offers
settings for responding to mutual need. Governments can make
people's willingness and capacity to respond individually and col-
lectively to mutual need more or less likely to happen. Governments can themselves be more or less responsive to the structural
factors affecting poverty, racism, unemployment, and health risks
in light of community members' commitments to addressing the
needs of others. Our arrangements for allocating responsibility
and protecting freedoms affect how much people seek freedom or
community, choice or commonality, consumption or democracy.
Yet we risk neglecting pervasive shifts until our daily landscape is
transformed.

Sorting out pros and cons about school choice and parallel
changes in other areas of social provision requires discovering
the patterns, explaining their causes, and determining their effect
on the polity. In *Partners, Not Rivals* I seek to identify the promise
and dangers in the shifting roles of public and private, religious
and secular, for-profit and nonprofit organizations in providing

schooling, welfare, health care, and legal services. Chapter 2 offers a view of the shifting landscape. Chapter 3 zeroes in on schooling and welfare. Chapter 4 turns to medicine and law. Chapter 5 considers issues of accountability while arguing for public debate over how resources should be deployed to meet human needs.

The events of September 11 give new urgency to the two linked questions motivating this inquiry: What combination of governmental and private action can accountably meet basic human needs while promoting freedom and pluralism? How can religious resources strengthen society without endangering tolerance and democracy? The stakes could not be higher. How we mix public and private, profit and nonprofit, religious and secular in providing for schooling, welfare, human services, medicine, and law will spell the future of our democracy. We could shape newly vibrant and caring communities of freedom or cauldrons for distrust and privation. Let's first see what's happening, without much collective deliberation, and then consider how best to join rivals as partners to meet human needs.

CHAPTER 2

What's Going On?

Yogi Berra said, "You can observe a lot by watching." If we start by watching connections between federal and state governments, religions, nonprofit organizations, and business, we can observe some striking shifts along each of the borders. Government and religion have always been more interconnected than is implied by the metaphor "a wall of separation," introduced to constitutional analysis in a letter by Thomas Jefferson.[1] But as the religious makeup of the nation has grown more complex, and as privatization efforts move across government areas, the connections between government and religion at least seem more visible. At the same time, religious organizations and nonprofit groups explore ties and activities with for-profit enterprises; governments make arrangements with a variety of nonprofits, religious and secular; and governments and nonprofit organizations increasingly use the techniques of private industries to enhance their own effectiveness as well as collaborating and contracting with for-profit entities to fulfill public and charitable missions. So many activities cross the conventional boundaries that the boundaries themselves seem to shift and blur. Let's look at these developments, explore explanations, and identify worries.

CROSSING THE BORDERS BETWEEN RELIGIOUS AND SECULAR, PUBLIC AND PRIVATE, AND PROFIT AND NONPROFIT WORLDS

Muslims and Hindus as well as Catholics and Jews now rotate with Protestants in leading opening prayers for the Congress. Government contracts and voucher programs in the areas of welfare and human services involve houses of worship as well as their affiliated but distinct nonprofit organizations. An emerging norm of neutrality and equal treatment brings more contact between government and religions. Religious schools now can receive public aid to buy computers if other schools can; religious student publications can receive public aid on college campuses if other student publications can; and religious after-school programs can be held at public schools if other programs can.[2] The debate over the place of religion in public school continues with new chapters addressing the teaching of evolution, prayers conducted at school sporting events, and the use of grief counselors brought in to deal with violent school tragedies.[3]

Besides new ties between government and religions, secular tax-exempt foundations have also recently invested heavily in religiously based social services. In 2001, the Robert Wood Johnson Foundation announced a plan to give $100 million through its Faith in Action program, which supports religious groups that mobilize volunteers, who provide social services as well as coalitions of faith-based organizations and others working in social services and health care.[4] The Lilly Endowment, the Pew Charitable Trust, and the James Irvine Foundations have made record-breaking grants to religious groups addressing volunteering and community service.[5]

Meanwhile, nonprofit enterprises engaged in delivering social services increasingly collaborate with and mimic for-profit business. To be a nonprofit organization does not mean never making a profit; it means that any profit cannot be paid out to a residual claimant, like a shareholder.[6] To be a for-profit organization does not mean making profits; it means being organized to permit payment of profits to a residual claimant, and it therefore can find fi-

nancing through equity capital. Recently, though, nonprofit social service, medical, and education entities have been pursuing
relationships with for-profit entities or activities—and for-profits
are also finding benefits from affiliating with nonprofits.[7] Harvard
Business School Press published a notable book by Shirley Sagawa
and Eli Segal addressing the burgeoning field of business and
social sector partnerships. *Common Interest, Common Good,*[8] complete with an introductory note by Hillary Clinton and a foreword by Rosabeth Moss Kanter, describes, defends, and advances
partnerships where businesses discover social values and social
purpose organizations discover business principles.[9]

For example, Home Depot joined with a nonprofit group
committed to building playgrounds in low-income neighborhoods. With cash and in-kind contributions from Home Depot
and an insurance company, the nonprofit—named KaBoom!
—has built twenty playgrounds and is now massively expanding.
Home Depot has not only improved its public relations, it has also
helped to build a sense of teamwork and pride among employees
who have volunteered. KaBoom! ensures that the projects run
smoothly and benefit the company's community ties while gaining moneys, volunteers, and technical advice.[10]

Profit/nonprofit collaborations go far beyond corporate
volunteering and financial donations to nonprofit social agencies.
They go beyond even the growth of charitable organizations large
enough to resemble bureaucracies and businesses, traveling a path
from founding saints to unscrupulous bureaucrats, described criti-
cally by George Bernard Shaw in his 1896 preface to *Major Barbara.*[11] Indeed, Sagawa and Segal claim to find a new paradigm that
"eliminates barriers between the sectors while preserving their
core missions"[12] and allows the creation of new value for both the
for-profit and nonprofit members in the alliance.[13] A business may
affiliate with a social service organization to build its capacity to
produce a good or service or to promote its image in a direction
favored by its clients or potential clients.[14] Particularly after a scan-
dal or adverse publicity, a company may donate money or expertise to a cause or group that has a positive public image.[15] Such

involvement can be justified to shareholders even in a highly competitive climate, because profits themselves are tied to public image. Through a relationship structured as a sponsorship, the company can obtain an exploitable commercial potential—whether through media exposure or joint branding of products. BankBoston's sponsorship of CityYear, Denny's restaurants' sponsorship of Save the Children, and many corporations' sponsorship of AIDS and breast cancer runs illustrate how sponsorship can be used to improve a corporate image and increase brand awareness.[16] Annual sponsorship spending in North America grew from $850 million in 1985 to approximately $6.8 billion in 1998.[17]

Cause-related marketing—through which a company encourages sale of an item by pledging to donate a portion of proceeds to a charity or social agency—can raise visibility and resources for the cause while also benefiting the for-profit entity with revenues and positive public relations.[18] Thus, high-end kitchenware manufacturer Calphalon designated a two-quart sauté pan to co-brand with Share Our Strength, an anti-hunger organization, and directed $5 from each sold pan to the charity.[19] Over time, the two entities also involved high-profile chefs in joint events and in return found ways to showcase them and their restaurants.[20] Working Assets recruits customers for its Visa card by donating a portion of the interest and return to nonprofit enterprises voted for by cardholders; increasingly, retailers offer to donate a percentage of revenues or other resources if customers shop with them.

These are classic win/win collaborations. The nonprofit groups get financial support and visibility while the for-profit groups gain reputations as "good guys" among valued consumers—while also often making a profit through consumer purchases of the goods or services linked to the cause. Yet, unless the for-profit firms turn over 100 percent of the profits attributable to the involvement of consumers attracted by the cause marketing, the nonprofits are in fact subsidizing the returns to the for-profit entities by offering them a bigger client base.[21]

In another variation, the nonprofit runs a for-profit business by providing a desired good or service and directing the profit to the cause.[22] Many nonprofits are turning to for-profit activities because the demand for their charitable help exceeds their funding sources. Meals on Wheels, which brings free food service each day to homebound individuals, receives $500 million from federal and state governments and private donors, but still the demand exceeds the available resources.[23] In 2001, the organization reported the biggest waiting lists in their history and yet predicted escalating need as the number of elderly people will double in the next thirty years. The organization therefore has launched a catering business and in some locations also has tried to charge those who can pay for the home-delivered meals.[24] One publicly traded $300-million business and another very profitable business are subsidiaries of a nonprofit community development organization.[25] Large publicly traded companies have become the dominant providers of services to people with disabilities. [26]

In still another variation, a nonprofit authorizes use of its name and logo in a licensing agreement in exchange for a share of revenues; the nonprofit then implicitly endorses the product. The American Medical Association ran into trouble with such an agreement with Sunbeam home health care products because it did not undertake a process to test the effectiveness of the products; consumer and professional groups expressed outrage that the AMA would nonetheless grant its reputation in endorsement. It breached the deal, losing millions for public health and public educational programs, five staff members, and $9.9 million paid in a damage settlement to Sunbeam. [27]

Similar difficulties can arise as international nongovernmental organizations with humanitarian or human rights purposes collaborate with multinational corporations. Defined roughly as entities that are neither governmental nor market-based, nongovernmental organizations gain legitimacy from this definition and from purposes such as humanitarian aid, building civil society, and promoting human rights.[28] Especially in emerging democracies, such entities may play a crucial role in economic, social, and democratic development.[29] Yet the boundaries between NGOs and governments on the one side, and for-profit enterprises on the other, are crossed in complex ways in many settings. Many NGOs collaborate with governments, support political parties, and enter into competitive politics. And many operate as for-profit entities or develop partnerships or affiliations with for-profit entities. While some nations do not grant a tax-exempt status to NGOs, this is not simply a matter of form. In some instances, NGOs receive funding and sponsorship from multinational corporations that themselves seek to enhance their public relations around the globe or in a given region. By itself, this is not troubling, but the arrangement can indeed be disturbing when the NGO intended to monitor human rights, trade, or environmental matters is affected by corporate conduct. In other instances, NGOs themselves engage in profit-oriented businesses such as printing, trading in bond markets, and marketing cellular phones, which can compromise their own credibility.[30] Recent media attention and conservative advocacy groups challenge international and domestic nonprofits for taking unfair advantage of their tax-exempt status.[31] Yet nonprofit organizations are also touted as a vital check on governments and on international corporations.[32] Whether nonprofits should be subject to antidiscrimination laws as corporations are is another complex question, especially when their activities cross into commercial territory.[33]

Nonprofits cross into for-profit territory often simply by learning from for-profit business how to revitalize their efforts and enhance their effectiveness. Growing numbers of entrepreneurs and heirs to accumulated wealth indicate a desire to make their own choices, rather than defer to professionals, and to develop "their own private visions of the public good."[34] With the extraordinary opportunities open to new millionaires to invest in the public good and with public spending increasingly restricted to nondiscretionary income transfer programs, private philanthropic efforts will play an ever larger role in shaping innovative responses to collective needs.[35] Social entrepreneurship is a new buzzword to characterize efforts by philanthropists to bring market-style ideas or business accountability methods to philanthropic investment. Some nonprofit innovators seek alliances with new philanthropists on particular initiatives and in the use of business methods to address social needs. Vanessa Kirsch founded New Profit, Inc., a venture philanthropy fund, to borrow the practices of venture capitalists for social service nonprofit organizations.[36] Her organization uses performance-based funding, emphasizing the creation of value for current and future consumers, to evaluate the enterprises it chooses to support and helps those organizations devise their own internal performance measures. The gamble is to apply for-profit business techniques to nonprofit settings while seeking to ensure social service and social change goals. The effort has itself become the subject of a case study by the Harvard Business School. The returns are not all in, but the model advances upon conventional nonprofit efforts by moving beyond good intentions to measurable results that themselves guide management and funding decisions.

Health care delivery within the United States is another case of activities constantly crossing the boundaries between public and private, profit and nonprofit—and secular and religious. Health care has long been a setting in this country that has joined public and private dollars and, increasingly, for-profit and nonprofit organizations. Health care providers use public dollars—such as Medicaid and Medicare—to pay for services delivered in private, and often religious, institutions. No one seems to worry when federal and state funds covering individual patients and programs support religious hospitals that infuse their care with religious symbols, prayers, and personnel.[37] The past twenty years produced an explosive rise in for-profit hospitals, nursing homes, and other health care providers and increasing mergers between profit and nonprofit providers.[38] For-profit health maintenance organizations even more than public regulations have driven cost-containment measures that have a worrisome effect on the quality of individual patient care.[39]

These days, in Massachusetts and elsewhere, the economic insolvency of the nonprofit health maintenance organizations makes for-profit suitors desirable white knights even if they would change the character and style of health care settings and jeopardize services to the most disadvantaged and most sick.[40] The choice of the for-profit form opens up equity financing while nonprofits can pursue tax-exempt debt financing. The for-profit organization has incentives to skimp on care while the nonprofit lacks incentives for cost savings and efficient delivery—and each therefore may risk jeopardizing quality care.[41]

Mergers between Catholic and public or private nonprofit and profit hospitals and health care systems remake the shape and scale of resources available to the uninsured. Health care institutions face cost squeezes, downsizing, and a scramble to consolidate and create bigger entities with trimmed practices.[42] In many communities, the Catholic health care providers are literally lifesavers; the Catholic health care mission includes a commitment to serve the poor, a mission which is increasingly rare and commendable as other public and private actors abandon those who are poor and lack insurance.

Yet a study of Texas hospitals indicates that public hospitals afforded greater charity health services than nonprofits, including Catholic hospitals.[43] Mergers that reduce the presence of public hospitals can lead to a net reduction in the provision of care for the poor, even when the new entities involve religiously identified organizations. In addition, mergers with specifically Catholic hospitals affects the availability of reproductive services and assisted technology, abortion, counseling for persons who are HIV positive about the use of condoms, vasectomies, and end-of-life choices.[44] In accord with Catholic teachings, Catholic hospitals do not provide or make referrals for pregnancy terminations, and this ban applies to any physician or resident working on the premises regardless of the individual's own religious beliefs.[45] Observers indicate that as a result of these mergers not only abortion but also family planning and sterilization services disappear from institutions that used to provide them.[46] One report indicated that in nearly half the cases studied, mergers eliminated all or some of the reproductive health services previously provided by the non-Catholic hospital.[47] These include sterilization and vasectomy procedures. In addition, Catholic leadership relies on religious teaching to forbid certain forms of assisted conception, including artificial insemination by donor and in-vitro fertilization, and to restrict some decisions to withdraw or refuse treatment to dying patients, even at the patient's request.[48] The National Conference of Catholic Bishops Ethical and Religious Directives for Health Care Services articulates these commitments and guides the content of health care services acceptable to Catholic institutions engaged in the fifty-seven mergers or affiliations with non-Catholic ones between 1990 and 1995 and the additional ones since then and into the future.[49] Increasingly, these mergers involve for-profit hospitals and health care systems, such as Columbia/HCA Healthcare Corporation.

In some instances, the resulting arrangement permits practices that depart from Catholic teachings to continue in a portion of the newly merged entity that is able to retain a non-Catholic identity or move to a new facility.[50] Yet in many other circumstances, all or most of the services related to reproductive freedom have been cut.[51] Especially in small cities and rural areas, the mergers reduce or even eliminate choice about health care providers and risk imposing Catholic rules on many who would not choose them. For example, mergers in Eugene, Oregon, eliminated all but one nonemergency abortion facility in the city and neighboring region where Catholics constitute only 4.4 percent of the population.[52] According to one study, there are forty-six communities in which Catholic hospitals are the sole providers.[53] The economic pressures to consolidate health services lead some observers to predict that most hospitals will not be free standing in five years but instead will be part of networks and mergers: How many will include Catholic entities? And how far will the Catholic partners spread their rules?

In a development that physically illustrates the connections between religious and for-profit activities, houses of worship in dense urban areas are selling development rights to for-profit entities. Churches holding increasingly valuable urban real estate explore opportunities not only to sell and relocate, but to sell air

rights and then come to coexist, physically, with structures housing commercial and residential activities.[54]

Colleges and universities in the United States have long combined religious, nonprofit, public, and private funds. Public dollars support individuals who enroll in private, including religious,
institutions. The GI Bill, in particular, has enabled millions of
people to gain access to higher education and allows the individual beneficiary to select the institution to attend.[55] These include
religiously affiliated schools, as well as other colleges and universities and job-training programs. The religious identity of many
private colleges and universities has paled over the twentieth century, but some have gained renewed vigor.[56]

Tax-exempt, nonprofit institutions of higher learning increasingly explore relationships with commercial ventures either
as partners or affiliates. Universities increasingly devise complex
rules to govern ownership of faculty and student work that is performed on campus, in light of exploding markets for biotechnol
ogy, information-technology, and the Internet. Many universities
enter into partnerships with for-profit entities to develop real
estate, patents, and educational materials; some institutions of
higher education aggressively facilitate student entrepreneurship.[57] Silicon Valley's economic explosion stems in no small way
from deliberate efforts by Stanford University administrators to
promote town-gown cooperation.[58] Yet the boom it launched—
the Internet juggernaut—potentially challenges the proprietary
premises about information and knowledge production behind
private universities.[59] Corynne McSherry argues that maintaining a sphere of knowledge that cannot be owned is the irre-
ducible task of universities, while managing knowledge that can
be known is the mission of intellectual property.[60] The two missions become blurred, to the detriment of each, when universities
use copyright, patent, and trade secrets law to gain ownership,
commercial benefits, and control over knowledge. Universities
have already acknowledged some of the dangers by adopting rules
against faculty investment in student enterprises.[61]

Some states forbid government agencies from engaging in

businesses that would compete directly with private businesses, however. This presents limitations on state universities that wish to pursue profit-making enterprises.[62] Meanwhile, many universities struggle to support commercial ventures and commercial outlets for faculty work if only to prevent faculty from emigrating to other universities or to full-time commercial undertakings.[63]

University presses offer a small but illustrative example. Once subsidized by universities to promote publication of scholarship, in recent years university presses have faced pressures to become self-sufficient and thus to publish more books capable of appealing to a broad general public and fewer monographs with readerships consisting of the small number of experts in the field and the authors' devoted relatives. Yet university presses cannot hope to compete with trade presses for most works with mass popular appeal. Indeed, few commercial presses survive today in the highly competitive world of million-dollar advances for a few hot properties and product placement and promotion budgets for those and only those few books each year. The dissertation study of a single medieval text thus is unlikely to find any publisher these days; even the study of a single modern poet will not. Instead, Web posting is the likely destiny for much contemporary research. With Web posting, the entire pretense of a market exchange can be dropped. Access to the posted text and data requires no fee beyond the user's prior investment in a computer, modem, printer, and software; and there is little incentive to create a turnstile fee for the author who chiefly hopes somewhere, someday, for a reader.

Why not, then, post the course syllabus, lecture notes, the course itself? Here, some universities providing students and faculty with subsidized Web access will flinch. For the entire livelihood of the university depends upon its ability to exclude people and thereby charge for its knowledge and knowledge production. The Massachusetts Institute of Technology, thus far, is the sole institute to choose to allow free access to course materials by posting on the Web materials by those professors who volunteer to participate.[64] Other universities are trying to find ways to charge admission on the Web to full fledged, for-credit courses.[65] Similarly, university presses are increasingly searching for more profitable publications, or at least reducing the number of publications that lose money. The University of Toronto Press has found a way to retire its debt in part by publishing journals and distributing books published elsewhere, by publishing at least some very popular books, and by owning the university's bookstore.[66] Other university presses lack this diversification as well as the uniquely prominent position within its country that the University of Toronto Press occupies.[67] Rivaling university presses in distributing information and on-line education services, many nonprofit, tax-exempt colleges and universities are establishing partnerships with for-profit entities and internal technology transfer units.[68] Meanwhile, these nonprofit institutions of higher learning are themselves facing competition from emerging for-profit universities such as the University of Phoenix and educational institutions and programs developed by corporations for their employees.[69]

Two enterprising students invited corporations to compete for the chance of supporting their college tuition and expenses in exchange for their services as "spokesguys"—and now Chris Barrett and Luke McCabe represent the credit card company First USA on campuses and in promotional campaigns.[70] A *New York Times* article commented: "In a world where kindergartners learn to count with books created by Cheerios, where Channel One beams commercials into classrooms, and where Coke and Pepsi compete for turf alongside hall lockers, this is the latest frontier. . . . Students are not just surrounded by marketing tactics; they are adopting them."[71]

Border crossing along the profit/nonprofit line characterizes the enterprise that still bears the name of "public broadcasting." Under old technologies of scarcity, public broadcasting emerged as a classic instance of a "public good," broadcasting with programming without commercial advertising and with the intention of serving the public interest.[72] Advocates successfully made the case for allocating some frequencies in each market to public television and radio in order better to serve the public interest with educational and cultural programming, with community access, and with noncommercial children's programming. Critics of public broadcasting have ensured that it has never received adequate funding in the United States, unlike comparable efforts in Britain, Japan, and Canada; and even the inadequate public funds have faced sharp cuts. In response, public broadcasters have pursued commercial sponsorship, allowing on-air identifications of corporate sponsors that increasingly resembles commercials; and public broadcasters have also promoted commercial tie-ins with public programs.

Notable among public television producers is the Children's Television Workshop, which supports itself with profits from sales of *Sesame Street* toys, videos, and other products.[73] Its success has also convinced commercial broadcasters to pursue new, related shows.[74] Does there remain a place for "public television" if private for-profit broadcasters and cable channels find paying customers for the same kinds of shows—and as new technologies challenge the assumption of scarcity used to justify the creation of public television? Perhaps yes, but the argument must be made in new terms that reestablish precisely what is public or in common about the enterprise. Free access may be one feature; public service content may be another. In any case, the very necessity that pushed public broadcasters to emulate commercial broadcasters may jeopardize their raison d'être.

In commercial broadcasting, the government has maintained the line between the secular and the religious through the prevailing public system of private licenses. Religious groups have secured their own licenses or airtime on other privately held channels. In some instances, religious groups themselves make profits through broadcast-related appeals; such activities potentially jeopardize their nonprofit status, though these are instances of abuse rather than shifting lines. Meanwhile, for-profit media have cut back on or eliminated public affairs programming, taking the cue from the 1985 decision of the Federal Communications Commission to stop mandating shows attending to political, civic, and community concerns.[75] Robert McChesney, a professor of communications, concludes, "There's more pressure to put on programs for the wealthy because they have more money to buy products. The bottom third of the community is not that attractive to advertisers. It's sad, but the idea that TV stations are a mass medium that serve the entire community doesn't exist anymore."[76]

The federal government borrows business techniques when it auctions off publicly owned electromagnetic spectra and when it invests in scientific and technological research. In both contexts, the government uses market-style reasoning, ostensibly to serve public ends, but the public ends in both contexts are in fact jeopardized. Thus, past governmental auctions of the spectra have not preserved the proceeds for any particular public purpose. Proceeds from spectra auctions could instead generate funds to finance libraries, museums, schools, and open up new digital technologies for public access, but only if the government returns to thinking about public values after using the market mechanisms to generate revenues.[77] As Lawrence Grossman and Newton Mi now argued in their 2001 book *Gift to the Nation,* this kind of proposal echoes the land-grant college system, which used resources created by the sale of public lands.[78] Ideas of that sort require attention to consistent efforts to advance public values even while using market techniques. Currently, revenue from the public auctions simply goes to the Treasury to help pay the federal deficit, much in the way that a commercial enterprise would sell an asset to help defray costs and debt. To think in public terms would require viewing the sale of the public asset as a resource with the potential for enhancing a public good—but only if the proceeds from the auctions are preserved for distinctive purposes.

Confusion between public and private methods can work the opposite way—but similarly neglect public values—when government invests in private research. The public-minded motives behind federal investments in scientific research too often neglect the resulting profit possibilities that government (and the public) could pursue, as the government allows individual scientists and their own institutions to take patents and devise commercial uses of research supported by public funds.[79]

Government ties to business also take the form of public contracts given through competitive bidding to for-profit entities. Construction of public buildings typically works this way. But increasingly, so do actual government operations. The Lockheed Martin Corporation, known for aerospace production, now works for thirty-eight states and localities arranging and processing welfare payments and enforcing child-support obligations.[80]

Justice institutions and legal services generate new relationships between governments and nonprofit organizations, governments and for-profit entities, and governments and religious entities. The federal government and most states are authorized to contract for private corrections facilities and management.[81] Managers in state and federal justice systems busily pursue public/private partnerships especially, but not only, in the field of corrections. Private companies, some of them publicly traded, now hold contracts to operate secure adult facilities and juvenile facilities around the country, and in some instances, private companies own the facilities as well as operate them.[82] One company indicates that its public/private partnership techniques "are used extensively with city, county, and state governmental agencies" for "virtually all facility and infrastructure requirements."[83] At least one religiously affiliated unit of public prisons involves nonprofit ministries in prison programs that segregate prisoners who are willing to be converted and offers them better living conditions and different programs.[84]

Private attorneys may be drawn into previously public roles of prosecutor and public defender. A growing number of civil disputes are handled by private mediation and arbitration services not merely as alternatives outside the formal justice system but also as adjuncts, linked to the formal system.

Religious figures and religious communities increasingly connect with prosecutors and courts to engage in dispute resolution.[85] The Victim Offender Reconciliation Program joins prisons and the Mennonite Church in conflict resolution and restitution sessions that allow victims and offenders to try to understand one another and work out responses to crime guided by spiritual values.[86] An Interfaith Mediation Project involves clergy in resolving child custody disputes.[87] Growing involvement of religious persons and institutions with the state's justice systems in a sense reconnects the search for justice to institutions and traditions that predate the secular state.[88] In a different and related development, increasing scholarly and professional attention is directed to what it means to be a lawyer or judge while belonging to a particular religious tradition.[89] And the newly appointed Attorney General for the United States instituted regular prayer meetings in his office at the U.S. Department of Justice.[90]

Stand back and watch the boundaries blur. Crossing the public/private division, nonprofit organizations perform important societal tasks in the fields of education, health, and social welfare with mixes of public and private funding.[91] Crossing the profit/nonprofit divide, nonprofits pursue partnerships, sponsorships, and other affiliations with for-profit entities and undertake for-profit activities of their own. Governments increasingly deploy market-style solutions and contracts, in some instances with for-profits, to perform public functions. Crossing the secular/religious line, religious nonprofits receive public funds, competing with other private entities, and take on duties at times performed by governments; houses of worship themselves get engaged indelivery of social services and building housing and profit-making enterprises quite beyond the weekly bingo game. When President George W. Bush declared at a National Prayer Breakfast, "Government cannot be replaced by charities, but it can welcome them as partners instead of resenting them as rivals,"[92] observers of the longstanding interconnections among religious, nonprofit, and governmental agencies that fund and deliver social services heard his comment as an ill-informed call for something that already goes on everywhere.[93] In recent years, government and large philanthropies have made it a priority to promote just these kinds of collaborations. Philanthropies subsidize collaborations among nonprofit service organizations, police, schools, churches, public health entities, private health providers, and business in order to promote social justice.[94] Public interest lawyers focus on these collaborations instead of test-case litigation for social justice work.

WHY THESE TRENDS?

It is not unusual for the boundaries between public and private to blur. The lines themselves are historical inventions. Nor is it unprecedented for governments to work closely with nonprofit and religious groups, but shifts do seem to be occurring especially around collective commitments to provide for the basic human needs for food, shelter, education, medical care, and justice. The use of explicit business techniques by nonprofits and governments does seem to be taking new forms. Governments and secular foundations are pursuing more ambitious and direct relationships with religious congregations. Why are these developments occurring? No doubt, there are distinct reasons for blurring each of the lines, but several common, underlying factors contribute to blurring the public/private, profit/nonprofit, and secular/religious lines. In a sense, the trends amount to a return to patterns that predated large government, but cyclical as it may seem, social practices, like clothing fashions, never return to where they once were, precisely because of the intervening changes. In any case, the questions remain: Why these changes? And why now?

First, policies calling for reducing the federal government role in social services both reflect and contribute to disillusionment with government solutions and faith in private approaches. In the 1980s and 1990s, the arguments of politically right- and left-wing groups converged in an assault on the dehumanizing operation of government welfare, even though those on the right prescribed eliminating it and those on the left sought to reform it.[95] Critics of government point to the inefficiency and costs of public programs, the bureaucratic delays and cumbersome practices, and the lack of accountability and responsiveness.[96] Western democracies are backing away from social welfare states created through democratic politics. In pursuit of stable currencies and promising positions in global markets, Canada and European nations have been cutting back on social welfare guarantees. In the United States, devolution of governmental responsibility to the states constitutes part of a larger withdrawal from the New Deal's federal commitment to provide economic relief for the poor. The private approaches themselves comprise the heterogeneous array of for-profit firms, nonprofits, and religious entities. Even formerly socialist countries like Russia are cutting back on basic social guarantees ranging from child care to police protection.

Arguments for devolution and privatization come together to support a framework that promotes pluralism, competition, and what some have called the "mediating structures" of civil society.[97] In response to diminishing faith in and resources of government, many religious and secular nonprofits themselves have greater burdens with fewer resources and find themselves looking for commercial partners or income from commercial ventures. International and domestically based nongovernmental organizations are constantly scrambling for funding and are thus drawn to corporate sponsors and partners. Both within the United States and elsewhere, nonprofits pursue market-based or market-style mechanisms for delivering services as a way to gain income and convince potential donors and partners that they have the efficiency and dynamism that government lacks.[98]

Faith in competition and consumer choice to harness the efficiencies of the free market and promote individual freedom animate movements to privatize government programs as diverse as Social Security, schooling, substance abuse treatment, and garbage collection. Faith in competition as a motor for efficiency contributes to government policies soliciting not only nonprofit providers but also for-profit partners, contracting agencies, or vendors of fee for service in fields ranging from familiar partnerships in social services and health care to the newer terrains of education and corrections.[99] For-profit providers meantime try to convince private investors that they can, indeed, find efficiencies and cost savings sufficient to generate a profit for shareholders and owners. The same trends can be traced to the fall of communism, which made market-based competition and private enterprise the solution of choice and reduced skepticism about markets and commerce even in domains previously separated from them.[100] A related trend is the extraordinary success of economics and related modes of analysis in colonizing other academic fields, such as law, politics, and even religious studies. Academics now discuss with no apparent squeamishness market-based distributions of pollution, babies, sex, and rational-actor consumer choice in democratic politics and in selection of religions.[101]

Yet parallel to the market-style criticisms of government are religiously informed criticisms. For some, the goal is not vindicating the market but instead cultivating religious and community-based organizations that nurture moral obligation, helping relationships, and human dignity. Here the charge is that governments fail in providing education, substance abuse treatment, welfare, corrections, and dispute resolution because governments neglect people's spiritual side and lack the power of religious teachings, traditions, rituals, and communities. Governmental programs do not generate the sense of "moral obligation" that is essential to education and social services, but community-based private alternatives do, claims Charles Glenn in his 1989 book *Choice of School in Six Nations* comparing government and faith-based education and social services.[102]

Others argue that government displaces efforts that otherwise would or could emerge especially from religiously inspired volunteering and nonprofit efforts. People holding these views increasingly press private religious alternatives to provide education for children and aid to indigents and substance-abusing individuals— but also push for rearranging public programs to pay for schooling and services provided by religious entities. Already, through contracts, and perhaps in the future through vouchers, churches and other religious entities are moving into corrections, housing, job training, and welfare provision. Yet note the tension here: government is criticized for displacing private commitments, and yet private providers continue to turn to government for support. This tension directly concerns many who fear that private, and especially religious, providers can be co-opted or their distinctiveness can be undermined if they embrace ties with government. The ties though are already there: 41 percent of charitable organizations providing human services receive government grants.[103]

Perhaps, paradoxically, a potential reason for the shifting secular/religious lines stems from growing comfort among religious groups with participating in a pluralist society. For some people within minority religious groups, such as Jews, this seems the greatest moment to date for sufficient comfort and security to imagine participating in school voucher programs. For Catholics, too, there may be a sense of relative security as well as a profound sense of religious duty to attend to those who are poor, disadvantaged, and in need—with or without government as a partner. For Evangelical Protestants, this may seem a propitious time to reclaim the terrain that had been occupied in recent decades by the secular state. The pressures to push religion into the private sphere suited a time—much of the twentieth century—dominated by a kind of Protestantism comfortable with that approach while it also allowed government to push religiously based intergroup conflicts out of the public spotlight. Yet multiculturalism challenges the pretense of uniformity in the public sphere—and now affords a framework for religiously identified people to join in political debate and policy decisions alongside people organized by race, ethnicity, region, and gender.

Finally, public arguments for privatization did not emerge without a lot of strategic planning and considerable resources. Well-financed groups have lobbied for decades to extend market ideals to social services and schooling and to privatize a wide range of government activities, creating more room for market-style activities and religious groups. Conservative groups converged around a vision of a limited state with an increasingly privatized administration, even as they disagreed about degrees of distrust of government and executive power.[104] Leading players include the American Legislative Exchange Council, the National Center for Policy,[105] the Heritage Foundation, the Cato Institute, and the American Enterprise Institute. Leading funders of these and related efforts are the Lynde and Harry Bradley Foundation,[106] the

Adolph Coors Foundation, the Koch Family foundations, the John M. Olin Foundation, and the Scaife Family Foundation. A recent report notes that the American Enterprise Institute, the American Legislative Exchange Council, and the Cato Institute in Washington, D.C., in 1996 had combined resources of nearly $46 million while leading progressive think tanks—the Center for Policy Alternatives, the Institute for Policy Studies, the Center for Budget and Policy Priorities, and the Economic Policy Institute—shared $10.2 million.[107] One journalist noted that "with increasing frequency, legislation, proposed and enacted, can be traced directly to think-tank position papers on such conservative agenda items as welfare cuts, privatization of public services, private options and parental choice in schools, deregulation of workplace safety, tax limitations and other reductions in government, even selling the national parks."[108]

Privatization of this sort does not require but is compatible with an increasing role for religious organizations. The market-based and religious critiques of government share the argument that private efforts would be more effective, less wasteful, and more likely to respect the dignity of individuals served even as the market and religious critiques differ about the specific forms and methods those private efforts should take. There are potential tensions between for-profit and religiously inspired alternatives. Yet even their differences can be submerged under general articulations of faith in the human spirit, as Jack Kemp, among others, argues.[109]

Indeed, the movement for privatization and free enterprise is well illustrated by philanthropic initiatives to promote entrepreneurship for people who are poor or disadvantaged. Rather than using philanthropy to support programs and institutions that operate on principles of care, charity, or beneficence, some individuals and groups seek to align philanthropy with the self-reliance assumptions of capitalism. As described by one businessman and philanthropist, such venture capital philanthropy makes sense because too many existing nonprofits share the approach pursued by the government, the approach that fosters people's dependency rather than promoting their independence, self-reliance, and capacity to engage in the for-profit world. Thus, philanthropist Joseph Jacobs lauds a young man who started Skid Row Access, a project involving skid row residents in making and selling wooden toys. In his 1996 book, *The Compassionate Conservative,* Jacobs reported this conversation:

> I said, "Chuck, your business is expanding and pretty soon you'll be able to cover your overheads. Who knows? Maybe you'll even be able to pay yourself and your partners a salary. Then what?" The answer: "I hate having to ask foundations like yours for grants, but we could not have come this far without that help. Perhaps we should become a profit-making company instead of a tax-exempt charitable group. What do you think?"[110]

And Jacobs then explained,

> My heart sang! "Chuck by all means, go for a profit-making organization. Just think what it will mean to those people in skid row to know that they are not only making a living, but that their work is valued enough to be worth more than just a subsistence for them. Isn't there an added source of pride when someone can say he is not only being paid fairly but is also producing a profit for those who had faith in him? If you want to give the profits away to help others in the community, then you will have a self-sustaining model of philanthropy."[111]

With specific individuals and groups working to spread their own faith in free enterprise and distrust of government, a particular for-profit, free market tilt informs critiques of government and arguments for privatizing the functions of a scaled-back government even while making more room for religious participants and an enlarging private sphere. To be somewhat simplistic, right-wing analysts think government crowded out private, voluntary, and nonprofit institutions, and that is why there should be less government and more diversion of government funds to private and nonprofit entities; left-wing analysts see volunteerism and civil society harmed by the excesses of the market.[112] They both converge in supporting efforts that blur the distinctions, whether they are government vouchers redeemable at religious institutions and other nonprofits, or efforts to urge more volunteerism and community service for employees in the corporate sector.

Ironically, the call for greater governmental partnerships with religious groups to meet basic human needs grows in the United States precisely as Canada cuts back its government financing of faith-based food, shelter, and social service programs.[113] With a different constitutional tradition, Canada has never had a barrier to government funding of religious-based services, and in fact, has specifically funded some programs that are limited to people who belong to a particular religious group as well as others without such limitations. But as the government reduces its budget for social services, the Canadian religious groups face continuing and expanding needs with shrinking resources. Caroline DiGiovanni, an executive at Catholic Children's Aid Society of Toronto and a former city council member, observed that the most pressing duty of the faith-based community "is to pressure the whole community for more government funding."[114] It could be that the deepest source of even these contrasting trends is the recognition, gained over and again by different people in varied settings, of the inadequacy of any response to human needs yet found.

WHY WORRY?

No one committed to the public values of freedom, equality, and fairness can watch these trends and simply cheer. Nor can anyone truly impressed by the nonprofit sector and religious organizations sit at the sidelines without concern for the autonomy and vitality of private and religious spheres. Conflicting missions and loss of accountability surface immediately as central problems when public and private, profit and nonprofit, and secular and religious sectors converge.

The specific virtues and defects of the current welfare reform, faith-based initiatives, school reforms, health care reforms, and media reforms deserve sustained attention, but that is not my focus. The worries I wish to address here stem specifically from the new activities that constantly cross and blur lines between public and private, profit and nonprofit, and secular and religious domains. Each line is, of course, a fiction, a convention of speech. Yet the lines embody ideas about good ways to organize society and daily life. Current activities and policies risk raising concerns about where responsibilities lie and how accountability can be demonstrated and ensured. They also jeopardize public values, including commitments to freedom, equality, and democracy. They risk government intrusion on religions and religious intrusions on the government. They challenge professional expertise without necessarily demonstrating why volunteers would be better. And they could undermine what it takes to cultivate a sense of mutual concern, mutual vulnerability, and mutual responsibility in communities and in society as a whole.

Blurring public and private risks both the vitality of pluralist traditions and the implementation of public values. Neither voter nor consumer sovereignty can secure accountability when public and private realms merge. Blurring profit and nonprofit may unleash massive nonprofit failures, instigate conflicts of interest and missions, and vitiate the vitality of the civic sphere. Blurring religious and secular may interfere with the religious freedom of individuals, the autonomy of religious entities, and the public peace.

Public and Private

The public/private divide, at least in the United States, is notoriously complex. As a purely analytic matter, we use "public/private" to refer at times to the distinction between government—the public—and everything else as private. Alternatively, we treat families as private, everything else as public. In the first view, with the line dividing government and all else, employment and market exchanges lie on the side of the private. With the second view, workplaces and markets become public because they lie outside the realm of the family. Even this set of alternatives is too simplified in an environment of pervasive governmental regulation. For when the government determines what counts as a family, what counts as a corporation, what counts as a religion, and what counts as a tax-exempt charity and establishes benefits and burdens from these determinations, the very identification of "the private" involves governmental acts.

Consider organizations established as nonprofits or charities that gain from the government tax-exempt status and the ability to receive gifts that in turn allow donors to take tax deductions. This exemplifies the critical approach to the public/private distinction. Generally viewed as private, such nonprofit organizations depend upon governmental recognition to gain their tax-exempt status. Moreover, many economists would view the tax exemption and ability to receive tax deductible gifts as a form of public subsidy. Similarly, even the quintessential domain of families could be understood as constructed by law. What is a family, who is a parent, who can marry are each decisions made by governments with important financial, reputational, and moral consequences. Even the traditional privacy accorded to families—a conception that historically shielded husbands and parents from otherwise prevailing criminal and civil laws against violence and abuse—marks public allocations of power to private actors. For families, workplaces, hospitals, and so many other settings, the interconnections between public rules and private authority permitted by public rules make it difficult to sort out what is a private realm and what is not.

Nevertheless, abandoning a distinct private sphere would diminish, not strengthen, human freedom and dignity. Whether conceived as a literal geographic domain like the workplace or the home or instead as a scope of autonomy for individual action, privacy signals and guards deep human needs for self-determination, control over the disclosure of information about oneself, seclusion from prying and interfering eyes, and latitude for creation, invention, experimentation, and variety. Commitment to some form of distinction between the public and private realm is also vital to a vibrant pluralist society, for the stringent demands of governmental order and regularity and public transparency and participation can squelch varieties of expression, practice, and belief associated with distinctive ethnic, religious, geographic, and individualist traditions and inventions. For private, including religious, traditions, insulation from governmental control, and even from the temptation to use government to dominate other groups, is vital to retaining vibrant distinctiveness and their own, religiously informed, paths of development. The private may be jeopardized if increasing involvement with public activities comes with heavy strings of public regulation.

The flip side of this concern for protecting the private realm, however, is the crucial importance of articulating and maintaining public values that a liberal legal order both demands and implements. Most notable are the public commitments to equality, freedom, fairness, and democracy. Translated in our legal system as antidiscrimination, freedoms of association and religious exercise, due process, and voting, these public commitments traditionally helped to undergird the public/private distinction itself, ensuring private freedoms by restricting public incursions. A private facility is not bound by due process, which only restrains governments. Will private prisons nonetheless comply with due process restrictions? Will a parochial school respect public guarantees of freedom of religion? Will a private social services agency fight racial bias among its staff?

The American legal system has made the distinction between government and other realms matter as a trigger for the constitutional protections guaranteeing due process and equal protection, and assuring against establishment of religion. These commitments operate only as a constitutional matter when the state acts, not when private parties act.[115] Other countries have adopted different constitutions that do apply fundamental rights to private actions. Yet in the United States, the Fourteenth Amendment's prohibition against deprivations of life, liberty, or property without due process is only violable by states.[116] Courts can, and do, find sufficient involvement of the state in private action to trigger constitutional protections where governmental resources or governmental powers are involved.[117] But the mere presence of public funds has not convinced the Supreme Court to treat a private school as a state actor.[118] Only where the government would be viewed as entangled with racial discrimination or where the pri-

vate actor is fulfilling a traditionally and exclusively public function have the courts found private conduct to constitute state
action.[119]

The pervasiveness of discrimination on the basis of race and
gender fueled effective and admirable social movements to establish public norms reaching into employment–that slice between
the public government and private family—and also reaching private schools and clubs to the extent that they enjoy any public benefits, including tax exemptions and books purchased with public
funds.[120] As a result, many civil rights laws at the federal, state, and
local level extend as a matter of statute or regulation into the com-
paratively private realms of commercial employment, housing,
and schooling. Many would argue that the resulting reforms extend equality to realms where it really matters. Others counter
that the reforms breach the public/private line and interfere,
wrongly, with private activity and freedoms.

This fight continues today especially with struggles against
discrimination on the basis of sexual orientation by, for example,
the Boy Scouts. If cast as a private organization, exercising its freedom of association, the Boy Scouts can avoid public efforts to
eradicate exclusionary practices.[121] Yet then the Boy Scouts face
decisions by public schools to exclude them in order to separate
the private associational activity from public support and endorsement.[122] By choosing to characterize itself as a private association
with private liberties, the Boy Scouts of America had to distance
itself from an alternative conception of the group as a federally
chartered preparation for citizenship, open to all.

Whatever one's view may be about these kinds of questions,
they have centered on what precisely is public and what is private.
It is not that these concepts have intrinsic decisional authority or
that they produce indisputable answers. But these concepts stand
in for liberal democratic commitments to extend the norms of inclusion and equality as common guarantees while also protecting
freedom for individuals and groups to express and define themselves safe from governmental control.

When government is a purchaser as well as a guarantor of both freedom and equality, the competing goals become difficult to reconcile. Should the scope of public obligations to combat discrimination persist when the government contracts with a private entity to provide social services, education, and incarceration? As drafter of the contracts, and the piper calling the tune, the government can set extensive and detailed public requirements. As the purchaser of services that uniquely speak for all of the people, the government should not be in the business of paying for programs that perpetuate exclusions or degradations of individuals because of their group membership. And, as a specifically public purchaser, the federal and state governments must not fund religious practices or else they surely cross over into establishing religion.

This is not the end of the discussion, however, when it comes to governmental subsidized services. For the government can also provide funding through means that involve no direct grant or contract. Instead, the government can convert public dollars into vouchers redeemable by eligible individuals at private entities. Should public prohibitions against discrimination and for due process extend then to these private entities if they receive financing—perhaps a large share of their financing—from such public vouchers? Electing vouchers rather than grants allows policy makers to avoid extending public obligations and reporting requirements to private partners, even though this device does not alter the fact of public aid. Critics charge that allowing private entities receiving public dollars to discriminate amounts to publicly financed discrimination. The underlying question of values cannot be resolved here by reference to a tangled and muddled distinction between public and private, but the underlying concerns that these words signal should guide debate and decisions.

Courts, but also legislatures, make such decisions. In both settings, policies to avoid public guarantees in the context of private provision should worry us no less than the burdens of bureaucratic compliance on private providers. In addition, although there may be by law sufficient latitude to allow public dollars to finance private organizations that do not comply with public norms, the permissible does not define the desirable. Citizens and public leaders can fairly argue in legislative settings that government expenditures should not be used to advance the kinds of discrimination that public norms reject even when conducted by private organizations.

Vouchers raise an additional worry about poor choices by uninformed individuals. In that light, Yale University professor Susan Rose-Ackerman has urged proxy decision making—by actors other than the ultimate recipients—when vouchers are used by government and private charitable organizations to subsidize access to a range of nonprofit, for-profit, and governmental suppliers of social services.[123] Whether or not that is the right solution, the important insight is that the accountability mechanisms assumed by market-style consumer choice are often misplaced when social provision is at issue. It is too often empirically false to assume the existence of sufficiently informed consumers who are also sufficiently free to shift choices based on dissatisfaction and to signal preferences to both providers and other consumers when we deal with aid to the poor, medical care reimbursement, schooling for children, and treatment of substance abusers. Assuming that consumers will "vote with their feet"—as private markets assume—is so unlikely to be realistic that accountability cannot be produced. Yet the use of vouchers and other market-style mechanisms for delivering social services, poverty aid, schooling, and health care also usually abandons the alternative techniques of accountability used by government, such as expert decision making, oversight, and supervision.

Most fundamentally, relying on private agencies and religious groups to address social needs—even with public dollars—risks cutting off the very wellsprings of public obligation to provide social services, aid to the poor, health care, and schooling. It is not just that conceptions of public investments as entitlements are at risk, as with the recent welfare reform of 1996. More basically, the collective commitment to meet the needs of the needy can lose strength when public dollars are disbursed to—and struggled over by—disparate private and religious groups. Rendering the arena of public support less visible, government reliance on pri-

vate providers may obscure how much those served face needs because of societal practices, as well as because of bad luck and bad
choices.

For example, the growth of Catholic hospitals—largely
funded through Medicaid and Medicare—substitutes in many urban areas for a public commitment to provide hospital care. One
commentator asserts that when a Catholic health care provider
becomes dominant in a community, at some point "it moves from
a private sphere into a more public sphere" and then "it is morally
unsupportable for it to limit medical services considered valuable
by the public,"[124] such as contraception, abortion, and end-of-life
case management. I do not find this a helpful mode of analysis;
their sheer scale does not convert Catholic health care institutions
from private into public providers. Preserving their status as private entities is vital to promote freedom for individuals and groups
to associate, express themselves, practice their religions, and promote and sustain a pluralist society. The simple receipt of public
dollars does not convert a private entity into a public one.[125]

The problem is not the growth of private, in this case Catholic, health care, using public dollars, but the fact that extreme
complexity in the relationships among public and private funding
sources and providers makes it more difficult to frame as public debates precisely what the scope of public responsibility for meeting
the entire range of people's health care needs should be. Government is indirectly involved in these shifts by failing to use regulatory and antitrust tools to prevent this kind of domination by one
kind of provider and by failing to ensure alternative public or private provision; but the central problem here is not government but
the interplay among private actors, rearranging secular and religious domains. In sum, both public commitments and private
freedoms are endangered by ambiguities in the line between public and private. Private enterprises funded by the public too often
lack both the accountability mechanisms imagined by perfect
markets and those developed by full-fledged governmental action.
And shifting activities to private settings shrinks the very scope of
public debate about how those activities should proceed.

Secular and Religious

Because religious activities fall within the "private" sphere under most conceptions of the public/private line, shifting and blurring the line there often involves religious groups. Yet the secular/religious line is itself governed by specific constitutional language and distinct public values. Even in realms beyond the scope of the constitution—which only restrains government action with regard to religion—blurring the secular/religious divide changes the character of broader civic spaces and social provision. For example, the distribution between secular and religious in the delivery of social services and health care may not directly implicate the government, but it does affect the character of civil society.

To return to the case of Catholic hospitals, economies of scale and other financial pressures increasingly press for consolidation and reduce the range of alternative health care providers. Hospitals implementing Catholic teachings restrict access to family planning, abortion, and certain kinds of end-of-life care while also implementing a religiously guided mission to serve those in need. In most cities, secular public hospitals have not been able to survive the current economic climate. Catholic institutions have merged with other entities and in many instances have become primary sources for tertiary health care for low-income and uninsured people regardless of religion. For-profit providers do not meet the need. The result alters the divide between secular and religious realms and subjects non-Catholics to the borders of health care governed by Catholic teachings.

Where governments are directly engaged—as in contracts with religious organizations and public voucher programs recognizing redemption at religious organizations—the First Amendment's guarantee of an individual's free exercise of religion and prohibition against the government's establishment of religion should come into play. Analysis of the constitutional doctrine, pursued in chapter 3, has its own import, but it signals deeper worries about what happens when the religious/secular relationship shifts.

Despite shifts and contests in historical understandings of the place of religion in society and public life, three underlying values remain central. First, individuals' freedoms of religious belief and practice need protection against government-backed preferences or interference. Second, religions need protection from governmental control or censure. Third, society needs protection against the kinds of religious schisms and conflicts that arise when government policies and benefits become subject to religious rivalries.

Voucher programs, from one perspective, enhance individual freedom of religion by allowing individuals to select schools, heath care, and social service providers that match their own religious views and affiliations. The government's role then is an enabling one, and its chief task is to attain neutrality about the means for fulfilling an end that the government itself endorses. Consider the analogy to the government stance toward the performance of marriages. The government alone issues licenses but it recognizes marriages performed within any religious tradition.

But from another vantage point, this approach holds real danger to individuals and to religious groups. Privatization that relies on faith-based groups to address people's basic needs interferes with individual freedoms particularly when there is no available school, health care provider, or social service agency matching a person's beliefs or tradition. A likely solution would be to ensure, always, the availability of a secular alternative of comparable quality to the religious schools, health care, or social service provider. In the case of schools, the comparability in quality has been precisely the problem, especially in large urban areas. In many urban areas, parochial schools often appear to provide better instruction[126] and yield better results than do public schools in the same neighborhoods, although these conclusions are confounded by the ability of the parochial schools to exclude and by the self-selection of participating families.[127] For social service providers, the mix between secular and religious and among different religious providers varies in different communities. But if the only disburser of food stamps in a particular region is a religious provider that engages in prayer and other religious ritual, individuals

who do not share that faith could indeed feel coerced or op-
pressed.[128]

The second danger is to religious groups themselves. In an era
of declining public commitments to the poor and needy, governments may expect religious communities to take on more than
they can do.[129] When religious organizations participate as providers of services under governmental programs, they risk becoming
subject to governmental control, censure, or influence that interferes with their own mission, identity, and self-determination.
They may even grow dependent upon the governmental support,
with further jeopardy to their independence and religious character. Yet extreme governmental solicitude, exempting religious
providers from requirements the government would otherwise
impose, risks undermining public values, including commitments
against discrimination on the basis of religion, gender, race, and at
least in some jurisdictions, sexual orientation.

In the past, the law has partially reconciled these risks by exempting religious entities from the public norm against discrimination on the basis of religion in the context of employment.[130]
But the law has not exempted religious entities from the norm
against discrimination on the basis of race even to maintain the
entity's tax-exempt status, let alone more direct government
aid.[131] More ambiguous is the treatment of gender and sexual orientation.

Equal protection claims mounted against gender discrimination have not yielded the same vigorous protections accorded
comparable claims on the basis of race. The courts have ruled that
public educational institutions cannot exclude women or girls,
but the courts also have permitted differential treatment that does
not reinforce outmoded stereotypes about gender differences.[132]
When claims of gender equality encounter competing claims of
religious freedom, the norm conflict is intense, and the current
courts may well prefer the autonomy and freedom of religious
groups if their gender-based practices are religiously informed.
Certainly the statutory civil rights laws exempt religious groups
from challenges to excluding women from serving as clergy or
performing other religious roles.[133]

Groups claiming religious freedom also seek exemptions from local and state laws banning sexual orientation discrimination. When a Baptist social service agency in Kentucky fired an employee after discovering she was a lesbian, she sued, and argued that the high percentage of government contracts (paying over 50 percent of the budget) rendered the agency public and thus subject to antidiscrimination norms. The judge dismissed the case on the grounds that the antidiscrimination norms in Kentucky forbade discrimination on the basis of religion, but not sexual orientation, and therefore the use of a behavioral code in the absence of religious requirements avoided running foul of the law.[134] Yet a dozen other states have adopted laws guarding against sexual orientation discrimination in employment, as have hundreds of cities and towns. In those contexts, similar antidiscrimination claims will not be so easy to dismiss, and private agencies largely funded by public sources will face more vigorous challenges if they claim that private associational or religious freedoms exempt them from public antidiscrimination laws.

The Salvation Army, the Roman Catholic Archdiocese of New York, and Agudath Israel, an Orthodox Jewish organization, legally challenged a New York Executive Order requiring organizations receiving city funds not to discriminate on the basis of "sexual orientation and affectional preference."[135] The groups denied that they engaged in discrimination but argued that this regulation exceeded the city's authority and interfered with the organization's control of their own hiring practices, consistent with their beliefs against condoning homosexuality. The New York Court of Appeals in 1985 agreed with the challenge, finding that the order exceeded the mayor's authority and left the question to the city council. The city council responded by allowing religious groups to make hiring decisions consistent with promoting the religious principles of those organizations.[136] In contrast, a San Francisco ordinance requiring city contractors to provide health insurance benefits to employees and their partners, whether married or not, initially produced protests by the local Salvation Army and Catholic Archbishop, but ultimately both informally agreed to comply.[137]

Charles Glenn, professor of education at Boston University, argues that such capitulation to government strings could undermine the religious character of sectarian organizations.[138] Indeed, he warns against the application of the same criteria and controls used by the government for its own operations, which can dismantle the autonomy, flexibility, and responsiveness of the religious nonprofit providers.[139] Especially in the contexts of schooling, Glenn suggests it takes a lot of nerve to require private parochial schools to conform to the floundering public model.[140] For Glenn, and others, it is not just governmental control but any outside interference that could undermine the mission and character of the religious schools, hospitals, and agencies. Even professional norms developed by teachers, social workers, and doctors and nurses jeopardize the special qualities of the religious provider.[141] This warning against professionalization matches cautions from feminists about battered women's shelters, which lost their self-help and empowering features when they gained public support and professional staffs.[142] Thus, blurring the religious/secular line jeopardizes religious autonomy. This mirrors dangers to other kinds of volunteerism. Government aid, and also professional mindsets, can crowd out the alternative spirit and practices developed by people offering help because of their distinctive beliefs and worldviews.

The third danger from blurring the religious/secular line is new risks of schisms and rivalries fueled by religious differences. The secular line and the secular state stem in no small way from the sober lesson of religious conflicts, notably the Thirty Years' War and other bloody European religious feuds.[143] These taught the lesson: Keep religion out of the public sphere; devise a conception of the abstract, reasonable social order. One corollary could be: Do not invite religious groups to seek influence with or benefits from the polity. Competing for government contracts and vouchers could trigger new rounds of religious tension.

Yet, curiously, the current political context invites leaders and members of quite diverse religious traditions to come together, against the old secular/religious line. The new schisms are as likely to emerge between secularist and religious individuals and groups, whatever their affiliations. The very effort to keep religion out in the name of the secular and the abstract contributes to what religious observers see as the sterility and coldness of public schools and public assistance. Especially after September 11, signs of religious cooperation and gestures of religious solace make objections to religion seem almost unimaginable.

Profit and Nonprofit

As nonprofits turn to profit-making activities and extended relationships with for-profit entities, three problems should worry us. First, nonprofits that undertake their own efforts in profit-generating activity should beware of the high failure rate of for-profit start-ups. Up to 70 percent of all business start-ups fail in the first eight years.[144] Many that have initial success have difficulty sustaining it. These serious risks can jeopardize a nonprofit's reputation, assets, and even its lawful existence.

Second, for-profit activities and affiliations entered into by nonprofits can produce serious conflicts of interest and conflicts of mission that raise direct ethical problems and long-term dangers to each mission. Perhaps the most extreme example of conflicting interests has already arisen. For-profit actors, in merger or take-over mode, in some instances have offered what amounts to bribes to board members and executives of nonprofit hospitals.[145] Sponsorship by a corporate actor can undermine the credibility of a nongovernmental organization, especially where the corporate sector decides to sponsor in order to overcome a bad public image on the precise issues handled by the NGO. Close ties can jeopardize not only the appearance but also the reality of self-determination by the nonprofit, especially if the two pursue joint decision making and management of shared activities.

Conflicting interests reveal conflicting missions. Increasingly, corporate managers restrict charitable giving of the entity except where it can justifiably preserve or increase shareholder value. When the corporate charitable giving is accounted for in strictly public relations or research and development terms, the result may, but also may not, advance the mission of the recipient groups. A for-profit that puts social service first can lose both customers and investors and, ultimately, its very existence. Conflicts in missions are more obvious when the profit and nonprofit agencies merge or undertake joint ventures. For-profit partners with nonprofit health care providers often cut costs by cutting care and dumping the unprofitable—that is, the charitable—care.[146] A for-profit health care, social service, or education agency can turn away those most in need because of the bottom line.[147] Granted, nonprofits can learn from successful for-profit enterprises.[148] For example, "For-profit managers contend that their attention to the bottom line creates incentives for them to provide excellent customer service and to keep costs down."[149] This longstanding debate over which form better serves those in need should be resolved on the facts in specific contexts. Facts do include perceptions, however. How will communities perceive profit-making providers of foster care or prison facilities?

Affiliations between profit and nonprofit entities may help but may also hurt both sides of the partnership. The effort to lend the credibility of the nonprofit organization to the for-profit may backfire, and the nonprofit group may instead appear to be "bought"—leaving the for-profit entity looking crass and manipulative. Or the nonprofit group's attempt to diversify sources of support by offering something in exchange for corporate or commercial resources may scare away traditional sources such as charitable individuals and foundations.

When the nonprofit undertakes its own profit-making activity or licensing agreement with a for-profit, it may scare away charitable contributions and government aid. Public and private grant makers and donors grow reluctant to give to an enterprise that makes money for shareholders and managers. If nonprofits license their name on a product, help with its marketing, and avoid paying taxes on proceeds, this becomes precisely the kind of boundary-blurring that could jeopardize the legal and political basis, and philanthropic base, for nonprofit enterprises. A technical legal problem also comes into play. Except for revenues from unrelated business income, most nonprofits have been presumed exempt from taxation under the Internal Revenue Code income tax provisions and from state property and sales taxes. The tax-exempt status of the nonprofit depends upon compliance with the tax laws, including the requirement of paying taxes on income generated for a purpose unrelated to the charitable mission.[150] As a result, the nonprofit's tax-exempt status could be jeopardized if it generates too many revenues unrelated to its core mission.[151]

Those running the nonprofit entity are not always knowledgeable and competent to forge a successful for-profit undertaking, which even in the best scenario often takes several years to become profitable. Yet seeking profits as a nonprofit organization has advantages; such an entity avoids sales taxes and worker compensation taxes, becomes able to raise money through tax-exempt bonds, gains access to discounts available to nonprofits, and can receive donations from benefactors who, in turn, can take a tax deduction for their gifts.[152] All of these features may create resentment and even political opposition as the nonprofits seem to be competing with for-profit organizations.[153]

The Internal Revenue Service has based its decisions on the scale of the profit-making activity, the destination of the profits, and the means employed to implement the rules, and nonprofits can run afoul of the rules. As a sector-wide problem, small for-profit businesses charge that the growing profit-making activities of nonprofits involve unfair competition.[154] Because the nonprofits enjoy tax-exempt status and tax-deductible gifts from private donors, small business—backed by the Small Business Administration—seeks to eliminate any tax exemption for profit-making activity by nonprofits.[155] Increasing commercial activities by nonprofits has generated arguments from these and other quarters for changing the tax treatment of nonprofits.[156] Congress has already withdrawn tax-exempt status from nonprofit organizations providing "commercial-type insurance."[157] There are proposals to increase taxation of investment income to business leagues.[158]

Yet charges of unfair competition ignore the ways in which the community and public service missions of nonprofits typically involve them in providing services where competitive markets fail. When a nonprofit organization produces revenues by employing and training workers who cannot get jobs in the mainstream labor market, it often faces higher costs.[159] Moreover, nonprofits do not have access to venture capital and equity investment, as do for-profit enterprises.[160] These defenses fade, however, the more the distinctive identity of a nonprofit dissolves through partnerships and other affiliations with for-profit entities.

Blurring the borders between profit and nonprofit organizations could undermine legal and political support for the nonprofit sector and eliminate, in practice, its distinctiveness. Yet nonprofit organizations offer ways to vitalize civil society, facilitate people's freedoms to associate and express themselves, enable people to participate in running their lives, and nurture traits vital to democracy. Loss of the nonprofits would weaken civil society and democracy. In the words of one scholar, "The nonprofit sector acts as a counterpoise against excessive displays of power emanating from the public or private sectors."[161] Nonprofits involve people in civic activity and service to others and thereby teach skills of self-government and inculcate habits of tolerance and civility.[162] Impairment of the nonprofit sector could exacerbate declining civic and political engagement.[163] Losing nonprofits would disproportionately hurt poor and working class people.[164] Nonprofits provide an array of collective goods that neither the market nor governments address because nonprofits proceed with distinct missions and willingness to take certain kinds of risks that the other sectors bypass.[165] Higher education, university presses, and public broadcasting enable pursuit of knowledge and culture, which purely private markets have never been able to sustain. Nonprofit social service agencies, advocacy groups, and civic associations offer modes of assistance and outlets for human generosity that in turn forge social bonds and defend vital liberties. If forced to compete with for-profit enterprises or required to become self-sustaining, each of these activities could falter. At the same time, for-profit enterprises jeopardize their duties to shareholders and consumers if they pursue charitable purposes instead of their primary mission. Yes, collaborations between profit and nonprofit activities can produce benefits—or in the jargon, win/ win solutions—for each, but only if the clarity of each mission and certainty of each accountability mechanism remain intact.

WHAT MATTERS

Through individual and collective efforts, society should respond to basic human needs and redress inequalities. Schooling, welfare, social services, health care, dispute resolution and corrections each represent institutional efforts to respond to human needs and to redress inequalities. The following is a rough statement of the values and goals that should guide the discussion and decision making on how society responds to basic human needs.

1. *Achieving Social Provision:* It is not by accident that a mix of public and private, secular and religious, profit and nonprofit providers emerged in the United States to respond to human needs and to redress inequalities. Plural approaches spur competition and enable rich variety in the ways to meet human needs and in the kinds of people drawn to help. Vital public values are at stake even in the mix of public and private providers, in the roles of profit-making, not-for-profit, and religious entities, and in the methods of governance and accountability used in and across each domain, but actual delivery of responses to human needs should not get lost in efforts to accomplish other goals.

2. *Freedom:* Given public values historically animating this nation, social provision efforts should be compatible with and in turn should advance freedom for individuals and for groups for self-expression, for religious practice, and for political action consistent with respecting the rights of others. Such freedom requires governmental protection and also government restraint to ensure no official establishment of religion, and no governmental action to prefer or disfavor religion or any particular religions over others.

3. *Pluralism:* Establishing and sustaining a vibrant but nontoxic pluralism is important for cultivating the virtues of participation, self-governance, mutual aid, and care for others that can

support a larger whole while also allowing escape valves and freedoms that counter the controlling force of a powerful nation state. To be nontoxic, the social, cultural, and religious groups must permit individuals to exit and to participate in multiple groups or no groups at all. A nontoxic pluralism also requires sufficiently overarching civic virtues, such as freedom of speech, equal opportunities for individuals in public and private settings, and democratic participation, to temper risks of prejudice, demagoguery, and group-based domination.

4. *Democracy:* Institutions and cultural practices should support democratic engagement and participation by individuals and groups in the tasks of self-government and the job of holding people in positions of authority accountable and responsive.

5. *Division of labor:* Social provision efforts should be undertaken at the level of community as proximate to those in need as possible while still remaining effective and should reflect both the insights of professional expertise and the energy of volunteer initiative.

6. *Accountability:* To prevent abuse, fraud, and waste, and to enhance learning and improvement, transparent and effective means of accountability, in the day-to-day administrative settings as well as through formal public elections,[166] should govern those who provide care, especially for people who are not ideally situated to monitor that care or advocate for themselves.

Some may think that these are not the right goals or that these values are expressed too abstractly, or too specifically. Surely, these kinds of values do not generate a formula for decision making. But they can guide public analysis of policies, proposals, and practices. For we can ask of any program or practice: Is it compatible with individual freedom? Does it protect individuals from unequal treatment? Does it foster or undermine community? Does it enable a sustainable pluralism? Does it enable public debate and accountability in the exercise of collective resources?

Even if this rough statement of values is inadequate or wrong-headed, it stands in for the debate over the public values that should persist no matter how the efforts for social provision shift. The most serious danger in blurring the boundaries between public and private, secular and religious, profit and nonprofit, I think, is the risk of losing a public framework through which we debate, implement, and revise public values. Accretions of individual governmental decisions to outsource, to downsize, to spin off, and to collaborate with profit-making organizations, secular non-profits, and religious groups could so remake the landscape of society as to render obsolete or impotent the very methods and scope for broad-based self-governance—and articulation of the scope and meaning of public values.

Across the globe, nations that formerly provided public social supports are cutting back. The limited public provision in this country is not only subject to cuts but is increasingly working through private providers, whether for-profit, nonprofit, or religious. It is neither the government's main strength nor the apparent will of the electorate to render direct social provision entirely a governmental task. Nor will private sources ever be able to fully meet the needs of children, poor people, people with disabilities, people with substance abuse problems, and prisoners. Public contracts, voucher plans, asset sales, and shared space will no doubt be joined by still other combinations of public and private efforts to meet schooling, health care, and social services needs as well as dispute resolution and corrections. The exuberant win/win enterprises joining profit and nonprofit and the inventive efforts of nonprofits to make profits will expand. Religious organizations will, in the near future at least, play larger, not smaller, roles in social provision and public life than in the past.

Yet no one committed to the public values of freedom, equality, pluralism, and democracy can watch current trends without concern. Nor can anyone truly impressed by the nonprofit sector and religious organizations sit at the sidelines without worrying about the autonomy and vitality of private and religious spheres. That joint ventures may involve conflicting missions is one problem. More severe is the dilemma regarding too little or too excessive accountability. For moving social provision entirely to pri-

vate settings jeopardizes accountability. Governmental accounting rules, attached to government funding, jeopardizes the autonomy of private and religious groups. New kinds of governmental
oversight and regulatory reforms, informed by other countries
with more experience giving public aid to religious organizations,
could reduce administrative burdens while adhering to vital
public values.[167] Industries and governments could collaborate in
flexible, self-monitoring regulations. There may be ways for religious providers to embrace public values without endangering
their own missions. Urban Catholic schools seem to take this path.
Most have dropped specific religious instruction and instead try
to teach tolerance and civic virtues to diverse—and increasingly
non-Catholic—student bodies.[168]

Religious providers and other nonprofits with distinctive
characters need to generate methods of accountability to offer as
viable alternatives to government regulations and professional
standards. Peer review and engaged involvement by governing
boards are two possible avenues.[169] On the specific worry that the
participation of Catholic hospitals will reduce or eliminate access
to reproductive services and end-of-life care management, political pressure and creative partition of responsibilities among
different providers looks more promising than lawsuits or direct
public regulation.[170]

Part of the difficulty in imagining new approaches grows from
the limitations of language. It is time for a new metaphor, not one
of lines and boundaries, but one of values and commitments. The
images of lines and walls simply do not describe what goes on and
therefore impair the urgent task of ensuring latitude for the private, the nonprofit, and the religious, as people work to fulfill public values, seek market efficiencies, and promote domestic peace.
A new metaphor must acknowledge how public encouragement
and support of private alternatives encompasses both for-profit
and nonprofit organizations, including religious, while at the
same time it enables observers to attend to the very different motives and interests of each domain. Notably, profit and nonprofit
undertakings both offer contrasts to government provision, but

they do so with startlingly different purposes, means, and measures of success. The new metaphor must enhance our ability to appreciate and sustain the plural associations, cultural practices, organizations, and beliefs that offer meaning and support for divers human beings. It is a distinctive feature of American philosophy to insist on plurality and the impossibility of a single frame to encompass all domains of human experience even while exploring the forms that unity can take.[171] Americans have struggled to permit a cultural pluralism that permits the preservation of each ethnic and religious group rather than a melting pot in which each group loses its distinctiveness,[172] a kind of political pluralism that makes the state simply one of many sources of normative affiliation and association, an E Pluribus Unum.[173]

Pluralism at its best generates creativity, tolerance, and variety. Making everything public or everything private, everything nonprofit or everything for profit, everything secular or everything religious would undermine these values and impoverish our lives. Yet sustaining plural sectors and activities requires delicate balancing of competing norms and methods, and rigorous internal methods of accountability for each.

After my colleague Bill Alford returned from a recent trip to China, he told me about a Chinese lawyer who agreed to an interview only if Bill would look over a contract in exchange. In the course of their discussions, it emerged that the lawyer's firm had joint for-profit ventures with a restaurant and with a local court. No hint of American-style concerns about conflicts of interest emerged. Instead, the ventures reflect China's rampant privatization drive, directing all enterprises—including the courts and the police—to become self-financing. As Bill told me the story, I shifted quickly from astonishment at that very different world to worry that ours is quickly shaping up in ways that will also render unfathomable our longstanding concerns about conflicts of interest and the borders between public and private, profit and nonprofit, and secular and religious.

A lot is happening. We *should* worry and keep in mind what really matters.

CHAPTER 3

Schooling, Welfare, and Faith-Based Initiatives

Private choice is both a slogan and a central cultural and legal value in the United States. So perhaps it is not surprising that private individual choice has surfaced as an organizing framework for important reforms of two public systems widely thought to be failing: public schooling and public provision of welfare. Proposals to extend private choice to other governmental programs invite newly intensive connections between government funding and religious organizations, as well as new markets for for-profit enterprises.[1] Private choice is roomy enough to welcome both marketplace competition and religious alternatives to public institutions. Social policies pressing private choice could enhance society's capacity to meet human needs while promoting individual freedom—but choice policies could also impair common purposes, equal opportunity, and sustainable relationships between religious and secular worlds.

For public schooling, the new, even faddish, solution is "school choice," a phrase that encompasses proposals both for vouchers to pay for private schools and for charters to start up new, entrepreneurial public schools. Under each of these plans, parents are permitted to select the schools their children will attend.[2] For public provision of welfare, the solutions already in place in federal law include both time limits for public assistance and "charitable choice." Charitable choice enables states to contract directly with private providers, including religious ones, for the provision of social services, as well as to issue vouchers to individual recipients redeemable for private assistance. Encircling both solutions is wary skepticism of public institutions and government.[3] Blamed for inefficiencies and an absence of values, public schools and public welfare need a jolt of competition, or perhaps they should be replaced by private, largely religious providers—or so voucher advocates suggest.

Reliance on vouchers for schooling and welfare indeed can promote competition, pluralism, and at least the appearance of private choice. However, such reliance risks diminishing the sense of "we," the collective to which everyone in the country should feel connected or responsible. Vouchers seem to convert public expenditures for public purposes into individualized consumer choices, and this shift to private providers shrinks the common spaces created by public schools and public assistance. Both recipients and providers can retreat from a sense of the collective good to commitments to smaller and perhaps more homogeneous groups, especially if the private providers are affiliated with a particular religious group. Even more troubling is the possibility that people who are neither providers nor recipients can come to see schooling and caring for the poor as outside their sphere of concern. Indeed, they can come not to see these increasingly privatized projects at all.

In a nation as diverse and complex as ours, the tasks of schooling and caring for the poor cannot be managed entirely, or even largely, by private institutions. Private institutions lack sufficient resources. Even if these private institutions are subsidized through public resources, they remain insufficient to promote the public purposes of social cohesion, equal opportunity, and respect for religious and ethnic diversity. Because schooling directly involves the preparation of each new generation for adult roles, concern about the large, encompassing good is vital to the establishment of public values in general. Even the provision of welfare deeply involves core values such as equal respect and individual liberty, not just for welfare recipients but also for the nation as a whole. These public values, embraced by the Constitution, require complex connections between public and private institutions, between general norms and individual freedom, and between secular and religious activities.

Paradoxically, the turn to vouchers in the current moment reflects both the triumph of the market as the preferred mode for social organization and the resistance to the market mounted especially by people attached to particular religious traditions. After exploring this paradoxical development, I will offer both legal and policy analyses of school and welfare vouchers. School vouchers are probably constitutional, but they raise troubling policy questions. On the other hand, welfare vouchers raise more thorny constitutional problems, but they may well be a good policy idea.

Whatever the difficulties of the current proposals, they nevertheless hold more promise for meeting the complex demands of constitutionality and good policy than the more simplistic alternatives for social provision. The end of this chapter sketches three simplistic alternatives that underlie policy debates: leaving each community to care for "its own," assigning responsibility for schooling and welfare support entirely to centralized government, or leaving these tasks instead in the hands of individuals and their immediate families. Each of these alternatives is unworkable, undesirable, and potentially unconstitutional. By urging resistance to the temptation to reach for simplicity, I seek to cultivate appreciation for deliberately complex solutions that combine individual responsibility with communal and governmental social provisions.

ASSUMPTIONS BEHIND SCHOOL CHOICE

When policies like vouchers emerge to alter public programs, their endorsers intend at least in part to harness the competitive efficiencies of the free market and to promote individual consumer choice. The rhetoric of competition and choice permeates reform proposals for numerous programs such as Social Security, where individual retirement accounts are the rage.[4] Choice rhetoric also dominates the traditionally public sphere of children's schooling.[5] The new ideal, at least as captured in slogans, seems to be maximal individual choice for students and parents regarding both the type of school attended and its location.[6] Schooling is increasingly viewed as a private consumption item, instead of a shared experience for children from all classes, races, and ethnic backgrounds. Decisions about schooling become a matter of consumer choice rather than citizen self-governance or public policy. Within the public school system, magnet and charter schools offer students options beyond the neighborhood school.[7] Public school systems experiment with parental choice of particular schools and programs for their children.[8] Public tax credits and vouchers stretch this expanding arena of choice even farther, so that even students whose families currently lack sufficient resources to opt out of the public system would be able to do so.[9] Fifteen states and the District of Columbia are considering additional programs to expand the school choices of either low-income parents or all parents through vouchers, tax relief, or other mechanisms.[10] The multitude of state legislative proposals for vouchers, scholarships, and tax credits to enable the selection of private schools indicates a genuine possibility of major revision in how society wishes to educate its children.

These market-based proposals seem to offer ways to cut through public bureaucracies. Business leaders and pro-market libertarians advocate vouchers not only because they believe in competition but also because they are suspicious of expansive government.[11] School choice seems to be the answer for parents and children who feel that they have had no control over what happens in public schools.[12] As education becomes ever more central to economic opportunity and job security, increasing parental choice may provide an important means of managing some kinds of anxieties about children's futures and frustration with sclerotic state and local bureaucracies. Advocates argue that by promoting competition and consumer sovereignty, school choice would force drastically needed changes and increase efficiency, even at the price of some failures.[13]

In addition, these proposals reflect growing disillusionment with public schools and increasing reliance on private and religiously affiliated schools to foster the moral, disciplinary, and group identity aspects of children's education. Although seldom discussed, the disillusionment with public schools began at just about the same time that these schools took on the task of educating all children, including those with disabilities and limited English proficiency, noncitizens, the homeless, and migrants. The rush of leaders toward choice proposals both in and beyond public schools may in no small way respond to the ambitious and troubled diversity in public school enrollments.[14]

However, the movement for school choice also finds support from those critical of market values and a secular, competitive world. Cultural conservatives of the Christian right generate one of the largest and most committed groups working for vouchers.[15] Religious leaders and others blame public schools for inculcating in children a culture of self-interest bereft of any obligations to society.[16] For some, religious values taught in religious schools can challenge the commercialization of everyday life, including the targeting of children as consumers. School vouchers thus may offer a way to rechannel taxpayer dollars to schools that instill values and discipline.

Similarly, many people criticize secular social services for failing to provide a moral framework in which to encourage more responsible behavior. The public welfare system, it is said, fails to forge social connections between those who are isolated and despised and those who are relatively comfortable and privileged. Moreover, public welfare is faulted for not respecting the individuality or humanity of people in need. To some, religious charities are more successful at inculcating values and discipline in the poor. Welfare vouchers thus provide a way to turn care of the poor over to such religious charities.

Academics and pundits, too, argue that a vital democracy depends on individuals engaging in mutual aid and recreation apart from the market or the polity. Robert Putnam's work is among the most renowned.[17] His research indicates that self-government and civic participation are closely tied to degrees of communal connection and involvement.[18] Without the kinds of ties forged by bowling leagues, volunteer groups, mutual aid societies, and religious organizations, civic engagement suffers.[19] Indeed, both Republican and Democratic leaders urge the strengthening of civil society, especially through nonprofit organizations and community groups to meet the needs of vulnerable and at-risk groups.[20]

Nevertheless, this call for more is often coupled with policies of less. Congress recently ended the federal welfare entitlement.[21] Local communities have widely rejected school levies and criticized the costliness of public education expenses, such as special education for students with disabilities.[22] Contemporary public debate thus reflects a complex mixture of confidence in market competition and efficiency, individual choice, pluralism, and private religious institutions and distrust or disdain for collective social provision. The political tilt of the voucher debates is therefore complex. School-choice policies, for example, seem to appeal to both suburban middle class parents and inner city, working class parents, who seek more control over the very different educational options available to their children.[23] School-choice programs are the perfect meeting ground for both market believers and market critics.

School choice actually encompasses many kinds of programs and proposals. Operating exclusively within the public system, choice can refer to modest opportunities for parents and guardians to enroll a child in one of a handful of specialized or "magnet" schools within the public school system. Or public school choice can refer to more ambitious efforts to disconnect residence from school assignment, such as the systemwide controlled choice plan of Cambridge, Massachusetts. In this approach, parents rank desired schools throughout the system, and a complex algorithm produces school assignments by combining private preferences with targets for racial and gender mixing, along with special weighting for families seeking to keep siblings in the same school or seeking to enroll in the neighborhood school. Choice within public systems might also involve limited cross-district enrollments, such as the Metco program offered in Boston to enable inner-city residents to enroll in participating suburban schools on a limited basis, subject to spaces in those schools.

The newest option within the public system is the charter school idea. Established by a chartering agency, such as a legislature or municipality, these independent schools are intended to operate with public funds but outside the usual regulations of the public system. Actually, the authorizing legislation in different jurisdictions varies considerably in the degree of autonomy granted to charter schools. Some schemes exempt these schools from otherwise prevailing collective bargaining agreements, curricular requirements, and spending requirements. Others impose some or all of these obligations. Typically awarded on a competitive basis to entrepreneurial groups, charters for such schools usually have a limited term. By the end of the period they must be either renewed or else terminated by the authorizing agency. Charter school arrangements also vary in the degree to which they specify how school admissions are to be governed. Some authorizing legislation does not address whether charter schools, unlike usual public schools, may select among applicants based on their abilities, disabilities, and other traits.

A different set of choice initiatives crosses the border between public and private systems. Typically using the device of vouchers, these initiatives offer public monetary payments to enable families to enroll their children in private schools. They may be given to low-income families only or to all families. One kind of program extends only to secular, nonparochial private schools.[24] Another—considerably more controversial—plan allows the vouchers to be used in any private school approved by the public agency, and these can include parochial schools. More than 3,700 students in Cleveland—about 5 percent of the public school enrollment—use public vouchers to pay for private schooling. The vast majority of these students attend religious schools.[25] The amount usually set for a voucher is insufficient to cover the costs of most elite, selective private schools, which typically charge five or six times the parochial school tuition. Instead, the voucher level approximates the tuition level set by parochial schools, a tuition level that reflects subsidies from other sources. Some parents gladly choose parochial schools precisely for the religious instruction and values they advance, others because they hope that the school will offer strong discipline or advantageous social mobility. But for others, the religious schools are simply the one available option to get children out of failing public schools.

Thus far, the scale of choice experiments is relatively modest. Yet the choice movement involves a radical challenge to the ideal of the common school that generated compulsory schooling laws during the nineteenth and twentieth centuries. As Yale University professor Seymour Sarason recently observed, "Charter schools rest on a devastating critique of the present system because it implies that for a school meaningfully to innovate to achieve more desirable outcomes, it must be free of the usual rules, regulations, and traditions of a school system."[26] In this view, the system itself is the barrier to real innovation and success. The choice movement thus represents a dramatic departure from almost all prior school reforms. Rather than aspiring to create the "one best system" of schooling run by experts and open to all children, proposals for charter, magnet, and voucher programs seek to multiply options, promote competition, and concentrate the mechanisms for evaluation and accountability in the hands of individual parents.

School-choice advocates, to varying degrees, make the following assumptions:

1. Competition will produce improvement in overall schooling; competition is well suited to the enterprise of educating children and youth.
2. Competition will generate sufficient, relevant, and comparable information for assessing the quality of each school.
3. Parents and guardians will seek out or otherwise obtain sufficient, relevant, and comparable information to enable them to make informed, responsive, and responsible selections from among schools. A sufficient number will do so, thus signaling the better choices and the better schools.
4. Good schools will attract more students; unsuccessful schools will lose students and either shut down, lose their charters, or change.
5. Competition will generate a greater supply of better schools.

Good schools will spread their methods; charter schools, in particular, will develop innovative methods and export them to remaining public schools. Effective schools will grow.

6. Competition will at the same time permit a desirable pluralism in teaching methods and in the values and traditions taught. The results will comport with American commitments to the free exercise of religion and to multiculturalism while also improving the overall quality of schooling; educational research indicates that quite different teaching philosophies can each sustain successful schools.

7. Competition will cut through burdensome public bureaucracies that stunt educational innovation and school responsiveness to parents and teachers.

Other reform efforts have not worked, and schooling is so poor that radical change is necessary, even if it jeopardizes features of the current system.

It is not just confidence in market-style mechanisms to generate quality—and the global triumph of markets—that explains the prevalence of these assumptions. Anchored in faith in consumer sovereignty, skepticism about experts, and the solution of pluralism in response to any dispute about the substantive good, these assumptions characterize what is distinctive in American political and economic traditions.

Yet there are significant gaps between these assumptions and reality. Competition may produce schools that offer superficial attractions without quality instruction. Unless admissions practices are regulated, schools are likely to skim for students based on their ability to perform on standardized tests.[27] Schools are also likely to "teach to the test" rather than provide deeper education. Schools may opt for glitzy appearances, such as gleaming computers, rather than quality instruction, which is more difficult to sustain and to demonstrate to one-shot visitors. College-level grant and loan programs have created a natural experiment showing the effects of offering school choice, backed by public dollars, and the experiment has troubling results outside elite educational institutions. Many post-secondary vocational and technical schools have sprung up; they over promise and still survive, even though students leave, because they keep drawing in new cohorts of gullible prospects. Similarly, despite bold promises, charter schools in unregulated settings have folded, especially in the less-regulated contexts.[28]

Yet not all inadequate schools close—and good schools do not easily expand or replicate. Inadequate schools often persist because of inertia. Inadequate public schools endure because of resistance to change by teachers, unions, and parents; insufficient numbers of talented teachers and administrators; and the absence of nearby alternatives. Rather than relying on competitive pressures, the Chicago public schools use a centralized administrative structure to put public schools on probation and to pair them with advisors under a tight time frame for required improvement.[29] The results there have been encouraging. In contrast, schools within a choice scheme can close abruptly with injury to children. In Milwaukee, Janita Hill School, one of the private schools funded by vouchers, closed its doors in the middle of its first year.[30] Its students were dumped back into public schools. The students returned to the settings parents had already found inadequate and suffered from dislocation and disruption to boot.

Enlarging the capacity of good schools is difficult, if not impossible, since both the scale of the school and class size are highly germane to patterns of success. The inability of successful schools to expand or scale up is the single most notable problem in prior reforms; reformers show how to improve individual schools but offer less evidence of spreading and sustaining improvement across entire school systems.[31] Schooling is a retail, not wholesale, business. Even if an excellent, replicable curriculum can be devised, the classroom teacher remains central to the student's education. The perpetual shortage of excellent teachers is compounded by the current shortage of teachers generally. Schools organized for profit are especially in danger of expanding before demonstrating success and then of cutting back abruptly as investors find the returns disappointing.

Experts predict the emergence of a two-tiered system: elite schools benefiting from competition and other schools declining in quality—but not shutting down—as their student enrollments shrink and resources accordingly diminish.[32] Diffusion of successful methods is not well demonstrated. Competition between charter schools and other public schools, and between private and public schools, presses against sharing information about what works. Changing this incentive structure and devising methods for sharing effective instruction and curricular programs could spread successful innovations, but this will require more deliberate and active effort than simply creating some choice options.

A central difficulty is the absence of reliable, comparable information about schools that are available for election. Parents use standardized test scores as the main criterion to compare schools. But standardized test scores are influenced more by parents' background and income than by the quality of school instruction. If standardized tests are the chief kind of information about school success, individual schools have powerful incentives to screen students at the admissions stage, to skim for the best test takers and to push out those who do not perform. In public systems that adopt high-stakes testing, linking student promotion and graduation to test performance, students pay the price for the failures of teachers and parents.[33] Prevalent use of standardized tests pushes competing schools to teach to the test rather than to develop inquiring, problem-solving minds capable of approaching issues with healthy skepticism—in short, to educate for the long term.[34] Deeper measures of instructional quality are costly, complex, and nonstandardized. They also take several years of evaluation to produce reliable assessments. Thus, adequate information is not likely to be available in the short term to identify quality instruction in new and expanding schools. Parental satisfaction has emerged as another measure to compare schools, but when used to assess voucher schemes, parent satisfaction levels may reflect a combination of hope and pleasure in the sheer act of choosing more than from discernment of educational quality.[35]

Comparable data is often difficult or impossible to obtain for comparative evaluations of public and private schools. Different school systems often administer different tests. Private schools have no obligation, and in fact disincentives, to share their results. Once again, richer measures of the quality of school programs are either absent or not comparable across schools. Even if adequate information were to begin to be gathered, not all parents and guardians would get it, understand it, or act upon it. Interest in becoming and capacity to serve as an informed advocate for one's children are not qualities evenly distributed among all parents and guardians. While motivated and competent parents will seek out information (to the extent that it exists) about the quality of programs, other parents will not do so, or they will be more influenced by matters of convenience (transportation, availability of after-school programs) or familiarity. The analogy to commercial markets assumes that competition among schools will engage a sufficient number of informed and motivated parents to make choices and signal to other parents so that they alter enrollment patterns powerfully enough to identify winning and losing schools. Yet the choice reforms may instead remove from existing public schools the parents motivated enough to improve those schools and disseminate messages about quality. Choice reforms may also reveal diverse parental preferences for different kinds of specialized programs rather than shared criteria for desirable schools. Law professor Molly McUsic puts it this way: "The irony of the school choice model is that it requires two components that are not in adequate supply: committed and interested parents, and empty desks in high quality public or private schools."[36]

One answer may be: Just wait long enough, and new, quality schools will start up. Yet basic structural difficulties involved in setting up effective organizations make this a remote possibility. One of the few reports on charter schools reviewed five charter schools one year after they started.[37] It identified barriers to success and implementation problems in six areas. The newly founded charter schools had difficulties developing effective school governance, particularly in defining roles and processes for decision making. Because teachers and parents often perform unfamiliar tasks in the context of a new school, role definition problems were intense. The new schools had problems creating cli-

mates and cultures of trust and respect. They also found it difficult
to devise manageable workloads for teachers and principals. They
had trouble gaining a stable financial base to cover fixed and vari-
able costs. They found themselves isolated; they found that isola-
tion hard to change. They also faced obstacles in presenting a
believable and attractive public image to outside communities.
Student diversity was either absent or a source of tension at the
schools. An experienced school researcher reviewed the report
and concluded, "The creators, the state [education department],
and the political leadership simply did not appreciate the *predictable* problems the new settings would or may encounter."[38] Ironically, perhaps, the choice movement reflects indifference to well-
documented difficulties of previous school reforms. Rather than
trying to learn from previous efforts, the new reformers want to
give people the chance to make their own mistakes.

One of the most emphatic claims by advocates for choice
is that bypassing central bureaucracies will improve schools.
Whether through charters or vouchers, or simply within existing
public schools, advocates seek greater managerial control located
at the school building level. This may bypass some features of centralized bureaucracy while opening new risks of fraud and cor-
ruption. Arizona, for example, adopted vouchers to bypass public
school bureaucracies and ended up with a full-fledged fraud scan-
dal, requiring the state to shut down schools in the middle of the
year.[39] In addition, new inefficiencies are likely to emerge, as each
school has to make budgeting and managerial decisions. There is
also the obvious danger that schools will misallocate funds by emphasizing public relations and marketing rather than programming. Devolving control to individual schools also dissolves economies of scale created in a school system. Because individual
schools will have more difficulty spreading the costs of educating
students with particular disabilities than would the system as a
whole, individual schools have strong incentives to exclude students with disabilities—or to specialize in one kind of disability,
jeopardizing the goal of inclusion and integration. (Parents who
prefer to select among private schools in finding the best place for

a child with disabilities are unlikely to secure vouchers large enough to pay for those private programs.)

The goal of promoting pluralism in teaching methods and philosophies may well be enhanced by "choice" programs. Absent some regulation, however, unregulated pluralism in education could produce self-segregation along the familiar fault lines of race, class, gender, religion, disability, and national origin. The results could exacerbate misunderstandings between groups and impede the goal of building sufficiently shared experiences, aspirations, and points of reference for a diverse society to forge common bonds. It is not just that the whole society is affected by the quality of each child's education; the whole society is shaped by the capacity of each individual to participate in their local and larger communities, to care about the good of others, and to help shape the future. Even a vision of pluralism, with mutual respect among religious, racial, linguistic, and ethnic groups, requires sufficiently common values to sustain the rights and institutions enacting that vision. Even a system of school choice requires sufficient common rules to establish eligible participating schools and freedom to move across them. The idea of choice, and the implication of private consumption, will not generate or support the necessary common institutions and values.

The fundamental assumption that competition will improve education is attractive. Competition, through vouchers or charter schools, could encourage teachers, administrators, and newcomers to schooling to innovate, to try to be responsive to parents and others who can evaluate schooling, and to develop programs with distinctive character and effective features. Yet a full-fledged market approach to schooling seems to misjudge the nature of the enterprise. Schooling has crucial features that depart from privately consumed goods and services. The choosers, or consumers, are parents and guardians, not the direct consumers. The direct users of education—children—usually are not well equipped to make crucial decisions about such important matters. The beneficiaries of education are not only the children, though. Nor are their immediate families the only ones to gain; the economy, the polity, subsequent generations, and even global relations each are linked to children's schooling.

Moreover, education has features like a public good, with externalities importantly affecting the entire population. Ensuring a good education for members of the next generation is important to the economic, cultural, and political well being of the entire society. The commitment to educating all children appeared more in rhetoric than reality until recent decades, but it has indeed come to characterize public education in the United States even more than in other nations. The capacity of schools to reach all children poses special public concern because so many children risk remaining in or falling into poverty; failing to obtain needed skills; never connecting with the political process; or drifting into crime, drugs, and violence. Students who do not learn well may become dependent on the community for support. Although a particular taxpayer may not see the direct benefits of public education today, failure to invest in universal equality schooling will affect national economic, political, and social conditions for decades. Improving the life prospects for the individual students matters to them but also matters to the rest of society, which will be affected by the students' capacities to become productive workers and responsible citizens—or instead economic failures and criminal justice risks. Creating effective, inclusive schools is a classic collective action problem, something individuals cannot do on their own that also involves inadequate information and large externalities.

Public education, furthermore, historically holds an important role in a diverse nation devoted to equal opportunity and freedom. Historians debate the core motivations behind America's public school movement.[40] Nonetheless, the basic point of the project of common public schooling in a democratic nation like ours is to forge commonality, promote civic engagement, and offer economic, political, and social opportunities on an equal basis. Academic achievement cannot be the sole purpose of schooling in a society bound more by civic ideals than by shared experiences or identities. Scholar and policy advisor Sheila Kennedy concludes:

If the "public good" requires more than the transmission of literacy and technical knowledge sufficient to support economic growth and individual self-sufficiency, if it requires instead the creation of a political community, a process of creating unum from e pluribus, then the utility of vouchers becomes problematic.[41]

Communicating the civic values of liberty, democracy, equality, and civility is as much a task of education as teaching reading and math. No less important is teaching how to take turns and respect others. The use of private, market models seems out of step with the civic demands on schooling children.

It is already an uphill effort to nurture schools as settings separate from markets with their commercial values. The entrance of for-profit school enterprises into the mix of schooling has introduced television with commercials to classrooms. Students encounter product placements—with ads for commercial products put into textbooks, cafeterias, and sporting events. Some textbook publishers follow the trend by voluntarily using brand names in their texts in order to attract student interest. Marketing experts survey children to locate the "coolest" kids and then use them to create a buzz around new products.[42] Although not caused by school choice, these developments reflect a shared trend, sweeping education and children into the ambit of competitive markets.

School-choice advocates embrace one further assumption, though, that deserves attention. They maintain that even at the risk of jeopardizing the existing framework of common schools, radical change should be explored because prior reform efforts have failed to remedy chronic public school crises. The assumption is overstated. On some measures, schools are better than in the past; there are higher graduation and literacy rates than in the past, and more kinds of students are taught more equitably in American schools today than thirty years ago.[43] Students who would have dropped out or faced exclusion from schools in the past are now often helped by special programs.

On other measures, however, there are real signs of trouble. American public schools are more racially segregated today than thirty years ago.[44] Extreme disparities in expenditures and quality mark American schools both within states and between states. The state in which a student lives has a profound impact on math achievement scores.[45] Student performance in the United States in math achievement falls below student performance in Taiwan, Korea, and Russia, although students in the United States perform better on reading comprehension evaluations.[46] Even ostensibly good schools widely underestimate their students' capacities. Many children with disabilities, while accorded rights to services and programs unavailable in the past, still fail to receive appropriate help even as disproportionate numbers of Black and Hispanic children are labeled as disabled and removed from mainstream classrooms. Urban and rural children risk spending stultifying years without learning much. Poor children of color are far more likely than white and middle-class children to fail to thrive in schools. We can, and should, do better. Hence, the energy behind the current reform movement looks welcome, and the chances that it will bring in new resources and new waves of committed people can justify at least some experimentation with reforms.

Thus, school choice looks most compelling as an idea to jump-start change. School choice is least compelling as a blueprint, predicated on faulty analogies and assumptions. Extreme versions of school choice deem public schooling a state monopoly marked by big government and collectivist (as in intrusive, anti-liberty) values. These claims distort the facts and obscure the vision of equal opportunity and civic good. Entirely replacing public schooling with private choice models looks like a big mistake, given the mismatch between the assumptions and the facts and the risks of losing at least a generation while educational institutions rebuild. Smaller experiments with choice and competition, within a broader public context including regulation and monitoring, make more sense. The project of schooling as a common enterprise should remain the norm while permitting alternatives within a generally shared rubric subject to public regulation. Limited experiments with choice within public schools and between public and private schools can enhance pluralism and justify innovation; more expansive rejection of public schooling cannot.

There is another reason that we should be cautious about large-scale school choice initiatives. Many school-choice reformers use the image of the inner-city parent, trapped in a terrible school system, and say that school choice will open up real options. Joseph Vitereritti is the school choice advocate who most explicitly pursues vouchers as a means to pursue equality; yet even he acknowledges that there is not yet evidence that school-choice programs will produce sustainable improvements in student achievement.[47]

Parochial schools are the most realistic options in these circumstances. But the number of available spaces would not accommodate all the school-aged children. Therefore, the rationale for vouchers that include parochial schools must be longer term; the availability of competition will spur changes in the public school system and improve education for all. Current school-choice reforms, to be candid, press for quality for some and assume that equality will follow.

Earlier reforms from the 1960s through 1990s, in contrast, emphasized equality as the first priority and presumed that quality would follow. Starting with racial desegregation, the push for equality expanded to gender equity, education for children with disabilities, bilingual and bicultural programs for English-language learners, school-finance reform, and even equal access to religious as well as nonreligious student activities in public school settings.[48] Each of these efforts reflects an underlying mission to ensure equal opportunities for individual students, regardless of their race, gender, disability, linguistic and national background, economic class, location of residence, or religion. These reforms extend the deep social struggles over group status and inequalities pervading other sectors of society.

People from many quarters criticize school desegregation, special education for children with disabilities, school-finance plans, bilingual education, and other equality reforms. The choice reformers do not explicitly challenge equality as a goal, but they reject the central features of equality reforms: centralized student assignment and top-down compliance mechanisms. It may be a coincidence, but the choice movement urges greater parental control over where and with whom each child will be educated on the heels of decades of desegregation orders and efforts to include children with disabilities in mainstream classrooms.[49] Whether the choice initiatives merely neglect equality goals or directly abandon them, they are flawed. Unless choice initiatives try to address the goal of equality along with quality, they will become illegitimate in the eyes of those still committed to the vision of equal opportunity through schooling. And they will likely generate yet another round of reforms. As Linda Darling-Hammond, a wise observer of schools, commented, "Schools chew up and spit out undigested reforms on a regular basis. This creates a sense within schools that whatever the innovation, 'this too will pass'—and that it probably should."[50] If school choice is to be more than a passing fad, it must address the public purposes of schooling, including the vision of equality and preparation for citizenship that schools have inspired in the United States.

WELFARE REFORM AND FAITH-BASED INITIATIVES

The 1996 welfare reform in some ways extended the 1960s war on poverty; both increased the role of private providers, using federal funds, to give job placement and education services to recipients.[51] Yet the 1996 reforms established new customs for the public/private relationship.

When Congress "ended welfare as we knew it," the Personal Responsibility and Work Opportunity Reconciliation Act of 1996 is well known for establishing time periods to limit how long recipients can receive benefits and for establishing work requirements. Yet it is landmark legislation also because it authorized the states to work far more closely with religious organizations in providing job training, welfare benefits, and related services than had previous governmental programs. This is the provision known colloquially as "charitable choice." This provision received almost no discussion in Congress or in public and media debates, which were occupied with other features of welfare reform.

The primary sponsor of charitable choice, then-Senator John

Ashcroft, stated that the provision "is intended to encourage faith-based service providers to cooperate with public welfare programs by ensuring that they will not have to attenuate or abandon their religious character or style of service."[52] By approving state contracts with religious entities—and protecting the religious character of those entities—the charitable choice provision of the law began to allow delivery of governmental services in religious settings.[53] Framed as an effort to prevent exclusion or discrimination against religious organizations, the legislation also protects the religious character of participating organizations by prohibiting the federal government and the states from requiring a religious organization to alter its internal governance or remove religious symbols or art.[54] These contracting relationships do forbid government expenditure on sectarian worship, instruction, or proselytizing[55] and also mandate that the religious freedom of individual beneficiaries should not be diminished by the private provider.[56] By selecting religious agencies for these purposes, states may not impair their religious expression or character.[57] At the same time, the provision mandates that the religious freedom of the individual voucher recipient not be diminished by the private provider.[58] The approved institutions receive reimbursement from the state for each aid recipient served.[59] The statute also allows states to issue vouchers redeemable at religious organizations.

Ideally, the provision of care by religious groups adds moral dimensions of expected responsibility and hope and facilitates relationships within which people can feel the pressure to change. Supporters argue that these relationships not only provide care and attentive connection but also offer models of the independence that can break the cycle of dependency.[60] Evangelical social ministries offer examples of the sort of work contemplated by the act. Critics question whether the service orientation of religiously based providers, operating on the implicit hierarchy of the helper and the needy, affords more mutual respect and reciprocal relationships than public service providers do. Alternatively, some may wonder whether religiously motivated employees at public agencies behave with any less caring or commitment to build a relationship within which personal change can happen than would someone working through a religious provider. Nonetheless, faith-based providers may seek to involve recipients in a face-to-face community of worship and social life, moving well beyond provisions of aid and social services.[61]

Congress has extended charitable choice to Head Start, to community services block grants, to children's health programs, and to other initiatives. While the 1996 welfare reform guarded against exclusion of religious providers from government programs, these more recent versions of charitable choice may depart from the historic practice of refusing to give government support to programs with a religious dimension. Outside the Senate floor, then–Senator John Ashcroft applauded charitable choice in the welfare law for shifting the setting of social provision from secular, public offices to religious organizations.[62] As chief sponsor of the Community Opportunities, Accountability, and Training and Educational Services Act of 1998, Senator Ashcroft announced that the law would allow "pervasively sectarian" institutions to receive public funds, while President Clinton expressed the opposite view when signing the bill into law.[63] After the change in administrations in 2001, Ashcroft became Attorney General and gained authority to implement his view while former President Clinton watched from the sidelines. But, under the Constitution, do the charitable choice statutes allow government to establish support for social services delivered intertwined with religious messages and rituals? The federal courts had used over several decades the phrase "pervasively sectarian" institution when assessing whether challenged government programs violated the Establishment Clause by directing public aid to a religious program. Nonprofit but religiously affiliated entities, such as Catholic Charities USA, Lutheran Social Services, Methodist Ministries, and Jewish Charitable Federations, epitomize the kind of organizations that are not pervasively religious and are therefore historically acceptable partners in providing secular services with government support. Because these kinds of organizations are established to operate separately from houses of worship, and because the content of the services they provide does not itself involve religious practices, instruction, or worship activities, their receipt of public dollars has not triggered Establishment Clause questions.

The charitable choice provision allows government to contract with churches and other houses of worship and protects the religious character of these organizations. By protecting participating religious organizations' religious art and symbols, and by exempting them from the federal civil rights ban on religious discrimination in hiring,[64] charitable choice approves spending government dollars on pervasively religious organizations and links public funds with the religious realm more directly than did past funding of human services. (The charitable choice provision did not relieve them from any state constitution or state statute limiting the expenditure of state funds in or by religious organizations.[65] The legislation remained silent about state and local laws forbidding discrimination on the basis of sexual orientation. As the federal civil rights law does not address this issue, it does not exempt religious entities from such bans.)

President George W. Bush wanted to take one further step by advocating for faith-based social services. Bush took his inspiration in part from Marvin Olasky, author of *The Tragedy of American Compassion*. Olasky argued that religious groups meet the needs of the poor, persons with substance abuse problems, and teens at risk of pregnancy better than government programs can.[66] Spiritual renewal can be as or more important than meeting material need. Consequently, provision of care for the most vulnerable should not be passed through the cold bureaucratic indifference of state-run programs but instead through face-to-face exchanges within a moral community. John DiIulio, first as a researcher and then as the first director of President Bush's Office for Faith-Based Initiatives, similarly emphasizes that people need caring others, not services.[67] In this view, religious organizations should not merely cooperate with government to provide social services, but replace government and its practice of dependency.

In July 2001, the House of Representatives passed the Community Solutions Act that sought to expand charitable choice to programs preventing and treating juvenile delinquency; preventing crime; and providing housing, job training, child care, community development, domestic violence services, hunger relief, after-school programs, and high school equivalency programs.[68] After the terrorist strikes of September 11, 2001, President Bush announced plans to pursue the idea of faith-based initiatives initially through tax credits while postponing the expansion of charitable choice.[69] The Senate then passed compromise legislation, the Charity Aid, Recovery, and Empowerment Act of 2002, jettisoning the most controversial features of the House bill and of President Bush's plan to advance faith-based initiatives, notably the provisions changing employment and civil rights laws. Besides offering tax incentives to spur charitable contributions, prohibiting discrimination against religiously affiliated applicants when awarding government grants, and assisting community groups in learning how to gain public funding and tax-exempt status, the Senate compromise would encourage subcontracts between large experienced organizations and small grassroots organizations. By permitting state and local governments to allocate funds to "intermediate grantors"—who in turn subcontract with other groups—the Senate bill may invite states impermissibly to delegate a government function to an intermediary religious organization. In addition, the Senate apparently leaves in place the charitable choice provisions of the 1996 welfare reform and prior social services block grants and the potential Free Exercise and Establishment Clause issues they raise. These include the scope of exemptions, if any, for religious organizations from compliance with state and local rules regulating employment discrimination, the rights of beneficiaries to avoid discrimination including denial of admission to programs supported through vouchers, and whether public funds could ever be used to support sectarian worship, instruction, or proselytizing—through direct or indirect channels of support.[70] No less important to future practice would be clarifying the requirements for audits and other accountability measures for entities receiving public funds; would the entire entity's budget require review or only those of a specific project? Direct contracts with religious organizations—even more than vouchers—generate questions about the proper lines between public and private, and state and religion, and these questions will persist as the federal and state governments explore new programs.

POLICY AND LAW

Vouchers seem to avoid some of the problems posed by direct public funding of religious activities, but they still raise questions about the relationship between government and religion and about what should be private and what should be public.[71] School-choice proposals for vouchers would allow people to elect private, even religious, schools. Public social-service programs designed as vouchers can be redeemed at private settings, including places of worship, as permitted under the charitable choice provisions of welfare reform and other faith-based initiatives. Fundamental but subtle policy and legal questions are raised in both contexts, for both involve continuities with as well as departures from past practices.

The option of private school has always existed for those who can afford it or otherwise gain access. Private schools predated public ones. The Supreme Court in 1925 rejected a complete state monopoly on schooling and required states to permit parents to select private schools to satisfy state compulsory schooling laws.[72] Only public schools received public funds; parents seeking an alternative had to pay for it themselves or find alternative forms of private aid. Experiments with publicly funded school vouchers are new and small; if they were to become widespread, they would dramatically change the character of schooling.[73] Private social services predate public ones; governments have continually contracted with private providers to assist in delivering public social-service programs. Yet vouchers introduce the possibility of government payments for programs that explicitly and specifically involve worship and other features of religious practice.

Would vouchers enabling individuals to purchase private, religious schooling and social services harmfully blur the boundaries between the public and private spheres? Would they offer more people exits from common life into private sectors divided by religion, race, and/or class? Would increasing activity by religious groups in schooling children and in providing food, shelter, child care, job-training, counseling, and treatment so alter the nation's fabric as to shrink what is public? Will government dollars go to schools and agencies aligned with some religious groups—only to alienate people not affiliated with those groups and alter the character of the nation and its religions?

The first response to such questions must be that the blurring of public and private, secular and religious, already exists throughout the United States. Private organizations, particularly those that are religiously affiliated, already play major roles in the provision of schooling, food, shelter, and social welfare services as well as health care.[74] Often such private organizations work closely with the state through contracts, reimbursement from public third-party payers, other material assistance, and referrals.[75]

Consider, for example, the roles played by Catholic Charities USA and Catholic schools, particularly in urban areas across the country. Local parishes have provided schools and assistance to the poor with no public support (beyond tax exemption) since colonial times.[76] Changing demographic patterns and the policies launched by the second Vatican Council in 1962 promoted a deliberate shift in church-run services and schools.[77] Rather than focus exclusively on serving Catholics, the services and schools now support a diverse population in need and work to advance a human society by modeling human cooperation for the common good.[78] Of course, these church-run activities may also have seeking converts as one of their goals. For many working-class people, including many non-Catholics, Catholic schools afford an avenue for educational advancement, moral development, and order in the midst of urban decay.[79] Furthermore, public school systems implicitly depend on the existence of Catholic schools to provide slots for children otherwise eligible for public schooling, depending upon the particular surges and declines in enrollments.[80]

In the contexts of child protective services, foster care, and health care, the functional and financial ties between religiously based programs and public commitments are even stronger.[81] Catholic agencies receive contracts from municipalities to provide child protective services and foster care, job training and drug counseling, and food pantries and homeless shelters.[82] Catholic hospitals serve Medicare and Medicaid patients, non-Catholic as well as Catholic.[83] Heads of public departments and agencies regularly rely on programs created and run by Catholic agencies (as well as programs created and run by other religious groups) in order to provide responses to human needs as authorized by their public mandates.[84] These programs historically have separated services from worship or other religious practices, but they have continually involved religious people in delivering publicly financed services.

Instead of trying to produce hermetically sealed boundaries between public and private, and between church and state, only to breach or ignore them again and again, it would be more sensible to determine how to allocate responsibilities in a world that continually mixes public and private, religious and secular. Indeed, partnerships between public and private already can and do enhance the actual delivery of services. Such partnerships can respect human individuality and group affiliations and also enlarge intellectual and moral resources for dealing with the potentially destructive features of global markets.

That said, the allocation question should not obscure the larger issue of responsibility. What matters is not just who delivers schooling or aid to the destitute, but who is responsible for seeing that it is actually provided. Religious groups enact their visions of responsibility, but they do not and cannot substitute for a broader umbrella covering multiple religious groups, as well as people neither choosing nor chosen by religious communities. On a more practical note, the financial bankruptcies of so many Catholic schools and agencies provide a clue as to why they cannot accept ultimate public responsibility for providing schooling and social welfare.[85] Religious leaders have been among the most outspoken in objecting to the prospect of turning social provision entirely over to private charity. Some form of shared responsibility, connecting governments with private groups (both religious and nonreligious), seems both most practical and most fitting.

But now we must face a second response to the question about the potential harms and problems of vouchers bringing public dollars to religious schools and social services. In this country, governed by the United States Constitution and its interpretation by the courts, legal constraints are vital to the acceptable methods of social provision. This means paying particular attention to the shifting judicial interpretations of the Constitution's protection of religious liberty and the prohibition against state establishment of religion.

The First Amendment to the United States Constitution sets limits on social provision arrangements involving the government. Specifically, the First Amendment prohibits the federal government and the states from conducting themselves in a way that amounts to either a governmental establishment of religion or a burden on individuals' free exercise of religion.[86] Mentioned first in the Bill of Rights, the religion clauses may overlap with but also remain distinct from other rights, including the freedoms of speech and assembly and the guarantees of due process and equal protection of the law.

Today's Supreme Court, however, must interpret the First Amendment in a world quite different from the one known by the Framers. As Justice William J. Brennan noted in 1963:

> [The] religious composition [of the United States] makes us a vastly more diverse people than were our forefathers. They knew differences chiefly among Protestant sects. Today the Nation is far more heterogeneous religiously. . . . In the face of such profound changes, practices which may have been objectionable to no one in the time of Jefferson and Madison may today be highly offensive to many persons, the deeply devout and the nonbelievers alike.[87]

Nearly four decades since Justice Brennan wrote, the nation's religious diversity is even richer, with more than 1,500 religious groups identified in a recent survey. The potential interaction between government and religion is now even more extensive. Though blatant governmental regulation of religion is unlikely today, the complex network of state and federal laws still carries great potential for adversely affecting religious exercise or preferring some denominations or sects or religion generally.

Interpreting the First Amendment has proved vexing for courts, legislatures, and commentators. Especially problematic is the relation between the commitment to guard against government establishment of religion and the guarantee to protect individuals' freedom to exercise religion. Do the two religion clauses of the amendment have independent meanings, or do they modify one another? Restrictions on establishing religion could easily collide with assurances permitting the free exercise of religion. If a state cannot close schools and businesses on Sundays or Good Friday for fear of establishing Christianity as an official or preferred religion, that prohibition burdens individuals' abilities to observe their Sabbath and their holy days. If the state cannot exempt a synagogue from municipal historic preservation codes, then public rules may infringe on a religious group's self-government. If a public school denies funding and space to an Islamic student group while granting resources to a stress-reduction meditation group, it prefers one group while burdening another. If the state accommodates the free exercise needs of a student enrolled in a public school by creating a prayer rug room, it may risk advancing Islam over other religions.

How should such collisions be treated under the law? Does the ban against establishment guard against government preference for any one religion, or for religion in general, as opposed to the secular? These questions remain open in contemporary jurisprudence, with clues provided only in the particular judgments of the courts. Simple guides or tests either fail to answer hard questions or else are easy to manipulate and unpredictable. Alternatives proposed by individual justices and scholars fail to secure widespread support and do not decide hard cases.[88] In the areas of schooling and assistance to the poor, free exercise and establishment issues often arise together and require joint consideration.

Predicting the Supreme Court's interpretation of the religion clauses is especially difficult at this moment. Recent decisions have split the Court, often yielding no single opinion even for a majority of the justices. Older judicial formulations of the relevant doctrine are in question, and no new formulation has emerged with clarity. Litigation results in high- profile cases that, if tabulated in a simplistic tally of pro- or anti-religion, yield no single trend. Nonetheless, I engage in prediction here. I also offer my own view about potential challenges to public subsidies for private religious schooling and governmental partnerships with private religious groups in the provision of welfare assistance, with a focus on the "charitable choice" provision of the Personal Responsibility and Work Reconciliation Act of 1996[89] and related faith-based initiatives.

DOCTRINAL FRAMEWORK

Despite its common use, the phrase "separation of church and state" neither appears in the First Amendment nor correctly summarizes the complex case law implementing the ban against governmental establishment of religion and the guarantee of religious free exercise. Indeed, the phrase nowhere appears in the Constitution and has never matched actual practices in this country. The much-battered doctrinal test for dealing with the governmental establishment of religion, developed in 1971 by the Supreme Court in *Lemon v. Kurztman*,[90] concedes that absolute separation between state and religious entities is not the goal of the First Amendment.[91] The doctrinal test set forth by the *Lemon* court considers: (1) whether the law or governmental action under question has a secular purpose; (2) whether the primary effects of law or government action advance or inhibit religion; and (3) whether the law or government action excessively entangles the government with religion.[92] Note how this last prong admits that entanglement of some sort is not only permitted but expected.

However, even *Lemon* has not supplied the basis for rejecting a law in over ten years, and at least five members of the Court think it should be replaced.[93] In a recent decision involving schools, four members of the Court joined a plurality decision sidestepping the third, entanglement criterion and asked instead whether the government program behaved neutrally.[94] The trend, if anything, is toward less stringent demands for separation of church and state than *Lemon* implied. For example, the Court in 1997 upheld the use of federal categorical funds to provide services on the site of a religious school to children otherwise eligible for federal services; this decision was a reversal of two prior Supreme Court decisions.[95] In 2000, the Court rejected the exclusion of religious schools from a governmental program making materials available to schools—although no single rationale gained the approval of a majority of the justices.[96] In 2001, the Court overturned a public school board's decision to deny a private Evangelical Christian organization's use of school facilities for weekly after-school programs for elementary school children, despite an Establishment Clause defense.[97]

The Court has not yet, however, fully rejected the *Lemon* test, nor has it approved a coherent alternative doctrinal framework. Justice Sandra Day O'Connor has proposed one alternative inquiry into whether the state's action could be viewed objectively as an endorsement of religion.[98] Others point to the Constitution's purpose in preventing social or political division based on religious differences.[99] Several justices have emphasized that the central goal is to ensure governmental neutrality toward religion,[100] but some have stressed that this is a necessary but not sufficient inquiry in enforcing the Establishment Clause.[101] Recent decisions have employed another aspect of the First Amendment—the protection of the freedom of speech. Under this lens, government exclusions of religious activities from otherwise available public support amount to impermissible discrimination on the basis of the applicant's viewpoint.[102] Each of these approaches suggests more leniency toward what some might view as establishment problems.

Regarding the free exercise of religion, the Court increasingly has rejected challenges framed as burdens on the free exercise rights of minority religious groups. Instead, the Court increasingly shields from challenge government action that is couched in a general form.[103] A generally framed state law denying unemployment benefits to people dismissed for job-related misconduct does not violate the free exercise rights of two individuals who lost their job with a private drug rehabilitation organization after they ingested peyote for sacramental purposes at a ceremony of their Native American Church.[104] If framed generally, a statute or rule that allegedly burdens someone's free exercise of religion now receives only minimal judicial scrutiny. Rather than ensuring the free exercise of religion, several justices make central to religion clause challenges an assessment of the potential coercion of the individual in the realm of religious belief or practice rather than burdens rendering religious practice more costly or difficult.

With less vigorous protection for the free exercise of religion and relaxation of previous Establishment Clause restrictions on public funding where religious adherents seek public benefits available to others, the Court is allowing a world with greater intermingling of religion and government support but less protection for members of minority religions, who are unable to convince majorities that "general legislation" nonetheless burdens their religions. This point may be elusive, given that the justices and advocates explain the shift in the Establishment Clause area as necessary to prevent discrimination on the basis of religion.[105]

Basing conclusions on a variety of grounds in particular cases, the Court seeks to steer a path between forbidden governmental establishment of religion and outlawed curbs on individuals' free exercise. More probative than any simple verbal formulation of the guiding principles for judgment are the actual actions taken by the Court in recent years. For example, in *Larkin v. Grendel's Den, Inc.*,[106] the Court struck down as unconstitutional a statute granting churches and schools the power to veto the grant of liquor licenses to restaurants within five hundred feet of church or school buildings.[107] In a more tortured opinion in *Board of Education of Kiryas Joel v. Grumet*,[108] the Court forbade New York from drawing school district lines to encompass only members of a particular religious group.[109] Here, some justices asked whether the government had delegated a public function to a religious group. Granting churches vetoes over liquor licenses for nearby restaurants and creating a special school district for a religiously identified community crosses into this forbidden zone.

Another line of cases deals with how much room public schools should allow for religious activities. The Court has invalidated school-sponsored prayer and religiously motivated Bible reading in public schools, at graduation ceremonies, and at sports events but has allowed the use of school facilities for religious after-school programs.[110] Additionally, monies generally available to support student speech on the campus of public universities must be available to support religious speech.[111] Student-initiated religious activities secure protection, while teachers, administrators, and commencement speakers must avoid appearing to endorse any religion.

In the context of aid to private schools, no discernible pattern has appeared in the Supreme Court's decisions affecting public financial support for activities related to private parochial schooling, and the current Court is deeply divided over how to analyze these questions. A particular tangle of cases approved some kinds of tax assistance and reimbursements for parochial school tuition but disapproved of others. Recently the Court has rejected, at least in part, some of its own prior decisions that forbade direct government payments at parochial schools.[112] Rather than forbid government assistance to pervasively religious schools, the Court has allowed governmental supply of resources, including monetary payments to sectarian schools to cover particular secular activities where the government also supplies such resources to secular private and public schools.[113] Perhaps, in the Court's view, the dangers of intergroup conflict seem more remote when religious groups are allowed to participate in universally available grant programs than when they are excluded from them.

The trend in the cases suggests that universally available assistance that does include aid to families using religious schools has a greater chance of surviving challenges. The Supreme Court has found expressly that governmental assistance that is neutral, and available to a broad spectrum of citizens, is more acceptable than programs assisting only some parents, or only parents pursuing sectarian schools.[114] Thus, public subsidies for textbooks used by students, regardless of their attendance at public or private schools, have been ruled constitutional.[115] Also passing constitutional muster is the use of public funds to support the transportation of children to parochial schools.[116] Public employees can provide remedial instruction and counseling to students on the site of parochial schools.[117] Yet, a state cannot supplement the salaries of teachers at nonpublic schools to approximate the salaries of public school teachers.[118]

The Supreme Court has moved toward permitting state financial assistance to students in parochial schools. In addition, the Court treats the private choice of parents and students as an act that severs any prohibited connection between the public funds and the religious institution. Thus, the Court ruled that a state can pay a blind student's tuition at a sectarian theological institution through generally applicable financial aid programs because the public funds are paid directly to the student, who then transmits them to the educational institution of his choice.[119] Similarly, a state may allow taxpayers to deduct from their state income taxes certain expenses incurred in providing education for their children, despite objections that this provision has the effect of advancing the sectarian aims of nonpublic schools.[120] Federal funds to assist students with disabilities, students from low-income communities, and students identified as presenting special risks of school failure may be used on the site of religious schools when they are distributed through a public agency to the eligible students, regardless of where the students choose to attend school.[121] Public provision of a sign language interpreter in a pervasively sectarian school does not violate the Establishment Clause.[122] Apparently, the Court has concluded that the parents' choice of a religious school should not deprive the student of services available to public school students. In this way, the Court has rejected broader challenges to any public dollars moving into religious schools even though such public support may free the religious school to have more resources to pay for religious activities.

The four conservatives in the present Court (Chief Justice Rehnquist and Justices Scalia, Kennedy, and Thomas) are not bothered by government support for pervasively religious schools; those in the liberal wing (Justices Stevens, O'Connor, Souter, Ginsburg, and Breyer) remain very concerned about this. For Justice O'Connor and Justice Breyer, the "swing votes" in the Court's religious jurisprudence, the interjection of private choice is vital. Where private individuals—the parents or the student —have selected the parochial school or the religious university, allowing generally available public funds to support that student's education seems different to the Court's majority than direct public payments to the religious institution.[123] It differs because the operation of individual choice makes it is less likely that anyone will perceive the government to be endorsing the religious mission or message.[124] The private choice also holds the line against direct public dollars to organizations that could divert that support to aid religious indoctrination.[125]

An unanswered question is whether the Court will maintain a line of inquiry into whether even a constitutional program that looks unproblematic on its face violates the Constitution in the manner in which it is applied. The Court provided for such an inquiry into the actual operation of a program funded by the government if, as implemented, it ended up using public dollars to pay for religious activity. In *Bowen v. Kendrick*,[126] for example, the Court rejected a facial challenge to statutory authorization for federal grants to public and private organizations, including religious ones, to assist counseling and research in the area of premarital adolescent sexual relations.[127] The Court nonetheless remanded the case for a factual finding about the actual uses of the monies and indicated that the grants might be unconstitutional if the funds assisted "pervasively sectarian" institutions or paid for "specifically religious activity in an otherwise substantially secular setting."[128] Thus, the Court acknowledged that constitutional violations could arise with particular uses of public dollars to support religious institutions, even though the Court generally permits religious entities to participate in universally available grant programs. Five members of the Court still seem concerned about public dollars becoming diverted into the religious activities of sectarian institutions, so this "as-applied" challenge could still be viable even if a general program survives constitutional attack.

The Court thus establishes that neither the mere presence of religious activity in a school setting nor the use of public dollars to pay for activity in a parochial school setting violate the Constitution if the larger context is a neutral, nondiscriminatory government scheme. The presence of public aid in the context of a religious school does not violate the Constitution. But a majority of the Court still indicates that public dollars should not be diverted into religious indoctrination.[129]

APPLICATIONS

The Supreme Court's recent jurisprudence suggests that government programs using public funds to pay religious school tuition will likely be upheld as constitutional, while government efforts to share or to turn over responsibilities in the welfare area to religious entities risk a greater chance of being found unconstitutional. The following discussion offers words of prediction and recommendation regarding both school and welfare vouchers.

School-Choice Programs
Public dollars can reach private schools through policies allowing tax deductions for school tuition and expenses, tax breaks on education savings plans, publicly funded scholarships, and school vouchers directing public funds to private schools. Because the vast majority of private schools are religiously affiliated, these programs may create impermissible interconnections between religion and the state.[130] Three cases recently considered by state courts highlight this issue. The Cleveland City School District case—which led to the first full consideration of school vouchers by the Supreme Court—arose when a federal district court in the city found the quality of the public schools so poor that it ordered the state to take them over.[131] In response, the state initiated a scholarship program to permit students to attend neighboring public schools and registered private schools.[132] Some 80 percent

of the private schools registered for the 1996–97 school year were sectarian; no neighboring public school districts participated.[133] A taxpayer group filed suit alleging that the program violated both the federal and state constitutions, and the state court of appeals agreed.[134] The Ohio Supreme Court, however, ruled that the school voucher program did not violate the Establishment Clause, except where selection criteria gave priority to students whose parents belonged to the religious group supporting the sectarian school.[135] Finding these selection criteria severable from the statutory scheme, the court rejected the remaining federal constitutional challenges,[136] while at the same time ruling that the statute violated the "one subject per statute" requirement in the state constitution.[137] This technical problem was fixed by the legislature in early 1999.[138] On August 25, 1999, a federal district court enjoined the voucher program on Establishment Clause grounds.[139] After waves of public protest over halting a school program just as the school year was starting, the district court stayed its order as to already enrolled students.[140] By then, over 99 percent of the participating students were enrolled in parochial schools. In 2001, the Supreme Court agreed to review the case.[141] Its conclusions will shape the future treatment of voucher plans across the country.

The Milwaukee Parental Choice program, initiated in Wisconsin in 1989, was amended in 1995 to allow up to 15 percent of the low-income students in that city's public system to attend private schools, including religious schools.[142] In 1995, eighty-nine of the 122 private schools eligible for the program were sectarian.[143] A state trial court enjoined the plan's implementation on Establishment Clause grounds, but the Wisconsin Supreme Court upheld the constitutionality of the program even though religious schools are the likely beneficiary of most of the public funds.[144] The United States Supreme Court declined to review this decision,[145] appearing to signal a green light to such experiments at the state level without giving explicit federal constitutional approval.[146]

In Vermont, the town of Chittenden authorized the payment

of private school tuition for its resident children in 1995, since the town did not have its own high school.[147] The Vermont Department of Education, however, disapproved of the town's plan to pay tuition to a nearby Catholic academy and threatened to deny Chittenden all educational funding.[148] The Vermont Supreme Court, declining to use an Establishment Clause rationale, ruled that the town's plan violated the "compelled support" clause of the state constitution, which forbids state support of religious worship.[149]

Given this history, as well as recent judicial decisions in religion-clause cases, I predict that courts will assess constitutional challenges to school choice by looking to the chain of decision making afforded under the program and by assessing how neutral and general is the scheme allowing monies to reach religious schools.[150] If the actual decision about where to spend the governmental money is given to private parties, such as parents and students, these programs can plausibly be understood as enhancing private choices in education rather than establishing religion through governmental means. This characterization would seem to satisfy the *Lemon* test: the purpose of promoting parental choice to improve education is a secular one, the primary effect arguably is to enhance competition and therefore overall educational quality, and entanglement between church and state can be minimized if funds pass from the state, to parents, to private schools. The state is unlikely to be viewed as endorsing religion or a particular religion when individual parents select the religious schools from a range of choices. Moreover, if these opportunities for selecting from a range of schools are afforded to all parents and students, including but not restricted to those choosing religious schools, it could not be said that the government was favoring only certain groups.[151] The legal system comfortably adopts this view about parents in other contexts. For example, a parent's decision to refuse medical treatment for a hospitalized child need not trigger any liability on the hospital because the parents make the treatment decision.

Indeed, if a state institutes a school voucher program allowing private selection of private schools, the program may be required to extend to religious schools. Otherwise, those who prefer religious schools could plausibly claim discrimination in public programs, amounting to a burden on their free exercise of religion or a violation of the Equal Protection Clause. Crucial to sustaining such claims, though, is the retention of public and nonsectarian schools as alternatives. The very success of parochial schools no doubt has something to do with their ability to select and to exclude;[152] the constitutionality of voucher plans that include such schools depends on the presence of genuine alternatives.[153] A plan that includes religious schools that select students on the basis of religion could violate the Equal Protection Clause. Surely a public voucher plan could refuse to allow use of the voucher at schools that discriminate on the basis of religion, race, or ethnicity.

The constitutional challenge most likely to succeed would attack the way in which a school voucher program is applied rather than how it is designed, but only if a majority of the Supreme Court still cares about this distinction. A majority of the Court is not likely to authorize courts to track the use of money to discern whether religious activities receive subsidy in practice. Yet a majority might well be concerned if all or most of the vouchers were used to select religious schools; especially if those religious schools were largely or exclusively of a single denomination, the voucher program might raise concerns similar to those the Supreme Court addressed in *Bowen v. Kendrick*.[154] Discerning such effects would require a factual finding about the actual operations of the scheme. Mere disparities between the number of religious schools receiving vouchers and the number of secular private schools receiving vouchers would not convince the Supreme Court that an Establishment Clause problem existed. Indeed, the Court has held that any unequal effect of a public program assisting private school choice "can fairly be regarded as a rough return for the benefits . . . provided to the state and all taxpayers by parents sending their children to parochial schools."[155] In so doing, the Court emphasized that it "would be loath to adopt a rule grounding the constitutionality of a facially neutral law on annual reports reciting the extent to which various classes of private citizens claimed benefits under the law."[156] So long as nonreligious options, public and private, remain available, providing school vouchers to help pay for religious school tuition seems compatible with the Court's emerging treatment of religion.

Conventional constitutional interpretation combines evidence of the intentions of the drafters of the First Amendment and analogies to prior Supreme Court interpretations of the amendment's Establishment and Free Exercise Clauses. Neither of these sources provides a convincing basis for rejecting public financial support for parental choice of schooling, given the Framers' commitment to education as a means for developing children's opportunity to be familiar with the Bible, as well as the pattern of Supreme Court precedents I have just described. I can imagine quite a different kind of a constitutional analysis—beyond any line of reasoning adopted by courts in recent years—that would stand back from the details of recent doctrine, and even the details of the challenged school choice plan, and ask about how the plan could affect the character of the polity and the purposes behind the Establishment Clause and the Equal Protection Clause. Such an alternative mode of constitutional interpretation would ask whether a set of social changes could so alter the assumptions underlying the context in which the Constitution operates as to place its premises in jeopardy. Under this imagined method of interpretation, television might warrant a reconsideration of what constitutes constitutional speech and political campaign practices; cyberspace might require reevaluation of property and jurisdictional rules; and the diversion of public dollars from public to private schools might require reassessment of the preconditions for a committed, tolerant, and equal citizenry. Calling for a holistic assessment of the Constitution's guarantees and preconditions, this mode of interpretation would also elevate facts about social change. How would school vouchers, redeemable at parochial schools, affect the nation's prospects for maintaining respect for religion without preferring any denomination or religion in general? How would school vouchers, redeemable at parochial schools, affect the chances that equality of opportunity would become a reality in a nation where the race and economic status of children too often predicts how long they stay in school and how well they achieve? Would allowing public funds to pay for the religious instruction interwoven into parochial schools make some families have to choose to subordinate their views on religion to their desires for better schooling? Would public aid to religious schools that segregate by religion undermine the vision of a civil society, open to all, in which schools help individuals become participants in an inclusive, tolerant democracy? Addressing these questions would be challenging, but they point to a kind of constitutional analysis that could preserve and deepen the commitments of our Constitution—and improve the chances to realize those commitments in practice. Nevertheless, no such constitutional interpretation currently guides the U.S. courts, and it is not my purpose here to propound and defend this alternative approach.

Absent such an analysis, school-choice plans can survive judicial challenge under the Supreme Court's interpretation of the Establishment Clause.[157] Then we are left with debates over policy. The courts may make voucher plans permissible; the voters and policy makers will have to decide if such plans are desirable. This raises some salient questions.

Would the inclusion of religious schools in voucher programs facilitate or undermine the important goals of preparing each successive generation for democratic self-governance and fostering the requisite qualities of tolerance, civic duty, and social cooperation? Many people think that the nation has much to benefit from private parochial schools and experiments enabling more parents to opt for them.[158] For example, a recent book argues that Catholic schools are more successful at fostering human cooperation than public schools, though public schools often were founded for that very purpose.[159] Contemporary American Catholic schools take as a basic purpose the promotion of cooperation for the common good and ground their work on a moral base with experienced teachers, communal organization, and a capacity to engage teachers and students.[160]

Yet, even if we admire the accomplishments of many parochial schools and appreciate their capacity to produce both good standardized test results and students imbued with a sense of purpose and coherent values, the mission of schooling in a democracy calls for inculcating certain public norms necessary to foster democracy.[161] Neutrality in message is neither possible nor desirable, but inculcation of the civic values of tolerance, equality, liberty, and democracy is defensible in a nation committed to and dependent upon these values. Schools that model these ideas are more likely to inculcate these values than schools departing from them. Such values are more completely modeled by the common public school, the school system intended to afford children from all walks of life equal opportunities and a shared experience, than by private, selective parochial schools.[162] Preserving the common school ideal enacts the commitment to equality and inclusion, even if a small percentage of families exercise their constitutionally protected right to elect religious or other private alternatives.[163]

Regrettably, the goal of the common school is a waning ideal, not a description of universal practice. Public schools across the country are marked by notable disparities in racial balance, and those disparities, sadly, track differences in school quality. Disparities in the quality of instruction mark divisions between white students and all others.[164] Social class and racial segregation thus impair the ideal of the common school. The real or perceived failure of so many public schools to afford genuine chances for education, especially in large urban districts, makes the turn toward experiments with competition in education a plausible, if not urgent, public policy development.[165] Unfortunately, if it relies heavily on private options rather than public charter and magnet schools, this very turn risks drawing so many students away from the public schools that the common school ideal will have no chance. New experiments should seek to strengthen, not to destroy, common public schools.

This potential dilemma points to a second policy question. Will inclusion of religious schools in voucher programs lead to such an exodus of motivated parents and children that the prospects for improving public schools will disappear? The flip side of this question is whether exclusion of religious schools from voucher programs will trap many children in failing public schools, despite the chance for a better education in neighboring religious schools. Resolving these problems involves a difficult balance of competing values, as well as conflicting views about what students and the nation need. Further, if religious schools are part of a voucher plan, how will their practices affect the socialization of children? Will the religious schools discourage enrollments of students affiliated with other religions, endanger equality norms, and invite self-segregation? Will members of minority religious groups face pressures to attend schools guided by a faith that is not their own? Or will the religious schools become so accommodating that, under public pressure, they lose their distinctive character and contribution to their own religious project?

Finally, there is the policy question of whether religious schools indeed can better educate all or even a substantial number of those who currently remain in substandard or failing public schools. It would be an enormous mistake to think that parochial schools or school-choice proposals can solve the problems of schooling for all of America's children. It is impossible to disentangle the success of parochial schools in retaining children from at-risk backgrounds and in generating good test scores from both the schools' ability to exclude and expel troublesome students and the involvement of the parents who select such schools.[166] If the competition with parochial schools is supposed to press public schools to improve, the public schools may seek ways to expel troublesome students and select students with motivated parents, as do many parochial schools. But the public schools will lack the subsidies afforded to many parochial schools through congregations or institutional religious aid or the in-kind contributions of religiously motivated teachers. And some public school still must take the troublesome students.

The belief that competition itself will elevate the quality of all schools has yet to be demonstrated. Even where all the schools are public, new charter or magnet schools do not generate improvements in all the system's other schools, although they may stimulate some changes. School systems have not found ways to learn directly from the emerging practices of magnet and charter schools, which often may have incentives not to share their strategies with their competitors. The vital ingredients of parental involvement and excitement about innovation characterize many new schools, although they do not ensure success or sustainability, or translate well into systemic reforms. Increasingly, even those "public"-choice options will include schools run under contract by private, often untested, management.[167] The deep problems of public education in America ultimately are intertwined with longstanding, complex problems in families and communities and with skewed economic opportunity structures. The immediate consequence of school-choice programs will most likely leave the most vulnerable children from the least-engaged and least-solid families in the worst schools.[168] The solution of school choice— either inside public systems or crossing over to private schools—is worth exploring in careful, controlled experiments, but only as one of many strategies to improve the real opportunities for all children.

Where pursued, school voucher plans must preserve public values in the schools found eligible for the vouchers.[169] Here, the Senate compromise in the area of faith-based initiatives provides a promising model: Allow public funds to be used by religious programs, but do not exempt those programs from public values, enacted, for example, in civil rights laws. The essence of this approach is: Public values should accompany public money. If public funding becomes available to private schools, those schools should abide by the same civil rights commitments as public schools. This means no discrimination on the basis of race—or religion. And the public aid must pay for schooling, not for religious activities. Rightly concerned about maintaining the distinction, Justice Sandra Day O'Connor asked Solicitor General Theodore Olson at the Supreme Court's oral argument whether the Cleveland voucher program made any "effort to make sure that the money that ends up in the parochial schools is not used for religious training." Even though the Cleveland vouchers go to parents who pick the schools, the city can decide which schools are eligible to receive the vouchers. Schools that will not allow students to opt out of prayer or other religious activities should not receive public aid.

Schools that find such restrictions too confining remain free to turn down public funds. Schools accepting those public funds must work to prepare students for the same academic standards set for public schools, and must share with public schools the mission of cultivating responsible and tolerant citizens. Working out these details will be challenging. The strength of many religious schools comes from their coherent mission and strong sense of community. Separating formal religious practice from other activities may not be easy, and in the meantime students may well feel pressure to participate in religious activities labeled "voluntary." But it would be better to spend our energy on these issues than on a simplistic "yes" or "no" to proposed expansions of school choice. Enlarged educational choices could help poor children and children of color gain access to better schooling and to real equality. Limiting public support so that it does not directly subsidize religious teaching and activities will keep us from sliding into a world of schools and communities divided by religion and belief.

"Charitable Choice"

The charitable choice provision of the welfare reform of 1996,[170] Head Start, and a variety of federal social service and housing programs that incorporate charitable choice,[171] look more vulnerable to a constitutional challenge, but may be less troubling on policy grounds. The portions of the provision that authorize the states to pay religious agencies directly for providing welfare services look especially vulnerable. If these services entwine religious teachings and practice with social services—rather than being simply a subcontract for secular social services—it looks like a forbidden government subsidy for religious indoctrination. The alternative device of vouchers, enabling individual aid recipients to receive welfare services from private nonprofit agencies approved by the state,[172] is less vulnerable to constitutional challenge because individual choice intervenes between government payment and religious practice. Yet the advocates' own stated purposes for the programs imply forbidden governmental endorsement of religious rather than secular programs. The conditions under which choice is inevitably exercised for those who are homeless, impoverished, hungry, or drug or alcohol-dependent do raise questions about whether the plans seek freely choosing individuals or instead seek to advance religious solutions.

Charitable choice represents a departure from previous governmental arrangements with religious entities in a number of respects that render it vulnerable to constitutional challenge. These departures involve the inclusion of pervasively sectarian institutions as recipients of public funds; the use of vouchers to connect individuals with religious worship and proselytizing in conjunction with social services; the direction, amounting at times to coercion, of destitute people to religious providers, thus interfering with their free-exercise rights; and the real risk that only an identifiable subset of religious groups will participate. Each of these features raise Establishment Clause concerns.

Pervasively Sectarian Institutions

Prior to the charitable choice reform, states and localities often used federal funds to contract with Catholic Charities USA, Methodist Ministries, Jewish Charitable Federations, and other religious organizations in order to provide child welfare services and other human services.[173] In the past, these religiously affiliated organizations provided exclusively secular services.[174] In contrast, charitable choice permits state contracts not only with religiously affiliated service providers but also with pervasively sectarian institutions, including churches.[175] Indeed, the statute explicitly directs that states cannot exclude religious organizations from voucher programs otherwise open to private providers.[176] A church itself, not merely its affiliated social service agency down the street, can receive a state contract to provide services and can be approved to accept vouchers from individuals eligible for public services. The statute also protects the religious character of the faith-based organization that obtains state contracts or receives vouchers.[177] Thus, these organizations are permitted to maintain the art, scripture, and other symbols associated with their religious order.[178] They are also exempted from Title VII's ban on religious discrimination in hiring.[179] The program's inclusion of pervasively religious organizations and the preservation of religious symbols link the public funds and the religious realm more directly than in past funding of human services.

By extending public funds to pervasively religious institutions, however, charitable choice may violate the Establishment Clause. Permitting public funds to be used directly to support religious institutions and their messages may have the appearance of advancing religion in violation of the second prong of the *Lemon* test for analyzing Establishment Clause challenges. Similarly, if the only local provider of services is a single religious organization in which prayer and other religious activities pervade its every feature, this may advance religion and present an excessive entanglement of religion in contravention of the *Lemon* test. If the organization receives public funds not by contract but instead through public vouchers, its status as the only local provider could still raise establishment concerns, for the individual choice would not determine the provider. Alternatively, each of these scenarios could also amount to a governmental endorsement of religion, running afoul of Justice O'Connor's test for Establishment Clause challenges. A federal judge recently found constitutional defects in a social service program that integrated religion and social services while receiving state and federal funding.[180]

The pervasively religious character of participating entities is precisely what commends them to supporters of charitable choice, yet this quality gives rise to an as-applied Establishment Clause challenge as described by the Supreme Court in *Bowen*.[181] Such a challenge would require a trial court to assess whether federal grants flow to religiously affiliated institutions that are pervasively sectarian. Even though four current members of the Court are untroubled if public funds flow to pervasively sectarian institutions, such a conclusion would depart from prior decisions, and five of the justices remain steadfast in opposition to this practice on constitutional grounds.

In addition, pervasively religious institutions project beliefs that may depart from public values and that enjoy protection from public regulation enforcing public values elsewhere. Particular religious views about the proper roles of women, sexuality, nonmarital parenthood, and interracial intimacy potentially diverge from public commitments to gender equality, privacy, and antidiscrimination on the basis of marital status and race. In the course of receiving help from a pervasively religious agency, an applicant for public assistance or social services may thus confront religious views and policies in direct conflict with public norms. In effect, the use of the religious agency for the delivery of services can supplant public values and erect religious ones. This could violate the prohibition against establishing religion or else heavily burden individuals' own freedoms of religious belief and practice.

Government Aid to Worship and Proselytizing
The voucher option opens up avenues for federal aid to worship and proselytizing. The welfare reform statute specifies that "[n]o funds provided directly to institutions or organizations to provide services and administer programs [under charitable choice] shall be expended for sectarian worship, instruction, or proselytization."[182] The important word here is "directly," for it leaves open the possibility that individuals will use vouchers to obtain services that include sectarian worship, instruction, or proselytization. Indeed, foreclosing these options vitiates the very argument that religiously based social provision holds special promise. Nevertheless, public dollars for such centrally religious activities would appear to advance religion and excessively entangle the state and federal governments with religion, as prohibited by the second and third prongs of the *Lemon* test. Thus, the individual who holds the voucher could be expected to pray as part of the church program; the provider-agency staff could pray over the recipient; or the recipient and staff could pray together. In each instance, government dollars would be supporting prayer.

As in the earlier analysis of school vouchers, the intercession of private choice could well immunize such expenditures from an Establishment Clause challenge.[183] The child whose parents use a voucher to select a parochial school exercises a private choice and does not thereby produce a governmental endorsement of religion. Similarly, an individual recipient of a voucher for temporary financial assistance who elects to redeem it at a local church expresses a personal, not a governmental, choice. The individual could then choose a program that includes, for example, prayer as part of the contact with the participating nonpublic agency.

Crucial to this defense is genuine individual choice, which requires both sufficient autonomy to choose and sufficient options for the choice to be meaningful. The mere fact that the matter at hand involves subsistence (as well as day care, substance abuse treatment, and other services crucial to daily survival) renders questionable the assertion that recipients are freely and autonomously choosing. Autonomous choice is in jeopardy when the individual has no money, food, or housing and is offered these necessities, which he or she might quickly refuse under other circumstances.

Consider a single mother who left home with her two preschool children out of fear of domestic violence. Upon arriving at the local church that has the city contract for providing temporary assistance, she may be too afraid to object to the religious character of the services. "Choosing" a religious provider under these circumstances may reflect duress not volition. Rather than an individual freely choosing, we would have a government manipulating and burdening the choice of the individual. Especially if any alternative program is farther away, less visible, or less convenient, a voucher recipient may end up with a pervasively religious provider of a particular denomination, despite a desire to receive help elsewhere. Faced with the power of a caseworker to deny eligibility for the voucher in the first place, a destitute and desperate person may be quite reluctant to voice concerns about the location and identity of the service provider.

Another Establishment Clause problem—the delegation of

state functions to religious groups—could arise if a state turned all charitable responsibility over to private, religious organizations and left no secular or public option. The statute in fact requires states to provide an alternative to an individual who objects to a particular religious provider,[184] but the alternative might simply be another religious provider, or even a secular nonprofit entity. The statute does not require preservation of a public governmental option. Elimination of a public, secular option for the distribution of human necessities such as food and shelter would pressure individuals toward a religious option they might not want.

The elimination of a public, secular option may be challenged as a delegation of state functions to religious groups that thereby creates an Establishment Clause problem. If a state chooses to turn all of its welfare activities over to one religious organization, this could amount to a delegation of state functions to a religious organization. Such a delegation was rejected by the Supreme Court in *Grendel's Den*[185] and *Kiryas Joel*.[186] Further, elimination of a public, secular option could expose a state to the kind of political divisiveness along religious lines that the First Amendment was meant to prevent. However, this objection could well fail to persuade a reviewing court, given the power retained by the states under the welfare statute to designate which contracting partners and organizations will be permitted to accept vouchers.

Religious Free Exercise for the Destitute
Voucher programs may directly burden the right of destitute and desperate individuals to exercise freely their own religion or non-religion, as the case may be. What if the closest provider of food and food stamps requires prayer before any food or food stamps are distributed? Even a staunch atheist who is sufficiently hungry and poor might end up praying. For those who believe in prayer, this could be a wonderful result, but it looks quite different from the perspective of one whose own beliefs take a different shape. It is possible that courts would find individuals seeking temporary public assistance, food stamps, emergency medical and disability assistance, and even substance abuse treatment vulnerable to coer-

cion, forced to engage in practices they do not support, or forced
to put aside spiritual beliefs they otherwise hold.

The statute prohibits discrimination against beneficiaries on
the basis of religion.[187] It also calls upon the states to accommodate an individual who objects to the religious character of the organization from which the individual receives benefits under the
1996 welfare reform law.[188] Notably, though, nothing in the law
requires states to notify applicants of such a right to object. The
absence of a statutory duty to tell applicants of their option to object to services provided by a religious organization reduces the
likelihood of such objections from economically and psychologi-
cally vulnerable people. The vulnerability of applicants in need of
financial assistance could profoundly affect their ability and willingness to object to the provision of aid through a particular religious organization.

An individual's freedom of religion might be powerfully constrained even by compliance with the statutory requirement that
an alternative provider be found within a reasonable time after an
applicant objects to the offer of a religious provider. If no prior arrangements have been made, it could take weeks or even months
to locate and to arrange for an alternative provider, and the state
could well characterize this as a reasonable time period. For the
destitute individual, however, the prospect of an extended wait
could lead to giving up on the objection, or suppressing it altogether, at the potential cost of conscientious belief. The secular alternative may be harder to get to or provide fewer hours of service.
Litigation may well test the amount of time that would be reasonable for providing an alternative, as well as what it would take to
make the right to object sufficiently protective of applicants' rights
of free exercise.

An Identifiable Subset of Religions

If charitable choice in practice promotes only one religion or
denomination, or an identifiable subset of religions, or even
religious organizations to the exclusion of nonreligious ones,
the program could be challenged as an as-applied Establishment

Clause violation under a *Bowen* rationale.[189] There is no comprehensive study as yet of how charitable choice works in practice,
but there is good evidence that only a limited number of identifiable religious organizations will agree to participate. The National Association of Evangelicals, for example, endorses charitable choice.[190] Moreover, Father Fred Kammer, the president of
Catholic Charities USA, has suggested that charitable choice can
help his organization in its work.[191] In contrast, Southern Baptist
Christian Life president Richard D. Land counsels against participation, because the organization's mission could be corrupted by
taking public monies.[192] Similarly, others warn that government
involvement might jeopardize the independence of a religious organization or its religious commitment to serve as advocates for
the poor.[193] Leaders of the Nation of Islam have publicly taken
this position in opposition to charitable choice.[194] The Baptist
Joint Committee on Public Affairs believes the charitable choice
provision is unconstitutional,[195] as does the American Jewish
Committee. Other religious groups may resist participation because they find the entire welfare reform problematic or even im-
moral. They can cite their already overburdened shelters and soup
kitchens as reasons to reject the premise that religious groups can
bail out the government.

If the level set for reimbursement presumes in-kind contributions by volunteers and religious congregants, charitable choice
could further sort religious groups in a predictable fashion that
would raise concerns about government preference for some
groups over others. A notable discrepancy in the types of religious
groups that seek participation could emerge. For example, store-
front African-American and immigrant Protestant churches in
urban areas are often less well off than Catholic parishes and suburban churches. With congregants struggling economically, their
time for volunteering may also be sharply limited. An as-applied
challenge could be mounted to demonstrate an unacceptable pattern of support for only one religious group or a select set of religious groups.[196] Advancing a limited set of identifiable religious
groups with public dollars and public duties would risk governmental establishment of religion and would also exacerbate community divisions over religion.

The public debate over President Bush's faith-based initiative raises the further specter of public disagreement over which religious groups should be allowed to participate. Reverend Pat Robertson surprised many when he publicly rejected the proposal because of the risk that it would provide support to the Church of Scientology, the Nation of Islam, Wiccans, and other minority religious groups.[197] Public opinion polls indicated that a majority of those interviewed would not support giving government funds for social services if Muslim mosques, Buddhist temples, or the Church of Scientology would receive aid under the program.[198] To avoid preferring some religions over others, the federal government would have to devise rules for state and local governments to guard against such discrimination in allocating contracts or approving organizations to receive vouchers. Once opened to public view, charitable choice could stir up serious conflicts among religious groups over the public dollars and over the acceptability of different religious groups.

In sum, charitable choice faces potentially formidable constitutional challenges by directing public dollars to pervasively religious institutions in a program that by design emphasizes the value of religious providers. The Establishment Clause may well find that both the contractual and the voucher versions of charitable choice unacceptably involve the government in providing public support for worship and proselytizing, that it burdens the free exercise of religion of vulnerable individuals, and that it advance an identifiable, limited set of religious groups. One federal district court in Wisconsin has already found a pervasively religious program in violation of the Constitution because the program "indoctrinates its participants in religion" and "it is not possible to isolate [religion] from the program as whole."[199] A state could also be charged with wrongly delegating a governmental function to religious groups if it turned the entire welfare task over to them. Indeed, all the points of potential constitutional vulnerability could grow larger as charitable choice is implemented. Consider the following scenarios:

> The only local provider of services is a single religious organization that requires participation in religious activities.

The only local provider of services is a single religious organization that does not require participation in religious activity, but such activities pervade every contact with the organization.

To comply with the statutory requirement of an alternative provider within a reasonable time after an applicant's objection, the state contracts with other providers or approves others to receive vouchers, but they are not located in the same town.

Individuals do not object to the religious character of the services because they are never informed that they may do so, because they are intimidated or threatened that they will not receive services if they do so, or because, like the single homeless mother of two young children fleeing domestic violence, they fear they have no alternative.

In each circumstance, charitable choice could violate both the Establishment Clause and the Free Exercise Clause. If the state directly contracts with the religious organization to provide welfare services, government funds could be seen as advancing and becoming excessively entangled with religion, and the free exercise rights of an individual applicant could be unduly burdened. If social services are redeemed on an individual voucher basis, the Constitution may afford more latitude for the governmental partnership with religious groups because private individual choice interrupts the flow of public money to religious organizations. Yet, the validity of that choice, given the individual's economic and potential psychological privation and actual set of options, could become a genuine question, exposing further constitutional vulnerabilities.

Still, as a matter of policy apart from constitutional concerns, partnerships between governments and religious organizations may offer better responses to human needs than government alone, so long as the risks of promoting a limited number of religions and burdening individual beliefs are minimized. Especially in treating substance abuse, there are impressive studies demonstrating greater success rates by groups that are either religiously affiliated or informed by religious belief systems.[200] Contracts with religiously affiliated social service agencies that agree to pro-

vide only secular service and vouchers redeemable at religious organizations that combine religion with social services could promote pluralism in the values and settings in which support can be
offered. These programs could also strengthen the work of people
who are devoted to assisting those in need for reasons larger than
a paycheck. Furthermore, religious groups helping those who are
impoverished, those who abuse drugs and alcohol, and those who
have been unable to put their lives together may be better able than
most government employees and even secular private providers to
address the individual in need as a whole person, with spiritual as
well as material needs and with the same spark of dignity as the
people offering help.

For many religiously inspired providers, it is a gift to have the
chance to help. This attitude can grace the encounters between
those who give and those who receive help with respect and atten-
tiveness. If compatible with the beliefs of the recipient, religious
messages and guidance can afford sources of strength, hope, discipline, and fellowship capable of producing long-term change in
the lives of those affected. The possibility of participating in a
voucher program could engage religious groups with people with
urgent needs and build political as well as personal support for
those who are impoverished and in trouble. It would be ironic, but
not unlikely, if charitable choice mobilized middle-class, suburban, and working-class religious congregations to lobby for a new
round of political changes supporting more substantial governmental commitments to redress the structural as well as personal
needs of poor and dependent people. Strengthening the ability
of urban congregations also to reach people in need would be
good public policy if the beneficiaries have real choices to go elsewhere.

Charitable choice holds promise if it is managed carefully to
ensure real choice and to avoid the appearance of governmental
endorsement of particular religions or of delegation of public
tasks to religious groups. Participating religious groups must
themselves be diverse, and genuine alternatives to religious provision must be available, even to recipients in rural or isolated set-

tings. In addition, it would be essential to retain public standards against discrimination on the basis of religion, gender, sexuality, and race; to ensure secular and public options equivalent in value and accessibility; and to make the exercise of such options a genuine possibility, even for very desperate people. Religious groups should not be exempted from state and local laws against discrimination on the basis of sexual orientation. Such laws are generally applicable and do not justify an accommodation under current views of the Free Exercise Clause. Injecting the federal government into the issue—and using its power to supplant state and local laws—would amount to federal subsidy for discrimination on the basis of sexual orientation and displacement of local democratic norms.

Many disagree with this position and argue instead that religious organizations should be exempted from public standards. Currently, private religious entities that receive no direct public aid enjoy an exemption from the federal civil rights employment law that otherwise forbids discrimination on the basis of religion. That exemption does not, however, extend to groups receiving public funds. Some maintain the federal law preempts any apparently contradictory state or local provision prohibiting discrimination on the basis of sexual orientation. As the exemption refers to religion, not sexual orientation, this seems at least an arguable point. Surely the exemption from religious discrimination does not protect racial discrimination, justified on religious grounds. Two senators convened a working group to develop consensus positions on these and related issues surrounding public aid for faith-based and community-based programs to address poverty and other human needs. The working group's report moves in the direction that I urge. It recommends that "[w]hen Government requires staff for publicly supported social services programs or activities to be selected without regard to religious beliefs or practices, it is appropriate that such restrictions apply to those publicly supported programs or activities and not to other programs or activities within the same organization," and "[n]o racially discriminatory employment policy should be permitted, even if that policy is ostensibly based on religious beliefs."[201] These recommendations remedy some of the problems with proposals for public funding of faith-based initiatives, although they would not guard against discrimination on the basis of gender or sexual orientation nor would they ensure secular and public options where faith-based services receive public aid. A more vigorous and complete commitment should guarantee that public values accompany public dollars even when private religious providers address public needs.[202]

At their best, vouchers for subsistence needs, social services, and schooling could promote effective partnerships between public and private sectors, between federal and local agencies, and between public norms and personal connections. In need of more intensive scrutiny is the role of for-profit providers as contractors or providers of public social services and benefits. These entities may introduce welcome efficiencies, but they may vitiate the very commitments to quality, community, continuity, and personal connection advocated by religious providers. For-profits may be helpful in a rich mix of providers under voucher schemes. The promise of vouchers, revised to ensure these dimensions of partnership, becomes apparent when contrasted with simpler solutions that underlie contemporary debates over social provision.

PROBLEMS WITH SIMPLER SOLUTIONS

As often touted in the rhetoric of private choice, vouchers create connections between public bodies and private providers. Those connections can be minimal, with the government simply serving as a pass-through agent, or they can be more complex, with the government affecting the content of programs and private entities affecting the government's priorities. The more complex arrangements may trouble people who yearn for simple solutions. Yet, this country has long rejected simple models of social provision and has embraced complex solutions that reflect its diversity and pluralism.

Consider three simple alternatives for organizing social resources to meet the needs of dependents, whether the poor or children:

Each "community" is responsible for "its own";

The largest unit of public authority—typically, the national
government—is responsible;

No one, or no one outside the immediate family, is responsible.

Implied by the contrast among these options is the persistent
debate over the causes of poverty. Does it stem from social mal-
function, from economic structures, or from character defects?
Without necessarily embracing any one of these explanations, the
options of community responsibility, governmental responsibility, and personal responsibility nonetheless select single solutions
for the complex problems of helping dependents.

The first alternative presents definitional problems—what is
a "community," and who constitutes "its own"? A community
could be defined in geographic terms, in terms of social networks,
or in terms of an affiliation with a shared religious, ethnic, or ideo-
logical experience or commitment. Society could then organize
its social provision by directing that each municipality be responsible for its dependent residents, or that each religious group fulfill
the basic needs of adults and children who are affiliated with the
religion. There can even be a combination of these geographic
and subgroup notions, as the Catholic and Mormon Churches
pursue through systems of parishes.[203] But aside from these crucial
definitional problems, this alternative reflects two deeply problematic assumptions.

Declaring that each community will take care of its own rests
on two assumptions: (1) that all comparable communities,
whether geographic, religious, ethnic, or otherwise constituted,
will perform the same roles toward dependents; and (2) that no
people will be left out of the pattern—no one will fall outside the
"our own" of some community. As an empirical matter, these assumptions are simply not accurate. Abundant historical examples
illustrate failed public efforts to require each community to care
for its own. The English Poor Laws embraced the principle of local responsibility for the poor.[204] The 1662 amendment to the
Poor Laws not only designated a period of residence as a requirement for receiving assistance, but also directed the return of a
newcomer even if he did not apply for assistance.[205] Several Amer-

ican colonies adopted versions of the English Poor Laws.[206] Plymouth, for example, ruled in 1642 that each town must support its own indigents.[207] Later, the Plymouth Colony adopted strict residency requirements and placed restrictions on bringing into town anyone liable to become a public charge.[208] Similar rules were adopted elsewhere in New England and in the Northwest Territories in 1795.[209]

Increased geographic mobility created difficulties in implementing the traditional principle that each community was responsible for its own poor.[210] Each town relied on a notion of "inhabitancy" rather than residence and used a system of "warning out" individuals lacking inhabitancy to lay the basis for removing them from the town if they became public charges.[211] Princeton University historian Hendrik Hartog noted:

> The harshness of a warning out system was presumably mitigated by the fact that some town somewhere would have to take in and care for the transient poor. . . . [B]y definition everyone had an inhabitancy somewhere, no matter how many towns from which an individual had been warned out. The problem was that inhabitancy might be virtually undiscoverable, particularly in a situation where there was no incentive for a town to volunteer itself as a poor person's home.[212]

Even people who had lived for twenty years in a town could be warned out and sent from their homes if they became destitute.

Perhaps in response to such problems during the eighteenth century, religious and ethnic groups organized charities to support primarily their own members.[213] The model of caring for the community's own persisted, but the unit for community was religious, ethnic, or in some cases occupational, rather than secular and governmental. Catholic charities emerged among Irish and Italian immigrant communities both to fulfill a religious duty and to serve as a form of mutual self-help against a difficult and potentially hostile larger world, just as other immigrant groups formed social and fraternal mutual aid societies.[214] The Italian Missionary Sisters of the Sacred Heart, for example, ran hospitals in New York, Chicago, and Philadelphia especially for Italian immigrants.[215] In general, Catholic hospitals, agencies, and schools paralleled public hospitals, agencies, and schools.[216] Private organizations also worked cooperatively with towns and counties on issues of relief.[217] Yet, these religiously and ethnically based efforts never reached the needs of all members of each group, and they never touched those who were not affiliated with groups that had sufficient resources and organization.[218] By the end of the nineteenth century, reformers criticized the reliance on a system of local charity because it defeated a principle of public responsibility and prevented the achievement of minimum standards in welfare and education.[219]

As state and federal programs developed in the twentieth century to meet the needs of indigents, localities and states increasingly set minimum residency requirements as a condition for eligibility.[220] The United States Supreme Court, however, set limitations on such residency requirements in the name of the right to travel. In *Shapiro v. Thompson*,[221] the Court rejected a one-year residency requirement imposed by local governments.[222] Similarly, the Court rejected as a violation of equal protection an Arizona statute requiring one year's residence in a county as a condition for receiving nonemergency medical care at county expense.[223] In 1999 the Supreme Court affirmed the rationale of these cases in *Saenz v. Roe*.[224] In a 7–2 vote, the Court rejected California's attempt to limit public assistance for the first year of California residency to the level an individual would have received in the state of his prior residence.[225] The Court reaffirmed a right to travel under the Equal Protection Clause, including the right to enter and to leave a state, the right to be welcome as a temporary visitor, and the right to be welcome in a new state as a permanent resident.[226] Moreover, newly arrived citizens are entitled to enjoy the same privileges and immunities as others who share their citizenship.[227] The Court thus soundly rejected the view, adopted by California, that each state should take care of its own dependents and that individuals should not be able to take advantage of higher levels of support offered in another state, at least during the first year after a move.[228]

The Supreme Court's record has been more mixed when dealing with certain requirements used to limit eligibility for public education. The Court has sometimes approved local residency requirements under the rationale that these requirements serve each state's interest in assuring that only state residents take advantage of state educational services.[229] In addition, localities typically have the authority to set tax rates used for financing public schools, thus producing dramatic variations in per-pupil expenditures across communities. This authority provides another way for local communities to express their commitment to take care of their own children, but not the children of others.[230]

In contrast, the Court has struck down citizenship requirements that limit eligibility for certain public programs. In *Plyler v. Doe*,[231] by a 5–4 majority, the Supreme Court held that Texas could not deny public education to school-age children who are not citizens or legally admitted aliens.[232] The Court found that the state lacked a rational ground for discriminating on the basis of citizenship status, noting that the children were not to blame for their presence in the United States and acknowledging the importance of education in assuring their economic self-sufficiency.[233] The Supreme Court has since refused to extend *Plyler*, emphasizing its unique circumstances.[234] Nonetheless, a federal district court recently revived *Plyler* when it considered California's Proposition 187, a voter initiative denying public education to undocumented immigrant children.[235] The court, relying in part on *Plyler*, rejected substantial portions of the proposition as unconstitutional and then approved an agreement between the state of California and civil rights groups to drop remaining portions of the suit.[236]

Thus, despite the attraction of reserving to local towns and states the primary responsibility for taking care of their own, localities and states have not been free to exclude individuals on the basis of residency or citizenship. The model of each community caring for its own has come into conflict with contemporary norms as well as judicial interpretations of the constitutional rights to equal protection of the laws, due process, and the freedom to travel. Even though majorities of those voting for state initiatives and legislation often revive the community model, hard-won and now-settled interpretations of the Constitution sharply limit the ability of states and localities to exclude individuals seeking aid.

The second simple alternative would place responsibility for social provision and education in the public, rather than the private, sector, pinning the ultimate duty on the federal government. This alternative does not require the federal government itself to create and to operate social welfare agencies, schools, food pantries, and the like. It only demands that the federal government ensure the performance of social provision and education, whether through direct service, contracts, or cooperative relationships with state and local governments, religious groups, and other private entities.[237] A paradigmatic example is Social Security, the federally administered and federal-based entitlement program for the elderly.[238] In contrast, the recent elimination of an enforceable federal welfare entitlement signals a rejection of federal responsibility for social provision for the poor.[239]

This country, unlike others, has also rejected federal responsibility for children's education.[240] It is true that the federal government subsidizes public education with specially targeted monies to assist programs for children in poverty and children with special educational needs.[241] The Supreme Court has also commanded equal availability of public education within a state that has chosen to provide it.[242] Despite this mandate, the responsibility for education has fallen mainly on the states and localities. All of the state constitutions guarantee public education for children, and school-finance litigation over the past several decades has produced court orders in some states specifying a right to an effective or adequate education.[243] Given the reliance of such lawsuits on particular state constitutional commitments, no uniformity has emerged across the nation. Consequently, massive disparities continue to exist in expenditure, quality, and opportunity both within and across the states. The democratic and constitutional processes in the country have treated federal responsibility for social provision and education as unworkable and undesirable. Indeed, the Supreme Court has construed the Constitution even to forbid state and local governments from holding a monopoly on education. Public compulsory schooling laws must permit parents to opt out of public schools for religious or other private alternatives.[244]

The third alternative—responsibility resting on no one, or at least no one outside the immediate family—leaves social provision and education to the voluntary actions of individuals. With regard to care for the poor, the homeless, or otherwise dependent individuals, this nation seems to be drifting toward this model. Our nation has rejected this model when it comes to schooling. Each state has adopted compulsory school laws and state constitutions include a provision assuring children some kind of access to basic education.[245] Therefore, at least by state law, the polity has designated public responsibility for provision of education through high school.[246] The remaining domain of private family responsibility in our system includes parental prerogatives to select home schooling or private schools, subject to the family's ability to pay or to obtain scholarships, and parental duties to supervise children's educational experiences, including homework. Preschool and post-secondary education, although publicly financed programs, can help families and individuals.

Actually, the potential exists for the third alternative to become a more salient feature of American education. As schooling moves into a more competitive model, either within the public system or across public and private options, parents are given greater responsibility for selecting schools for their children. As a result, children will become increasingly dependent on their parents' or guardians' exercising informed choices. The quality control for education then will be shifted at least partially from the public sector to individual parents. When parents or guardians lack the ability, motivation, or knowledge to fulfill this function, the third alternative, abandoning public commitment, becomes more germane.[247] Even if school choice is coupled with communal or federal obligations, such "choice" may take place in a world of insufficient numbers of quality schools, inadequate information about the stakes and alternatives, and large numbers of people unable to use the choice system effectively. This state of affairs means choice for some and not for others, and whether a child's educational needs are met will depend on his or her parents' ability to choose.

Abandonment of collective commitments is an emerging reality as welfare-reform time limits kick in and charitable responses to the needy fall short of mounting needs for shelter, food, and jobs. The hope that a growing economy would lift all boats looks increasingly unrealistic. Responses to September 11 revealed wellsprings of solidarity and rock-bottom faith in government to coordinate and backstop responses to disaster. Private charities, corporations, and religious groups stepped up admirably and immediately, although the Red Cross and other groups soon were overwhelmed both by the scale of the need and by the public demand for accountability. Hence, a complex partnership of public and private, secular and religious, nonprofit and for-profit efforts has had to emerge as the nation struggles to rebuild and heal. Moreover, the diversion of charitable dollars from other causes to September 11 needs demonstrated real limits on the sources of private giving in the country.

The other major private mechanism for social provision is markets. Advocates of school choice claim that market-style competition will favor those schools that deliver better results and that over time the bad schools will close and disappear.[248] It remains to be seen, however, if the system will work out a timely, practical mechanism for identifying and shutting down "failing" schools before their students have lost meaningful chances to receive education elsewhere.[249] Vouchers, in the meantime, may make liberty the only value—and in practice, liberty only for some. Combining vouchers with state or federal standards, however, could propel equality of opportunity as well as liberty, quality as well as choice, and central responsibility as a paradoxical correlate of local control.

As this brief discussion indicates, our country has properly resisted simple models for social provision and education.[250] We have embraced more complex solutions that combine notions of community responsibility, local government and private activities, and national standards. We should continue to do so. Voucher proposals for schooling and for charitable choice have the potential for fostering combinations of religious and secular providers in a general scheme of social provision. Public dollars can be accompanied by basic public standards to protect against the abandonment of each person and family, left always to provide for themselves. This political moment holds rich promise for reinvigorated public conversation about meeting human needs as federal governmental commitments decline. Religious and other private groups have always helped to meet the basic human need for food and shelter of people at the economic margins; they have also developed some of the best schools for children. As public welfare ends, the steadfast commitment of many religious groups to the poor and to children is notable and commendable. But religious groups cannot fill in the holes of a gouged public safety net; nor can they develop the capacity to educate all American children. Religious provision can never substitute for secular alternatives or ensure by itself fulfillment of public norms of equality and fairness.

How should we promote productive connections between religious providers and governments? Most helpful now would be enlargement of the commitment both within communities and within the nation to meet the needs of those who are impoverished, drug or alcohol dependent, or out of work and those children who are stuck in poor-quality schools. This calls for work internal to religious communities and localities but also for a public, civic space to connect impulses of compassion with democratic and constitutional norms. To this end, we need to conceive of partnerships and coordinate efforts to enhance the actual delivery of services and schooling, to enlarge respect both for human individuality and for vital communities of faith and tradition, and to strengthen intellectual, moral, and political resources to deal with the potentially destructive features of global markets.

Assigning exclusive responsibility for schooling and social services to governments violates constitutional protections for free exercise of religion, as well as good sense about the value of pluralism and the quality of programs infused with religious commitments.[251] Yet, abandoning to either private communal groups or individual families all responsibility for schooling and social provision is also unwise and contrary to commitments to equality, fairness, and individual dignity. A more complicated set of partnerships between governments and private groups, mixing public norms and individual action, may be less elegant. But it is more likely to preserve and to promote the crucial purposes of private choice, religious and ethnic freedom, social cohesion, and equal opportunity and respect across religious and racial groups for both men and women.

Pluralism, maintained consistently with and through public norms, can promote individual freedom, equality, and mutual respect among different groups. This nation has embraced pluralism nurtured by and conditioned upon guarantees of individual freedom and equality.[252] This pluralism must make room for entities, such as schools, social services, and providers of basic human needs that are religiously affiliated, but also for similar entities that are not religiously affiliated. This kind of pluralism should guard against the governmental establishment of religion and preserve free exercise of religion for individuals; it should also afford resources for critiquing and monitoring state alliances with global market forces. A robust independent sector and vibrant religious communities are thus worthwhile not only for their own purposes and for the immediate good they do for others, but also for nurturing values and relationships of care and responsibility, independent from the government and also from the market. Fostering public and private cooperation, where compatible with the Constitution, can promote mutual aid and preserve the distinct contributions each kind of entity makes to the needs of the poor, of children, and of the larger society.

Michael Ignatieff's exquisite book, *The Needs of Strangers,* captures two crucial yet potentially conflicting insights for societies that mean to be democratic, pluralist, and decent. Ignatieff first notes that "[w]e need justice, we need liberty, and we need as much solidarity as can be reconciled with justice and liberty."[253] Nations such as ours rightly endorse and celebrate liberty and justice as primary to human society.[254] Rights for individuals afford chances to break away from inherited social stations, as well as opportunities to challenge exclusions and degradations based on religion, race, or other traits.[255] Liberty and equality should guide political structure.[256] This includes religious liberty and freedom from discrimination on the basis of religious affiliation—or non-affiliation.[257] Alternatives that subordinate liberty and equality to solidarity, or any other purpose, are worse and undesirable.[258] Social solidarity too often comes at the price of foreshortened liberty, equality, and justice for the variety of human beings.[259] Even if it were possible to arrange a world in which "each community cared for its own," the enforcement required would constrain individuals intolerably.[260] Therefore, only the forms of social solidarity compatible with these watchwords should be promoted in constitutional democracies.[261]

Yet, here is Ignatieff's important, additional insight: "It is because money cannot buy the human gestures which confer respect, nor rights guarantee them as entitlements, that any decent society requires a public discourse about the needs of the human person."[262] The welfare systems that many democracies have produced are demeaning and inadequate; too many public schools across the nation deserve the same adjectives. Neither money nor entitlements administered by a bureaucratic state can guarantee the basic human needs for respect, care, connection, and genuine opportunity to flourish. Placing primary responsibility for those in need with the national government is highly unlikely to achieve these goals. Nor, of course, would abandoning all public responsibility for those in need. It is important to resist the faulty assumption that local, private (including religious) initiatives can or always will afford the human gestures that confer respect and also the basic social provision that is necessary for the destitute to survive. Choice might help improve schools and services, but not if exchanged for the public norm of equal regard.

The movements for school choice and for charitable choice

reflect the admirable belief that we can and therefore must make better schools available to more children and provide more meaningful public assistance with strong community ties. These movements also embody fair criticisms of too many schools and too many social service programs as dehumanizing and incompetent. However, general norms should remain to guide local schools and human services. Ultimately, it is a collective responsibility to ensure that no one is abandoned to starvation, privation, or to a dead-end, dismal school.

Even with the best motivations, private groups, including religious groups, can demonstrate biases against individuals or members of other groups. They can perpetuate longstanding lines of exclusion or degradation on the basis of race, gender, or religion. They can leave untouched or exacerbate legacies of intergroup conflict and stigmatized group memberships. They can fail to build sufficient capacity to reach all with comparable needs. More basically, beyond including private religious groups as options in the delivery of education and human services, the shift to choice may come to mean shedding public responsibility for social provision. This would be a costly change, potentially devastating to the very fabric of society. Even individually attractive choices cannot add up to a shared context for pursuing the common good. Without that shared context, there is no setting for debating what everyone deserves, no method for ensuring that choices are real for everyone, and no coordination of the information and accountability standards, which private individuals and groups cannot ensure.

The push for using public dollars to pay for private and religious schools poses a challenge to the shared context that connects private and public lives. Although the commitment to pluralism, religious freedom, and parental rights has long promised parents the authority to opt out of the common public schools, that option has remained until now just that: an alternative, leaving in place public schooling as the norm. Only the public schools have received direct public support, although nonprofit private schools remain eligible for the more modest assistance of tax exemption and incidental aid for transportation and books. The current school-choice movement calls for directing the funds set aside by society to educate youth outside of this public system. Channeled by parents to a variety of schools of their own choice, the funds may not, in the eyes of the courts, violate the existing constitutional scruples against direct public aid to religious schools. Nevertheless, this very channeling dismantles the idea of a common school, open to all, capable of integrating students from a variety of backgrounds, and committed to inculcating a shared American tradition. However elusive that ideal has been—given racial and class segregation and implicit preferences for particular versions of the American tradition—the ideal itself has both symbolized and fertilized the shared context that binds diverse Americans together. Without that ideal, the prospect for a common language and for a public domain in which citizens grapple to frame the common good becomes far less certain. If private schools join as partners in fulfilling this public mission—and abide by public values in so doing—the ideal would not be jeopardized. But that is not the dominant argument for school choice plans, which instead focus on academic achievement.

The injection of private religious options into the delivery of welfare services is perhaps less worrisome because food and shelter, job training, and drug treatment do not hold the place of civic and cultural meaning that schooling does. Here the risk lies more in unwitting, or witting, exclusion and coercion that violate the freedoms that have inspired the nation.

Recognizing the power of policy arguments for school choice and charitable choice, I do not think that constitutional law should prevent small-scale initiatives in these directions. These areas need experiments, new ideas, and renewed commitments. However, the details of any initiatives will profoundly influence the prospects for commonality, respect among different groups, and inclusion. To ensure continuity with public norms, four kinds of federal and state regulations should frame any options that become eligible for public funds in the contexts of schooling and welfare reform.

First, no private school or program should be eligible for payment through public dollars or vouchers if it excludes individuals on the basis of race, religion, ethnicity, or nationality.[263]

Second, any religious school receiving public funds or vouchers must engage in educational programming to address the legacies of intergroup hatred and conflict and to promote tolerance and respect across religious, racial, and ethnic groups. Such programs should include not only in-class curricula but also extracurricular music, sports, or other activities directly connecting students with peers from other schools of different or no religious affiliation. Here it would be important that students from different schools join in the same teams, orchestras, and theater groups—not merely participate in opposing or competing groups—so that students have the chance to work together on common projects and to get to know one another in that context.

Third, neither charitable choice nor school voucher programs should be allowed to eliminate a genuinely accessible and attractive secular option for people who do not want to deal with a religious provider of services or schooling. Schools receiving vouchers should also work to ensure that government funds do not pay for religious practice.

Fourth, all participating programs and schools must supply comparable information to watchdog and public groups to permit comparisons of their operations and outcomes. These requirements offer a minimal guard against segregated, self-confirming enclaves and the erosion of the shared public space necessary to a complex, pluralistic society.

Although some private religious providers may find these conditions too intrusive or onerous, they can always opt out of participation. Moreover, none of these conditions dictates how a private entity should run its services; they simply identify basic criteria for eligibility.

Would such requirements be politically feasible?[264] If adopted, would they be capable of being carried out? These are fair questions that I hope will be aired and addressed if religious groups and others participate in a broad public debate about how to arrange for social provision in a pluralist society committed to tolerance, liberty, and equality. That debate could, and should, be informed by the failure of simple solutions and the efficacy of complex ones.

Initiatives that work involve complex mixtures of resources: public and private, federal and local, professional and lay, legal and cultural. Consider, for example, Head Start. A federal program with roots in the religious activism of communities of Southern women, Head Start has always combined federal and local norms as well as federal and local representatives.[265] Mandated roles for parental involvement make Head Start an unusual but intriguing example of the way in which national law can support structure, enabling people to provide care and encourage respect for those who are otherwise constructed as the needy. Public and private agencies collaborate in training, delivery of services, and evaluation. There is nothing simple about it, yet it is widely viewed as successful across the country, with long-term studies attesting to its benefits for participating children and adults.[266] Another example is the Indianapolis Front Porch Alliance.[267] The city, led by a Republican mayor, initiated work with community organizations and religious congregations to create a kind of "civic switchboard connecting private and appropriate public resources with grassroots leaders" to meet community needs while helping to shape values, to instill hope, and to honor virtue.[268] The city's public role involves monetary support and symbolic endorsement, as well as matchmaking and information-sharing.[269] As a result, the community organizations and religious groups reach far more individuals—not merely those whom they see and identify on their own—because the government has engaged, and enhanced, but not displaced these local and rooted resources.[270]

Perhaps there is some comfort in messy realities that defy simple models.[271] Ours is not a nation that has ever abandoned, or is ever likely to abandon, the complex mix of authority, responsibility, and community found in the parallel realms of the public and private, the religious and secular, the local and regional, and the state and federal. In responding to the poor and in educating children, ours is a complex and untidy system. As Henry S. Kariel said in 1961 in *The Decline of American Pluralism,* "America, it would seem, is miraculously both singular and plural, organized and scattered, united and diffused."[272] Can this complexity be preserved alongside commitments to justice, liberty, and as much solidarity as is compatible with each? Can our traditional pluralism be strengthened by collective discussions of human need? The public square should be filled with people with boisterous, conflicting views about how to address these questions. Decisions on schooling and services for those in need deserve democratic deliberation and public attention. This is not merely a matter of private consumption. Public debate on the issues should also sustain and deepen the commitment to enlarge the "we," the sense of who is in this life together and who is within the ambit of concern and the community of participants. Ensuring this is the challenge of the current moment.

CHAPTER 4

Medicine and Law:
Profits and Prophets

"Nothing is more important than your health." "Law is the civil religion of America." The familiarity of these sentiments helps explain why medicine and law assume such importance as vehicles for meeting basic human needs in this country—and as vital missions of government, nonprofit organizations, for-profit enterprises, and religious entities. The enormous challenges of meeting the health care needs of every person and implementing their legal rights, protections, and punishments certainly make room for a variety of providers. Government has never been and probably never could become the sole or even primary provider or funder of health care and legal services. Yet public values, including fair access and fair treatment, demand attention even if the providers of health care and legal services are private. How can the demands of public values be addressed when providers are organized to make profits, to serve their own boards or constituents, or to advance a religious mission?

Recent developments in medicine and law involve greater scope both for profit making and for religious organizations and values. It is a good time, therefore, to consider how these shifts affect access, fair treatment, and liberty for disadvantaged people, and the prospects for democratic participation.

Profit-making entities and religious and nonprofit organizations offer distinctive strengths in delivering health care and legal services. Can governments learn from them and work with them while preserving the neutrality, independence, and public values of the state? Public values here include access for the poor to health care, to legal services, to liberty of choice over reproduction and end-of-life matters, to due process protections in dispute resolution and incarceration, and to democratic participation. How are these values faring, and how can they be advanced amid privatization, profits, and religious values?

These questions should not be new to anyone who knows about health care in the United States. Health care delivery is largely done by for-profit and religious organizations. Yet these institutions vitally depend upon public financing through public health insurance, public research funds, and publicly subsidized professional training, as well as private employer-based insurance, which is itself supported through governmental tax policies. Because employer contributions to employee health insurance are exempt from federal income taxes, the government has massively subsidized health care in the United States.[1] Public dollars support health care through veterans and military hospitals and health services; block grants to the states for maternal and child health, mental health, and other programs; state and county hospitals; and most important, federal Medicare (for retired and disabled persons) and state and federal Medicaid programs. For those whose income is below specified levels and for members of families with dependent children, public dollars from Medicaid programs regularly pay for care in private settings, whether they are nonprofit, for-profit, religious, or secular.

The daily mixture of public dollars with religious and for-profit health care is a long-standing and uncontroversial reality. This provides a striking counterpoint to current concerns about such organizations in schooling and welfare. The contrast deserves some attention and helps to highlight differences across fields of social provision, historical accident, and the contours of our nation's commitments to equality and individual liberty.

Privatization and the growing presence of religion also characterize developments in law and affect access to legal services and the shape of legal institutions. Legal services for low-income and impoverished people are often vital if they are to obtain or keep housing, employment, public benefits, and custody of children; legal services are also central to protecting people charged with criminal offenses. The public institutions of courts and prisons are resources for all people in advancing and exemplifying public values. The emergence of for-profit prisons and private dispute-resolution organizations are the most visible elements of the increasing privatization of previously public legal institutions. Private dispute resolution on the civil side offers an alternative to the courts. In a variety of decisions, courts have also made it more difficult for people to have access to the public court system when their employers or partners have required them to sign agreements to rely on alternative dispute-resolution techniques. Although these developments potentially offer efficiencies and innovations, they also may jeopardize public values of equality, due process, individual liberty, and democracy. There are risks to public values from shifts in the provision of both medical and legal services.

PRIVATIZATION AND MEDICAL CARE

Health care can be provided by private religious and for-profit entities; that is how the medical profession and hospitals developed. In addition, the enormous public insurance programs of Medicare and Medicaid each assume and support the market-driven structure of health care delivery in the United States, while public regulation surrounds both insurance and private health care delivery. The heavy use of public insurance dollars in religious hospitals, nursing homes, and other health care facilities generates no legal challenges grounded in the Establishment Clause or concerns about separating religion and state, while public vouchers for religious schooling generate vigorous objections.

Is there an important difference between governmental payments through insurance for individuals receiving services at religiously affiliated hospitals and government payments through vouchers to individuals receiving education at parochial schools? The first is uncontroversial while the second is highly debated. The difference lies more in the apparent consensus around the science of medicine and dissensus around the values and modes of education and socialization than in the concerns about apparent governmental endorsement of or entanglement with religion. In both instances, the money is directed to individuals who choose where to go. The integration of religious values in education may make government subsidy appear to more directly aid religion than it does when subsidizing medical care in many religious hospitals. Similarly, some would view the provision of welfare and social services in religious settings as more likely to engage individuals' beliefs, relationships to others, and relationships to faith than provision of medical services in religious settings would. But the presence of crosses and other indicators of religion imbue the atmospheres in each setting; nursing staff at religious institutions pray at the bedside. As a matter of logic, though, it is not obvious that there should be strong constitutional concerns about establishing religion regarding school aid or welfare but not regarding health care.

Provision of health care does not merely offer a contrast to debates over schooling and welfare provision. In health care, changing relationships between public and private, for-profit and not-for-profit, and secular and religious dimensions affect the prospects for the public values of equality, liberty, fairness, and democracy. Restricted access to health care for those who cannot afford it and who are not eligible for public health insurance jeopardizes the public values of antidiscrimination and personal liberty. This jeopardy affects not only the poor, as defined by official public criteria. Often, people priced out of the markets for professional services and yet ineligible for assistance to the most impoverished face even greater difficulties. Religious providers committed to meeting the needs of the poor and uninsured cannot match the need and, for religious reasons, may decline to provide particular medical services.[2]

Increasing privatization of the already limited number of public hospitals and responses to increasing market pressures by private hospitals risk diminishing care for those who are uninsured. Most hospitals in the United States are organized for charitable purposes as private nonprofits, but an increasing minority of hospitals have converted to for-profit corporate form.[3] For-profit hospitals are less likely to value provision of care to the poor and more likely to seek to minimize the amount of such provision.[4] Therefore, the switch in organizational form has implications for public values, even though it may not generate public debate or involvement. For-profit hospitals make money more by efficiently billing and exploiting loopholes in public insurance reimbursement.[5] Even if conversion to for-profit status does not significantly diminish quality or provision of care for the poor, the movement toward for-profit status does not begin to remedy the massive gap between health care provision and health care need.

Payment for health care remains largely in the private sector through private health insurance. The nation's reliance on employer-based health insurance has always left the unemployed at risk. Yet three-fourths of all uninsured adults are employed; because they work for small firms, or part time, or in agriculture or construction, they do not receive health insurance through their workplace.[6] In 1999, 42.1 million Americans were uninsured. Estimates in 2001 peg the uninsured nonelderly at one out of every six persons.[7] Uninsured adults are likely to have no ability to see a physician when needed; nearly 70 percent of those in poor health reported in 1998 that they had not seen a physician in the previous year, because of the cost.[8] One quarter of long-term uninsured people did not receive a routine checkup in the previous two years despite being in high-risk groups.[9] States with higher rates of uninsured individuals tend to have disproportionate numbers of low-income, unemployed, Hispanic, and immigrant residents.[10]

In the past, uninsured people have depended upon charitable care and public aid. Charitable care is shrinking in scope as public hospitals privatize and as private hospitals reduce their willingness to provide unfunded care. The tumult of economic reorganization in the health care industry over the past two decades has not only shifted the identities of the providers but also jeopardized the already slim public commitments to serve the poor and uninsured. Religiously affiliated hospitals maintain commitments to serve the poor and uninsured, but they cannot meet the large-

scale need. In addition, their own missions in many instances lead
them to decline to offer certain kinds of health care services. This
is exemplified by Catholic hospitals, which do not offer reproductive and abortion services. Some medical care professionals' own
religious beliefs affect the scope of care they are able or willing to
provide. Privatization and market-based pressures, combined
with religiously based restrictions on the kinds of care provided
charitably, can seriously impair access to preventive care, treatment, and palliative care and yet do so subtly, invisible to public
scrutiny. Increasing privatization in health care threatens already
limited access to health care for the uninsured, and religiously inspired missions cannot and should not fill in all the gaps. Thus, the
numbers involved are too large for private charities to address, and
the gaps produced by the religious teachings of those offering
charitable care reflect failures of public commitment, not short-
comings of the religious providers.

Medicaid is the country's largest means-tested program for
financing health care, and it both assumes and supports the market-driven structure of health care delivery in the United States
while also trying to meet an apparent market failure.[11] It has
helped reduce infant mortality and improved child health for low-
income children.[12] Because Medicaid provides insurance coverage for indigents, many people are neither poor enough to qualify
for this nor able to purchase private insurance.[13] Some efforts to
expand Medicaid to cover low-income working families have become federal law. Programs to extend public health insurance to
uninsured children have had some success, with a decline in the
share of children who were uninsured from 15.4 percent to 13.9
percent between 1998 and 1999.[14] This is the result of deliberate
efforts by state and federal governments to build on Medicaid, the
major public program for assisting low-income individuals with
health care financing.[15] But continuing implementation problems
mean that many of those eligible still do not receive insurance
coverage.[16] Many people who leave welfare for work have been
dropped from health care programs even though they remain eligible for them.[17] Low-income adults without children remain

largely unable to obtain insurance through employment or purchase. Frances Miller explains:

> As America moves even further into a non-unionized, small-business, service economy in which health care coverage is less likely to be provided as an employment benefit, and as health insurance premiums continue their dramatic escalation in cost, this group finds it increasingly difficult to afford private insurance.[18]

So what are the options? Universal, state-subsidized health care is politically infeasible whether or not it is wise. Forgoing health care altogether is a major option pursued by many low-income people. Uninsured people typically forgo regular check-ups and preventive services. They tend to wait until problems arise—and uninsured people are hospitalized at least 50 percent more often than the insured for avoidable hospital conditions such as uncontrolled diabetes and pneumonia.[19] Many uninsured people depend on public hospitals, which are required to serve those who cannot pay, and on charitable nonprofit hospitals, which receive their charitable status in exchange for a promise to serve those in need. Hospitals organized by legislation to serve as public entities typically have general duties to serve the poor. Charitable nonprofits receive their status by filing with the state a mission statement, such as assisting poor people who need medical treatment. Legal rules over time have diluted the requirement to serve those who cannot pay. Nonprofit charitable providers now must only report on how they have fulfilled a community-benefit requirement.[20]

Beyond these obligations of public and nonprofit charitable entities, the responsibilities of hospitals to serve the poor are quite limited. A common law doctrine and federal statute require facilities that offer emergency care to provide stabilizing treatment regardless of a patient's ability to pay.[21] When public and charitable nonprofit hospitals privatize, their commitment to serve those who cannot pay may diminish or disappear. Hospital privatization studies provide an overview of the significant scope of privatization activity, even though there are conflicting data on the effect of mergers and conversions on the availability of charity care. Indeed, scholars disagree over the rates and patterns of mergers and purchases of nonprofit hospitals by for-profit buyers.[22]

Even if the numbers are disputed, privatization and consolidation have characterized the hospital world over the past two decades. Take rural public hospitals, the chief source of acute medical services in rural areas.[23] Since the 1980s, many have closed, converted to provide only subacute care, or become privatized. For the rural poor and elderly, transportation to other facilities is difficult or impossible. As a result, these trends sharply reduce long-term access to health care services for these rural populations.[24] A reorganization of a public hospital into a private entity may provide greater efficiency and flexibility, especially in purchasing and personnel policies. Although this change opens up venture capital sources, it forgoes the ability to impose a tax to support operating expenses and to issue tax-exempt bonds for capital improvements. It also diminishes public control and public accountability.

Some states have explored lease arrangements through which the private entity agrees to fulfill the public commitment to the indigent.[25] One court, in a strikingly restrictive decision, rejected a plan by a nonprofit hospital to lease its facilities to a for-profit hospital corporation and apply the proceeds to create outpatient medical clinics for the poor on the grounds that this departed from the charity's incorporated purpose in maintaining a hospital.[26] Other courts have been more willing to allow nonprofits to explore leasing options.[27]

Those public hospitals that do not simply close or shift focus but privatize may do so by selling their assets, contracting out management or other tasks, or merging with a private entity. A state may by statute require that any private entity assuming control over public hospital assets continue serving those who cannot pay, but how will the private entity pay for such services?[28] The assumption that private entities can produce sufficient efficiencies to cover services for those who cannot pay is not established in fact, and the effects of private competition on providing care for those who cannot pay is especially uncertain with regard to quality.[29] Arrangements to privatize public hospitals may be challenged in court, and courts may require some degree of continuing public oversight of transferred public assets.[30] Plans to care for those who cannot pay must be made before the conversion of a public hospital into a private one, but figuring out how to ensure financing and quality of care is precisely the problem.

Similar difficulties accompany the conversion of charitable nonprofit hospitals into the for-profit form. Most hospitals in the United States are organized as nonprofit, tax-exempt organizations. Yet between 1970 and 1995 about 7 percent of the nearly 5,000 nonprofit hospitals converted to for-profit status.[31] The numbers may seem relatively modest and the rate of conversions has tapered off, but in the affected communities, the transformation can be severe, for the conversion often sharply diminishes services for those who cannot pay. Raising separate concerns, buyers or executives may abuse their position and strip or divert the assets, further limiting the availability of care to those who cannot pay.

What devices exist for public involvement in conversions of not-for-profit hospitals into for-profits? The chief option is oversight by state attorneys general under state trust law and corporate law.[32] In addition, as with conversions of public hospitals, conversions of nonprofits into for-profits can be challenged in court under state laws that govern incorporation and charitable trusts. State courts, interpreting trust law, may declare that nonprofit hospitals cannot switch missions as they became private.[33] Although this might seem a way to protect access to care for those who cannot pay, sticking to a narrow mission may impair such access if assets must be used for expensive, hospital-based care rather than less expensive clinic care or health-promoting subsidies for housing, nutrition, and education.[34] One observer notes that the cost of providing nonurgent care in an emergency setting is almost twice its cost in a nonemergency setting.[35] Yet review of a proposed conversion does not permit the state attorney general to push for the most rational way to redeploy assets to meet health care needs. Instead, attorney general review—the only legal check—is essentially limited to requiring continuation of the prior mission as outlined in the founding documents.

An attorney general may push for provision of charity care by the newly formed private entity as part of the agreement to sell the assets.[36] Yet there are problems here, too. When it comes down to enforceable agreements, the parties may not agree to do more than ensure the access to emergency care services required by law, or they may agree to goals that are so general that they are unenforceable. For-profit hospitals in some settings already claim to meet their charitable duty through videotapes and pamphlets.[37] Actually, charity care may be less of a problem than meeting the needs of the uninsured, most of whom are employed, or providing access to preventive care. Even a firm, enforceable commitment to maintain the preexisting level of care for those who cannot pay can be counterproductive if it hampers the ability of the new entity to raise capital.[38] Reformers suggest that adopting laws creating tax exemptions or other incentives for provision of charitable care by for-profit health care providers could help.[39]

In addition, some states have closely monitored conversions that created foundations formed with the proceeds from the privatization.[40] The foundations then are designed to aid health care, sometimes for charitable health care purposes. This device can preserve some resources for increasing access to health care for those who cannot pay, but the resources often can simply be spent on medical research and education rather than providing for those who cannot pay.[41] One reformer urges the creation of foundations dedicated to uncompensated care.[42]

Without imposing regulations preventing conversions, greater transparency and disclosure would enable meaningful public debate about the complex relationship between public regulation and health care finance. The Treasury Department has concluded that the value of the tax exemption to nonprofit hospitals exceeds the costs of the uncompensated care they provide.[43] If this is the case, why can't the nonprofits stay in business? And if privatization looks appealing, maybe it is because of this kind of valuation.[44] Then the duty to continue to provide uncompensated care should be required of the private, for-profit converted entity.

Concern over the medically uninsured takes us to hospital privatization and to the highly complex processes, largely veiled from public view, that diminish the already limited avenues for medical care for uninsured people. In the absence of vigorous public oversight, democratic debate, and movements for reform, access to medical care becomes even more difficult for those lacking insurance or resources. Yet the very way that privatization occurs—through the technical operations of for-profit entities with minimal public review—restricts the prospects for any public oversight, democratic debate, and movement of reform.

Opening access to insurance for those who make too much for Medicaid but too little to purchase private insurance would be a more direct and more easily described political initiative. But because this idea would shift costs to a public program, and hence to taxpayers, this route is even more politically difficult than pressing for public scrutiny of privatization. Another approach would develop ways to combine public and private underwriting of the safety-net providers of care to the uninsured.[45] New political coalitions would be needed to make sure that the public debate on health insurance addresses access at least as much as it attends to capping costs. Some observers see grounds for hope in the Oregon health plan, too easily described as a rationing plan, which has triggered sustained political attention and enlarged public commitments to expand coverage.[46] Oregon's plan seeks to provide cost-efficient and comprehensive health care to a broad range of uninsured people.[47] Working mainly to reimburse fee-for-service managed care, the plan increases eligibility for Medicaid and until 1996—when the federal government declined a state request to waive relevant Medicaid regulations—required employers to make available the basic Medicaid health care package to workers who are not entitled to Medicaid. The Oregon plan includes mental health and chemical dependency services, but through managed care practices, excludes coverage of some expensive treatments.[48] It faces practical implementation problems, such as flawed screening and budget shortfalls that require limitations in coverage and controversial state-set prioritizing of reimbursable care.[49] The plan has succeeded in expanding enrollment in Medicaid and over time has expanded the services that are covered but has failed to fully reach those who are working but not insured. The state's definition of services that deserve reimbursement generates criticisms that it is a rationing plan relevant only to the poor and a clumsy tool often out of step with best clinical practice.[50] It is certainly an experiment worth watching, for it demonstrates how rationing health care reimbursement can be an alternative to excluding large numbers of poor people from access to any insurance coverage. Yet the Oregon plan has not triggered a wave of similar reforms. Finding ways to engage and sustain public attention to health insurance and health care will remain especially difficult because it so often involves technical language and choices that can obscure the impact on access issues.

PRIVATIZATION AND LEGAL SERVICES

Access to law means access to lawyers and paralegals. It also requires entrée to dispute resolution institutions, including courts, administrative agencies, mediation services, and other alternative dispute processes. To be comprehensive, legal representation should also encompass lobbying and testifying in legislative settings and addressing the media on legal issues. That is what large corporate law firms offer their clients: full-service representation before any venue where the clients' interests may be advanced or hindered. Few individuals without lots of money can hope to find access to that kind of legal representation.

Delivery of legal services to all but the poor has been handled through private attorneys who at least hope to make a profit. Yet public rules governing awards of attorneys' fees to winning plaintiffs and class action suits, and private norms, such as pro bono service by the private bar, have commingled public and private dimensions to enhance access to legal services. So the very rules enhancing legal services are often accompanied by tight restrictions that may themselves jeopardize public values. Assessing the impact of these developments on the public norms against discrimination raises questions about the racial and gender impact of the current arrangements.

Competitive pressures within the private bar, as well as changes in rules governing attorneys' fees and class action suits, restrict the already limited access to legal services for those who cannot afford to pay for them. Experiments have also pressed for competition among private attorneys for public legal services dollars. Public provision or subsidy of legal services has never met the scope of the need. Less than 1 percent of all attorneys are legal services attorneys who provide free services to eligible persons.[51] This means there is one lawyer for every 9,000 persons eligible under the law, and one lawyer for every 14,200 poor or near-poor persons.[52] Legislation authorizing public provision of legal services imposes firm restrictions on the scope of advocacy that can be funded,[53] and private attorneys who offer pro bono services are typically ill-equipped to undertake, and fund, long-term advocacy in litigation and legislative settings.

Thus, privatization affects access to legal services in ways that are both less and more subtle than similar trends in medical services. Less subtly: for twenty years, federal subsidy of legal services for the poor has been a political tug-of-war, and budget cuts have sharply reduced funding, services, and the numbers of people who can access help.[54] The imposition of managed care on Medicaid is somewhat similar, but there the policy is to develop pressures to contain costs in the service delivery process, not to reduce absolutely the dollar amount of public commitment. Between 1980 and 1998, the budget for the Legal Services Corporation fell $21 million in non-inflation-adjusted dollars.[55]

Changes in market pressures, billing and compensation methods, and the ethos of private law firms are subtly shrinking the "public" commitments of the private bar.[56] Somewhere in between subtlety and bluntness are the limits on judicial awards of attorneys' fees, mandated use of alternative dispute resolution, and class action suits.

Public provision of legal services has developed through three obvious routes and three less obvious ones. First, the obvious: Under constitutional law, as initially established by the Supreme Court in the 1963 *Gideon* decision, individuals facing loss of liberty through criminal sanctions are entitled to public provision of legal representation—and the states and federal government have to come up with a way to meet this requirement. By statute, the Legal Services Corporation subsidizes legal assistance for eligible indigent individuals, and other public and private funds contribute to this cause as well. And by tradition, the bar's public service commitment admonishes lawyers to offer some portion of their time to pro bono service.

Each of these avenues commingles public and private commitments. The constitutional mandate to provide legal services to criminal defendants facing loss of liberty enables a court to appoint an attorney. But the courts do not have authority to conscript an unwilling attorney to perform this service.[57] These attorneys can be private individuals who sign up as volunteers for court appointments, and they can serve purely as volunteers or receive a minimal statutory fee and reimbursement for out-of-pocket expenses.[58] The statutory fee, of course, requires legislative action and appropriation. The attorneys can be salaried public defenders who receive their support from public funds. Either way, the attorneys often forgo income they could generate with fee-paying clients, so donation of attorney time is involved alongside public dollars.

Legal aid can be provided in both civil and criminal matters by salaried attorneys who are paid through a mix of public and private funds. It is the federal source of funding—through the federal Legal Services Corporation—that has attracted intense political fights over the past twenty years. In fiscal year 2000, the corporation's federal funding was cut from $400 million to $300 million.[59] Legal services offices engage in triage. Nonemergency matters—including housing, child custody, public benefits—get deferred or never served. Legal services offices in some communities must be staffed by attorneys who visit part time from other communities; others close down.[60] In community after community, legal aid for the poor has been reduced despite unmet needs.[61]

There remains the traditional pro bono service expected of all attorneys. While the pro bono duty predates the other two avenues, its insufficiencies helped to create them. Pro bono services have always been limited because they are not mandatory;[62] even if they were, pro bono legal assistance does not only serve those who cannot pay but any cause or client whose representation can be seen as offering a public service. For many attorneys, the pro bono obligation has a religious as well as a professional source.[63] Yet the competitive pressures at law firms have made it more difficult for many attorneys to find the time for pro bono services or to get their law firm's approval for spending much time on it.

There are three less obvious but still potentially powerful forms of access to legal services. Attorneys' fee rules and practices, such as statutes directing the losing party to pay the fees of the winning party and contractual contingency fees, give attorneys incentives to offer services because they can share in the client's success. Reducing the formality of the conflict resolution procedure—using mediation or small claims court rather than standard litigation—can expand access to dispute resolution for those without lawyers by offering methods that a layperson can navigate, although a lawyer's advice may still be very helpful. The aggregation of individuals' claims, in class actions and administrative processes, permits consideration of claims that individuals acting alone could not pursue because they could not afford legal representation. Aggregation allows individuals to pool resources or makes it attractive for lawyers to pursue the case because contingency fees or statutory fee-shifts become large enough to warrant their time. Through aggregation, individuals may get help as part of a larger group or as beneficiaries of decisions affecting others.[64]

Yet emerging restrictions on access to lawyers and legal remedies appear in each of these contexts. The Supreme Court has found no barrier to settlement offers that involve a waiver of the statutory attorneys' fee—and lawyers would be duty bound to recommend such settlements if they benefit the client.[65] States have considered and some have adopted caps on attorneys' fees in some contexts.[66] Contemporary arguments for tort reform— pressed largely by corporations—have helped to generate caps on damages, which in turn cut contingency fees and therefore the willingness of attorneys to take such cases.

Alternative dispute-resolution mechanisms such as mediation, and even small claims court, may open avenues to dispute resolution procedures for people who cannot afford lawyers—but people often find that lawyers are crucial even in these settings. Especially when the other side has a lawyer, proceeding without one can produce serious disadvantages that even rise to unfairness. Small claims court, intended to operate without lawyers, can disadvantage individuals who appear against banks and creditors that are much more familiar with the process. Indeed, banks or corporations often appear in small claims court through a "highly trained non-lawyer employee while the other party navigates the judicial system alone and for the first time."[67] Observers have identified systematic abuse of indigent parties when lawyers for the other side seek to negotiate with the unrepresented individual even before he or she gets into small claims court.[68] Working through small claims court and mediation, people who lack resources may feel pressured into compromising their rights or the claims they could have preserved if they had access to legal help. Some courts have pressured women to mediate family law matters even in the face of evidence of domestic violence.[69] In recognition of the inherent unfairness in this situation, some jurisdictions have barred mediation in criminal cases involving family violence, yet similar dangers arise in mediating any civil case.[70]

A troubling development is a recent Supreme Court decision upholding employment contracts that make signing away access to court over employment-related disputes a condition of employment. The agreement requires employees to submit employment-related disputes to arbitration even though the arbitrators often work regularly with the employers and provide lower recoveries than would juries.[71] By ruling that employers can require employees to sign such agreements, the Court significantly curtailed access to the kind of public justice to which employees would otherwise have recourse. Informal mediation with hospitals can raise similar concerns when the hospital provides the mediator—and the mediator then appears to be or actually is biased in favor of the hospital.[72]

Aggregation devices have also met resistance and curtailment. Courts and legislatures have made class action suits increasingly difficult to pursue, especially in the context of consumer and tort claims.[73] Plaintiffs' lawyers have nonetheless explored new routes for aggregating claims by going to state instead of federal court and by exploring techniques other than class actions for combining many small claims.[74]

A profound limitation on individuals' abilities to be heard and to enforce legal rights can arise with the privatization of governmental programs and services. Many legal protections, such as the Due Process and Equal Protection Clauses of the Fourteenth Amendment to the Constitution, apply specifically and only to actions by the government. Even if the financing of a service remains largely or nearly exclusively public, if the provider is private, due process and equal protection claims do not apply.[75] Sometimes, courts are willing to view even private contractors as fulfilling state functions and acting under color of state power and therefore liable for violations that would arise were they state actors.[76] Courts have imposed some public obligations on private prisons that are working under state contracts, for example.[77] Once over the hurdle of establishing that the private contractor is engaging in state action—and thus is subject to constitutional norms—there may even be greater liability for the private institution than for a public one, which would have recourse to certain governmental legal immunities.[78] Yet whether and when private institutions are responsible under constitutional and other public obligations remains a complex and unsettled legal question, which affects the degree to which the private institutions feel obliged to live up to those standards. Decisions to allow private contractors to deliver public services—including prison medical care, welfare and food stamp distribution, and legal services for the poor—raise matters of public concern and yet remain largely shielded from public scrutiny. Articulating enforceable standards of care within government contracts with private providers would be a vital way to protect individuals,[79] and yet this too remains typically outside the purview of public debate or participation.

New forms of privatization jeopardize realization of legal rights as older mechanisms for facilitating access to lawyers and courts and law enforcement face new restrictions. These shifts occur through decisions that are often veiled from the public or made in small steps, rendering them nearly invisible and removed from public debate or accountability. Access to the means for enforcing legal rights becomes constrained even as the forces limiting access to the law remain obscure and unaccountable to those most affected by them.

PUBLIC AID AND THE NEED FOR PARTNERSHIPS

Public aid might seem to be the ultimate answer to meet the needs of those who cannot pay for health care and legal services. A serious, steady, and substantial public commitment—one that may be fulfilled in partnership with private providers—would reflect my own judgment of what a rich society like ours owes to those who cannot secure medical and legal services for themselves.

What may be surprising, given this judgment, is how much private partners can and should supply to this solution. For, as a practical matter, reliance on the public entirely is inadequate. It is also undesirable. Reliance on public support is inadequate, practically, because it will not be enough and because struggles over the scope of public aid to the poor pit competing visions of the good against one another and against individual liberties.

To be concrete: Medicaid will not cover family planning advice that includes abortion as an option, and the Supreme Court has ruled, in *Rust v. Sullivan,* that this political decision does not violate women's rights or discriminate unconstitutionally among viewpoints.[80] The government—acting on behalf of the public and reflecting political debate and compromise—can choose what to fund and what not to fund. This is a practical reason why it is inadequate to rely on the government to meet the medical needs of those who cannot afford to purchase insurance or services. It leaves the vulnerable to the vagaries of politics. And it makes their exercise of their own rights contingent on government largesse.

Intriguingly, the Supreme Court came out the other way in 2001 in a seemingly parallel case involving legal services. In *Legal Services Corporation v. Carmen Velazquez et al.,* [81] the Court considered a challenge to conditions imposed by Congress on funds used by Legal Services Corporation grantees. Congress had prohibited legal service providers that receive federal funds from initiating any form of legal representation involving an effort to reform federal or state welfare systems. The Supreme Court overturned the congressional restrictions on the grounds that the program was intended to subsidize legal services, not a governmental message, and the legal services lawyer speaks for the private client, not for the government. Foreclosing the kinds of speech and activities lawyers can pursue for their clients might interfere with the lawyers' performance of their duties, distort the legal system and the functioning of the judiciary, and interrupt ongoing representation of clients.

Perhaps the Supreme Court rejected this congressional restriction and not the one limiting Medicaid funded family planning because members of the Court understand law better than medicine. In the decision affecting lawyers, the Court reasoned that "the statute is an attempt to draw lines around the LSC program to exclude from litigation those arguments and theories Congress finds unacceptable but which by their nature are within the province of the courts to consider."[82] A comparable sentence easily could be drafted regarding the restriction on family planning advice at issue in *Rust v. Sullivan*. How about: "The statute is an attempt to draw lines around the Title X family planning programs to exclude from medical and family planning advice those options Congress finds unacceptable but which by their nature are the province of patients and their health care professionals to consider"? But such a sentence seemed beyond reach. Hence reliance on public provision—whether as a legislative matter or even as a matter of judicial review of legislative choices—is simply inadequate.

Private provision—through philanthropic, voluntary, religious, nonprofit, corporate, for-profit, joint venture, or other alternatives—can fill gaps that public provision cannot or will not reach. But an overarching framework of public obligation remains vital to make sure public norms of nondiscrimination, fairness, and pluralism are preserved in efforts to meet the needs of those who cannot pay for themselves. Public obligation in this context should not be viewed as something the government has imposed on the rest of us. Instead, it is the expression of collective commitment, organized through government—and potentially involving both governmental and private actors.

Over the past two decades, most debates favoring collective commitment and public values have lost to arguments for privatization, subcontracting, and market competition. Market ideas and privatization have affected medicine and law in ways that affect discussions of public duties, redistribution, public benefits, and service to those in need. John Donahue, a professor at Harvard University's J.F.K. School of Government, deems it a mythology, which points Americans to "market solutions to public problems, from providing housing to improving education—especially with a fumbling, inefficient governmental program cast as the alternative."[83] The myth of market solutions may be tempered somewhat after September 11. Calls for public funding and federal oversight of airport security after that national tragedy may make some room for similar arguments in other areas of human need.

Health care and legal services should rank high. Reinvigorating public debate and mobilizing support to extend health insurance to the uninsured, to protect existing rights, to open courts to those who cannot afford lawyers—these are worthy, even urgent goals. But even explicitly and unabashedly public and governmental strategies will not be enough. We cannot leave the needs of those who cannot pay to the vagaries of politics and to the preferences of those who can command legislative and judicial majorities. We need public and private partnerships to ensure access to health care and legal services to meet unmet needs, to generate innovation, and yes, to challenge inefficiencies.

But even highly mobilized and coordinated public and private providers of, and contributors to, medical services and legal representation will be insufficient to meet the scope of the need. Access to these services reflects deeper issues, issues that come to the fore if we seriously examine public values. For law and medicine are themselves means, not ends; improving access for the poor should not be only to these means but to the ends of justice and health. As Larry Gostin wrote in his 2000 book, *Public Health Law,* "Medicine is only one contributor to health, and probably a relatively small one at that. Virtually all of the national health expenditures (excluding environmental funding) are devoted to medical care; only a tiny fraction is allocated to population-based public health initiatives."[84]

An equally emphatic argument can be made that law is only one contributor to justice, and we should approach population-based justice initiatives very differently than one-by-one reactions to illegalities and conflicts. How many landlord-tenant conflicts could be avoided if housing and safety codes received better public enforcement? How much family violence could be averted through serious and sustained educational, social, and religious campaigns against it? We should each remain mindful of the profound social changes needed to produce better ground rules that will enable just and more effective social preconditions for health, even as we seek to expand professional assistance for people in the world as we have currently made it. Improving access to medical care and legal services is only one dimension of the effort to address basic human needs.

CHAPTER 5

"A Daring System"

It should not be controversial to insist that public values follow public dollars. When the government funds programs, the government should be able to set terms and conditions. Not only does this match the age-old idea that "he who pays the piper calls the tune," it also fulfills the particular trust granted to government to act on behalf of—and with the resources of—the community. That trust must not falter when the government chooses private social service agencies, hospitals, schools, prisons, or mediation programs to carry out the work it funds. The widespread practice of government contracting for services, in particular, should not exempt the resulting activities from adherence to public values, even if it may remove them from the specific supervisory techniques governing work performed by government employees.[1] Even a government agency that gives a private entity by contract the power to decide which other private groups should deliver local health and human services should retain, within the government, responsibility for the resulting practices.[2] Yet it is often difficult for governments to set precise contractual terms to measure performance by private contractors in a meaningful way.[3]

Matters become more complex when the government chooses to fund or subsidize private choices. Then, the public trust is fulfilled in part by returning choices to individuals. Yet vouchers should not relieve the government of its entrusted duty to advance and protect public values. When the government gives individuals vouchers, they are redeemed for services at sites approved by the government. The resources are still public: financed by the community and allocated there rather than elsewhere. The structures surrounding a voucher scheme are also public, because the rules govern where a welfare or school voucher can be redeemed.

Even more subtle links between government and private choices arise when tax credits and tax deductions are the tools used by government to accomplish policy goals.[4] Should the money saved by individuals through these public policies be deemed "public money," appropriately tied to public values, or simply treated as the individual's own money, sheltered from taxation? This question stumbles into a territory of political and academic debate, yet all that is necessary is to recognize that it is a governmental decision how to sculpt the tax deduction or credit and hence which public values follow the resources that result. Public rules govern what kind of investment or charitable contribution receives a tax credit and what kind of nonprofits can receive contracts with state and federal authorities. Even the ultimate mix between public and private, religious and secular, profit and nonprofit reflects ground rules established and maintained by government. The public dimension of these ground rules reveals public power to influence nonpublic matters—and public responsibility even in the patterns that do not overtly reveal it.

Demonstrating this public dimension means that the government should be held responsible for the consequences of contracting with a publicly traded corporation to run a state prison, for example, or permitting redemption of vouchers for welfare benefits through Lutheran Charities. Privatization in many ways expands rather than contracts the government and yet risks removing governance activities from public scrutiny and accountability.[5] Expanding government also jeopardizes the integrity and autonomy of private, especially religious, efforts, and thus potentially violates public commitments to protect religious freedom. Thus, ensuring accountability faces three difficulties: the usual problems of implementation in line with goals, the special prob-

lems of respecting private freedoms while pursuing public purposes, and the emerging difficulties of generating sufficient visibility in public/private relationships to permit public oversight.[6]
We are all responsible, and we must all be permitted to join in evaluating the content and application of public values that should
apply when government and private groups work together. The
difficulty of our current moment is the invisibility of the decisions
that shape this work. Rendering greater visibility to the decisions
joining and blurring public and private, religious and secular,
profit and nonprofit institutions and sectors has been a central purpose of this book.

PUBLIC VALUES

The problem—or the opportunity—comes with defining the
content of public values. I have pointed to several candidates for
such values, and I will advocate them here. But two of them
underscore why my list cannot and should not be conclusive. The
first is the value of democracy. In a democracy, no one person can
or should define public values. They must emerge from debate and
deliberation in public settings that allow mutual education and
accommodation. They must be open to revision and critique.
Hence, my list is one of many contributions to what should be a
vigorous exchange, over time, in legislatures, school board meetings, Internet chat rooms, union policy committees, religious organizations, newspaper opinion pages, and dinner table conversations.

I defend a second value that also demands viewing all my other
statements of values as partial and tentative. That is the value of
pluralism. By this, perhaps not surprisingly, I mean many things.
Many philosophers have insisted on the plurality and distinction
of things and the impossibility of a single law or frame for encompassing all domains of being, even in explorations of unity.[7] This
philosophic pluralism is related but not identical to the norm of
pluralism I advance here, a norm that acknowledges that the state
is only one association to which a person belongs and from which
a person finds meaning.[8] As Harold Laski and Robert Cover have

suggested in different ways, the state is only one among many sources of ideas of right and wrong. A similar idea, though couched less as a description of our human condition than as a normative position on the nature of moral truths, takes the appellation "moral pluralism." Under this view, there is not a single good for every individual or a common measure for evaluating all that is good, but it does not abandon an ethical commitment to identify conditions and actions that should be viewed as objectively good or bad. Another way to pursue this notion would emphasize that although there are some practices that are wrong and unacceptable, there remain many kinds of practices that could be right.

Finally, pluralism can refer to the persistence of different ethnic and religious groups within a society, groups that maintain distinctive identities while shifting and influencing one another over time. One could value this variety for the richness of life experiences it permits or because of more particular assessments of the virtues of different cultures. Or one could instead stress the values of toleration and mutual accommodation either as virtues in themselves or as practical solutions to the risks of antagonisms framed in group terms. Mark Moore, director of Harvard University's Hauser Center for Nonprofit Organizations, points out that "[r]eligious participants in public debate must recognize that they lack absolute moral authority over the view of others."[9] The plurality of our worlds counsels similar advice to secularists as well. To fulfill their own commitments to tolerance and skepticism, and to manage, realistically, in a world of differences, secularists should recognize that they lack absolute moral authority over the views of others. Thus, there are plural reasons to respect pluralism. Embracing this value makes my own statement of additional values tentative, subject to reflection in light of the views and responses of others.

With this preface, a list of basic values deserving public endorsement and enforcement can be identified and defended as guides when government and private groups work together. Their sources lie in American legal and political traditions. They are, of course, contestable both as generally articulated and as interpreted in particular contexts.

First on the list is *individual freedom of belief and expression*. This includes religious and political beliefs and the opportunities not only to hold and express them but to hold and express them without coercion or systematic pressures to give them up. Individuality and conscience deserve respect as the fundamental sites of liberty and as the necessary source of and restraint against collective power. This value supports the provision of social services, health care, legal services and education by people who engage in those activities as part of their religious or political commitments. Effectiveness in secular terms may pale in importance to religiously inspired educators and service providers given their conceptions of more eternal goals.[10] But if they receive public aid, the freedoms of those on the receiving end (for example, welfare recipients, subsidized students) also must be respected and protected.

A second value is *government neutrality toward religion*. The government should not use its force or resources to elevate one religion over others or religion over nonreligion; doing so endangers individual freedoms, jeopardizes equality, undermines pluralism, and invites intergroup conflict. Accordingly, it would be permissible for a government to contract with religiously affiliated providers of social services only if such contracts are open to all bidders—including any religion and those without religious affiliation. If public subsidies through vouchers or tax benefits are available to parochial schools, they must be available to all parochial schools and also to nonreligious, nonprofit schools.

Third, there is *the rule of law*. This encompasses procedural opportunities for a fair hearing by an impartial decision-maker when governmental authority is involved in dispute resolution, for example, and opportunities to enforce existing legal rights when the government contracts with private providers to run prisons. The rule of law also represents the commitment to treat like cases alike and to be governed by rules rather than by personalities. It guards against whim; it promotes respect for public order; and it implements the commitment to fairness.

Fourth, there is the value of *freedom from discrimination, exclusion, or inferior treatment on the basis of race, national origin, language, gender, disability, religion, or sexual orientation.* To be treated the same as anyone else would be treated under similar circumstances: this is what fairness, respect for individual dignity, and commitment to overcome and prevent mistreatment on the basis of characteristics beyond an individual's control means. Government should ensure freedom from discrimination, exclusion, or inferior treatment on the basis of race, national origin, language, gender, disability, religion, or sexual orientation when it provides schooling, health care, and legal and social services. These same values should proceed when the government subsidizes or collaborates with private providers. There may be reasonable arguments about what implementing this commitment entails. Separating men and women for drug treatment may well not be discrimination; the programs should be comparable, but not identical, as it makes sense to devise special programs that accommodate pregnant women or women caring for young children. These issues can be worked out in specific contexts, subject to challenge as part of public accountability. Public commitments against discrimination should extend to those who are employed to provide the services or programs when government pays for or subsidizes them. Religious providers who disagree with these principles should not seek or receive public subsidies.

Fifth, we have *provision for basic human needs.* In a land of great wealth, there should be no one at risk of dying for want of food, shelter, or basic health care. In the domain of politics, the first obligation should be "to avoid extremes of suffering."[11] This is not a call for direct governmental provision of food, shelter, or health care for all people. More sensibly, legal rules and government structures enable the development of economic, social, and cultural institutions that make it possible for people's needs to be met by themselves or by others. Legal rules and government structures—including those that affect private markets—should be assessed at least in part by this measure. Religious and voluntary efforts bring many vital ingredients to the task of meeting basic human needs, but perhaps none are more impressive than the motivation to go beyond the call of duty.[12] Where the basic building blocks of society—including voluntary and religious efforts— leave identifiable people in desperate circumstances, with their basic needs unmet, government should provide for them, directly or by fixing the institutions and practices that have produced that circumstance.[13] Whether governmental administration is the best way to alleviate poverty or accomplish other social welfare goals is quite a separate question from whether these should be public commitments.[14]

The sixth involves *respecting pluralism*. As explained earlier, this value has many different rationales, whether they stem from tolerance and respect, skepticism about singular truths, or the practical desire to avoid antagonisms. It can also advance competition and innovation as religious and other groups offer different kinds of schooling and services.[15] Pluralism can justify creating rules that allow private organizations latitude to opt out of public values so long as they do not seek public dollars. Pluralism can also accommodate private organizations that want to avoid dependence on public funds in order to cultivate their own members' commitments or to remain free to vigorously criticize public policy.[16]

Here, it is useful to see a continuum of potential relationships between government and private groups. On one end of the continuum would be government bans or prohibitions, as with criminal sanctions for criminal conspiracies. A bit farther along the continuum, the government allows the group activity but does not subsidize it in any way; there is no exemption from taxation, for example. In this context, the expression of public values chiefly takes the form of permitting the activity, even if it does not advance public purposes, and prohibiting it only if it offends criminal prohibitions. Even farther along the continuum, the government subsidizes the private activity through tax policy, by exempting the activity from taxation and by allowing tax deductions or credits for contributors to the entity. Such tax policies express and implement public values, even if they leave to private individuals the choice whether to donate to the entity. Next on the continuum is governmental approval of the group or activity as a locus for redemption of government-funded vouchers for particular services. Because individuals choose to redeem the vouchers, the policy operates one degree removed from public direction—and yet public power is still deployed in selecting the approved sites for redeeming the vouchers. A school voucher system has to approve the schools where the vouchers can be received. Not only are public dollars used but the public selection of eligible schools also implements public policy. Further on the continuum would be government contracts, through which a government body selects a private entity to perform services specified by contract; further still on the line pointing toward closer governmental control are more comprehensive partnerships. On the farthest end lies state-established religion, which sits beyond the map of government/private relations within the United States.

This continuum suggests that, from the vantage point of the government, even the decision to permit a private activity to proceed while denying it beneficial tax treatment involves government policy and the capacity to implement public values. A commitment to pluralism as one of those public values would ensure equal chances for any legitimate religious group to receive a tax exemption or other favorable tax treatment. It would also permit groups to opt out of some otherwise prevailing public norms—say, against discrimination on the basis of sexual orientation—if they forgo the formal public support of tax benefits, vouchers, contracts, or partnerships. At the same time, pluralism viewed as a value within which government is only one vehicle defends private options in health care, social services, and schooling because public ones can fail or fall short; pluralism values public, secular health care and schooling options because private religious provision does not meet everyone's needs.

The last value is *democracy.* As noted earlier, the value of broad participation in the project of self-government is that it advances equality and freedom while also pressing for accountability and limiting abuses by those who wield concentrations of authority. As government and public functions proceed through private means, the transparency of public decisions and actions is diminished. This pattern reduces the avenues for public participation and renders less accessible the information necessary to enable active public involvement in policy making and in evaluating how the society operates.[17] For democracy to work under these conditions, people must find or invent access to the information through which they can watch activities in the private sector and evaluate their implications for public values. Hence, democracy here includes demands for open debates and visible decisions over privatization and the development of the kinds of information that would allow people to assess whether the mix of private and public efforts over time serves public purposes.

Political theorist Benjamin Barber has argued that terrorism forms a challenge to democracy—evidenced by the events of September 11—in part because "economic reductionism and its commercializing homogeneity . . . have created the climate of despair and hopelessness that terrorism has so effectively exploited." Barber maintains that democratic values require responses not only in the name of retributive justice and secularist interests "but also in the name of distributive justice and religious pluralism."[18] As his comments suggest, what we identify as public values reflects not only a sense of what is right and just but also strategies to protect human security and chances to flourish.

ACCOUNTABILITY

Whether the particular values I have listed offer the right values for public endorsement, the critical condition for public values is accountability. How will we even know if these values are violated or fulfilled if complex patterns of public and private, religious and secular, profit and nonprofit efforts proceed in schooling, healing, representing, and feeding people in need? In a purely public setting, public methods of accountability include voting for leaders who have to explain and defend their positions and their records and using courts and regulatory agencies for enforcement and implementation. In market-based settings, the bottom-line return on investment offers accountability—best measured over the long rather than the short term and tested by private choices to consume and invest. In nonprofit settings, accountability falls to boards of trustees to whom the employees and volunteers are responsible and to government oversight to ensure charitable purposes. Religious groups may operate that way while embracing as more authoritative a theologically informed conception of accountability.

In recent decades, public and nonprofit managers have pursued market-style reasoning to introduce internal competition, consumer choice, and cost-effectiveness methods within broader public or nonprofit missions.[19] For-profit enterprises explore partnerships with nonprofits and justify these efforts in terms of marketing, while the nonprofits justify them in light of the resources provided to underwrite nonprofit missions. But when efforts cut across these domains, there is a risk of a mismatch in methods of accountability. When for-profit companies create nonprofit subsidiaries, and when nonprofits have spun off for-profit companies, the lines and methods of accountability become even more confusing. As governments privatize public functions through contracts, partnerships, and voucher programs, should accountability methods match those of for-profit industries, nonprofit organizations, or government administrative and legal rules? When for-profit companies manage transition-to-work programs under a state welfare program, do they seek to cut costs by diverting people from helpful services?[20] If public and private school alternatives compete for consumers, should the consumers remember that they are also voters and evaluate the results for the entire community, not just their own satisfaction? Matching accountability methods to each enterprise poses intellectual, political, and normative challenges that vary across specific fields.

Consider how to evaluate state experiments that privatize coercive force by subcontracting policing, incarceration, and other punishment and confinement activities.[21] Many critics warn that for-profit prisons lack incentives or commitments to treat prisoners decently. In response to litigation, courts have subjected private prisons to even greater legal liability than the state for abuse.[22]

Here's a perfect example of the enduring significance of public, albeit judicial, monitoring of private behavior. At this point, indifference to liability for maltreatment of prisoners is a lesser risk than the dangers posed by the profit motive. For-profit prisons are accountable to owners and shareholders and therefore may respond to demands not only for greater short-term profits but also for more business over time. Hence, the Wackenhut Corrections Corporation of America, according to some reports, lobbies to make more conduct criminal and thereby increase the demand for its services.[23]

Misalignment between accountability structures and the purposes of a program easily occur elsewhere. When a state contracts with a religious provider to help individuals deal with alcohol and drug addictions, the state's goal of reducing recidivism could well diverge from that of a religious provider that aims to save souls. Legislators authorizing privatization may be seeking political gains or campaign contributions rather than more effective methods for meeting public purposes.[24] Private schools receiving public aid may undermine the common school ideal embraced by many state laws.[25] Outsourcing government work often depresses wages and salaries. This may secure immediate cost savings to the government while spurring political pressure for a living wage. Divergent criteria of success are especially problematic when public and private institutions collaborate as partners, sharing the financial risks.[26]

But there is an even greater danger that privatization will shield activities from public view. Then public accountability can easily drop out. No one seems specifically responsible. Outsourcing service work often shrinks the health care and retirement benefits available to the workers, but shields these changes from public view.[27] A private management company hired to fix a public school bypasses the school board's supervision except on the overall decision to hire or fire the management company; decisions previously subject to public review slip behind the private company's doors.

To expose what otherwise would be invisible changes and de-

cisions as public and private boundaries shift, disclosure and monitoring devices to generate information become crucial. The clients and workers who are immediately affected and the broad
public need help understanding the shifting relationship between
governments and private entities, whether nonprofit or for-profit,
religious or secular. Of central importance is information about
decisions to contract out public services, about the selection of
performance measures used to evaluate private providers, and
about the conditions placed on private organizations that use public resources.

Information is essential for any form of accountability. Albert
O. Hirshmann's classic study identifies exit, voice, and loyalty as
the three vital methods of accountability.[28] None of these are
meaningful unless the relevant players base their actions on information about the actual performance of governments, private enterprises, or other activities. Consumers and investors have power
to hold others accountable because they can vote with their feet,
but they cannot exercise this power if they do not know how or
even whether to judge. Citizens vote with ballots, petitions, and
speeches, but they too cannot pursue these actions meaningfully
if they do not know what is going on.[29] When allocations of resources are at stake, as with government contracts with service
providers and school vouchers, competition among different providers is intended to produce better options.[30] Yet competition
works only if the results become known to people who can use
their exit, voice, or loyalty options. Hence, public rules should
create incentives or requirements to report information on
government contractors and organizations receiving government
vouchers. Techniques to monitor actions by government and
private contracting partners or voucher recipients become indispensable to any accountability strategy.[31] Some private entities,
perhaps especially religious institutions, will find disclosure requirements invasive. We should reconsider the burdens of paperwork imposed by government regulations and partnerships to
test how much of it produces information that is actually useable
for measuring and improving practice.

Even if full, reliable, and useable information emerges, accountability remains a problem when public goals pursue a mix of public and private means. Little is known about how to make—and how to evaluate—the very decision about what mix to use and what tools of governance to adopt. When should vouchers, or tax credits, or contracting, or grants be pursued? When should the government proceed as a partner with private organizations, a co-investor, rather than the boss hiring others by contract? Are there some functions best kept in house and some better provided by private organizations?[32] Should competition between public and private providers be promoted? How would we know when a good mix has been achieved? Is that to be assessed solely by outcome or performance measures or also by judgments about the effects of the mix itself on the quality of the workforce entering the field, or by the character of the society? When there is consensus around goals and around measures of success these issues are less difficult, but governments often contract out or use tax incentives or other tools even in the absence of such consensus.

An obvious starting question for assessing school vouchers, charitable choice, or public/private partnerships in community economic development is how well the strategy achieves the underlying goals. But who defines those goals, and how? Efforts at social provision seek multiple goals. For example, schools seek to improve student academic achievement but also aim to promote intergroup relations, good citizenship, gender equality, social skills, work habits, and job-related skills, while assuring students safe places to learn. Specifying the relative importance of these goals and the measures appropriate to each is complex and controversial.

Even when we restrict discussion to the goal of improving students' academic achievement in reading and mathematics, remarkably intense technical and political debates arise over which tests to use; how often to test; how to accommodate students with disabilities or whether to exclude them; whether to collect test information by students' race and gender; whether to mandate comparable tests across all schools within a district, a state, or the country; and whether the test information should have consequences for individual students, teachers, administrators, schools, districts, or states. Minimum competency tests would not enable teachers and administrators to understand what steps to take to improve both student and teacher performance. For that, teachers and administrators need to focus on internal diagnostic indicators, attending to areas where partial improvements can accumulate into real differences.[33] The "No Child Left Behind Act," a federal education reform championed by President George W. Bush, mandates yearly tests but leaves most of these questions unanswered, endangering the comparability of gathered information and prolonging the debates over testing methods.[34]

This example merely hints at the problems of crude assessments and the tyranny of numerical measures. It is much easier to frame evaluations in terms of what can be counted than it is to identify and use qualitative indicators, even though the quantitative measures are often clumsy and reductive. Moreover, their very use is likely to distort behavior, as teachers teach to the test and administrators process cases to meet their quota. Quantitative measures are sensible elements of educational evaluations, but they are too often where evaluation ends, with misleading and even counterproductive results.

Devising sensitive and sensible measures for accountability is especially challenging when the goal is to provide individualized treatments or responses. For example, in education for children with disabilities, federal and state laws call for individualized education plans, tailored to address the particular child's strengths and limitations. Schools nonetheless tend to assign students to the programs and services that the schools have available. Implementation problems lead outside monitors to focus on what can be counted, such as how many children have received a plan, and how many services called for by plans have been delivered, even if these give no real sense of whether children are learning or whether the services suit their particular needs. No wonder parents of children with disabilities often want more control and choice—and therefore seek public payment for private placements.

Individualized processes—including meetings to review the

child's situation and hearings to challenge the placement—are easier to implement than individualized instruction plans. It remains difficult for the classroom teacher to understand, monitor, and help improve the individual child's learning style. It is harder still for parents, principals, and systemwide administrators to keep track of the progress of individual students with special needs, and even more challenging to adjust the learning environment to enhance the learning of each child with special needs. Diagnostic tools that are nuanced and yet easy to use should be keyed to instructional materials suited to the student's particular needs and strengths. The individual's needs, strengths, and actual learning must be reassessed periodically. Standardized testing complicates matters. Excluding students with special needs from standardized tests wrongly removes accountability for teaching them the general curriculum, but including them may wrongly skew results, with serious consequences. Individualized education plans may call for accommodations or tailored scales for interpreting the results. Yet individualizing the evaluation runs counter to the very conception of standardized testing.

FOSTER CARE: A TOUGH CHALLENGE ILLUMINATES THE PROBLEMS

Foster care, including private family homes, group homes, and institutional options for children removed from their own families, also presents similar accountability difficulties. Foster care also illuminates the difficulties of accountability when combinations of public and private agencies intend to meet the needs of vulnerable people. The promise of foster care is already a second-best promise. Since we cannot promise every child, at all times, a safe home with loving parents, we have arranged public support as a backup when children are not safe at home or parents cannot provide care. That backup is often private, not public. Temporary alternative homes have long been provided by extended family members, religious groups, and through other private methods, and the current public support programs directly grow from and remain intertwined with these private efforts.[35] State agencies approve and subsidize relatives as foster care providers; the states also contract with private, often religious, agencies to assist with the lion's share of placements and services.

In the early 1970s, eleven-year-old Shirley Wilder appeared before Judge Justine Wise Polier of the New York Juvenile Court. It was a propitious encounter. Judge Polier's mother had founded a leading, religiously affiliated social welfare agency to serve children. Polier was tough, courageous, and willing to rock the boat, even if it meant challenging the child welfare community. Polier learned that Wilder had no place to live. She had run away from an abusive home. A year later, while under the jurisdiction of the state and held in a juvenile detention center, Shirley Wilder gave birth to a child she named Lamonte. At twelve separate hearings, Judge Polier heard that no agency had a placement for Wilder. Frustrated with the welter of public and private agencies unable to find a safe and supportive home for Wilder, Judge Polier prompted the child's law guardian to bring a class action suit against the private agencies for rejecting nonwhite children for foster placements.[36]

The 1973 suit—*Wilder v. Bernstein*—challenged the way that New York City contracted with religiously affiliated child-care agencies to provide placements for children. At the time, it placed 90 percent of the children in the system through sixty private agencies, most of them religiously affiliated. As directed by state constitutional and statutory provisions, the city's arrangement called for matching children by religion, where possible, with the religious agencies. The suit, brought on behalf of the class of non-white foster children, alleged that the city's practice wrongly entangled the state with religion. It also claimed that the city's practice resulted in long delays in placing Black and Hispanic children because the Catholic and Jewish agencies, which tended to provide better services than the others, took disproportionately few of the nonwhite foster children.[37] Judge Polier herself gave a deposition in the case as evidence of the failure of the system in which she participated as a judge: "Over and over again I was forced to recognize that if this child had been white, the child never would have stayed in a shelter, never have stayed in detention that long, and would not have been rejected by these agencies. I say this on the basis of my experience over the years."[38]

The suit was settled, with judicial supervision maintained for its implementation. The settlement required the city to restructure its procedures. It could use religious matching in foster care when requested by the child's biological parents but only when consistent with an overriding commitment to assure placement of children on a first-come-first-served basis. In reviewing the settlement, the district court and the appellate court struggled with the proper relationship between the government and the religious agencies. The courts indicated that the agencies could display religious symbols unless they had the effect of impermissibly chilling the free exercise rights of the children in their care.[39] Judge Polier, by then retired from the bench, met with the lawyers for the foster children and decried the settlement for its failure to separate religion and government and to ensure vigorous public supervision of the private agencies. The lawyers reported that the settlement offered more services for children than they could get from a court order.[40]

Failures in implementing the settlement and continuing problems with foster care kept the courts involved in the case for many more years. Again, the individualized nature of the problems and the solutions contributed to the difficulties of implementing effective programs. Neither exit nor voice work as methods of accountability because the public and private programs serve children—who are typically presumed to be unable to speak for themselves—and impoverished, often substance-abusing, adults. Further, genuine difficulties in knowing what is the right result or even right intermediate steps arose because of conflicts in philosophies and disagreements about what kinds of risks are wise to take.

How can public and private efforts succeed when people disagree about what counts as success, when the need far exceeds the capacity to help, and when basic tools for improving practice are still underdeveloped and unknown by front-line staff? In child welfare, disagreement about overarching policies and about how best to apply them in given cases is simply the first layer of difficulty. Some people think that the overriding goal is to preserve biological families—to keep children with their biological parents or return the children as soon as possible after they are removed in the face of abuse or neglect. Advocates of family preservation successfully secured passage of the Adoption Assistance and Child Welfare Act of 1980. It emphasized that the most desirable place for children is with their own families. It also required states receiving federal funds to make "reasonable efforts" to prevent unnecessary out-of-home placements and to make reasonable efforts to return a child to the family of origin. Its supporters stressed that the racial and class biases of governmentally employed social workers lead to extreme misuse of the removal option. Poverty and socially created stress contribute to problems within the home. Rather than blame, parents should receive support. Foster care should be used sparingly and the focus should be on strengthening the home and the biological parents' ability to care with support from day care, Head Start, and other programs.

But critics of this policy argue that giving parents second, third, and fourth chances wrongly minimizes the effects of abuse and neglect on children and turns the children into means rather than primary objects of concern. They emphasize that the focus on family preservation led child welfare agencies, lawyers, and judges to try to preserve families at all costs—and the costs fall on children when families are hopelessly dysfunctional and when children suffer severe and extended abuse. The critics successfully pressed for the passage of the 1997 federal Adoption and Safe Families Act, which specified that reasonable efforts are *not* required in those kinds of cases.[41] Many who favor removing children from abusive and neglectful parents claim that the high correlation between their conduct and substance abuse makes the prospects for parental improvement small, given the failure rates of substance abuse programs. Fundamentally, each new chance given to parents postpones the moment when the child will need a permanent placement. Not only does this make it harder for children to move and adjust, it also means that the children will be older, more scarred, and less attractive to potentially permanent adoptive parents. Then the children will be more likely to remain in foster care, with the temporary placement becoming a permanent one. Yet this very fact exposes many of these children to shifts in placement as temporary caregivers find themselves unable to provide long-term care.

To ensure that foster care remains temporary, federal law now requires states to devise plans for permanent placements for each foster child. This often involves public and private agencies working simultaneously to try to reunite biological parent and child while also searching for a permanent, adoptive home. If the goal is a permanent home, how long should efforts to reunite the child with the birth parent proceed? Adoption becomes more difficult as time goes on. As crude as it may be to talk this way, prospective adoptive parents operate like consumers with preferences. Infants are more desirable to potential adoptive parents than older children, especially older children who have experienced trauma and retain attachments to other people. Extended periods of disappointment and movement between biological parents and foster parents can impair the child's chances for building trusting relationships.[42] The majority of children in foster care are children of color; most prospective adoptive parents are white. This racial difference informs the desires of the parents and the practices of state agencies, to the disadvantage of the children.

Can a particular child hope to return to her mother after her mother completes a drug treatment program? The answer depends on the mother's progress and the child's needs, which each require particularized inquiry and assessments. Yet systems of foster care often have trouble doing more than keeping track of all the children in state custody and keeping tabs on the location of their parents. Meantime, individual children get lost in the system. Many never get a chance to return home or to find a new permanent family. Others become injured and even die while under state supervision, either in the care of their biological parents or foster parents.

Until fairly recently, New York was one of many child welfare systems that could not, on any given day, report how many children were in foster care. That day is gone. In one major reform, New York City's Administration for Children's Services adopted an information management system to equip the state to keep better track of the children in its care. But still there is an astonishing lack of data. This makes it almost impossible to manage or evaluate staff and programs. Today, supervisors in New York can find out which social workers have been reporting their case records on time, but not how long the children they are responsible for stay in foster care or what proportion of the families they serve are successfully reunited.

Lawyers challenging such systems have often concluded that the only hope is to seek outside management, under judicial appointment and supervision. In litigation that lasted for twenty-six years after the launch of Shirley Wilder's case, lawyers for the American Civil Liberties Union settled a new suit and the remaining portions of Shirley Wilder's suit challenging New York City's foster care practices. The settlement required the city to agree to the direct involvement of a private group of private experts, funded by a private foundation, to scrutinize, monitor, and evaluate the reforms planned by the public agency.[43]

The public interest lawyers settled because they were heartened by administrative changes already taking place and because they despaired of further chances for progress through direct judicial management. Progress within the public system in New York included the adoption of unusually clear principles by the Administration for Children's Services to address the tension between reunification and adoption planning. The city directed that "[a] child who can be protected within his or her own family and home with the support of community services should not come into foster care," and "if placement into foster care is required to ensure a child's safety, the family should be fully engaged in planning for services and the child's safe return home as soon as possible."[44] Indeed, even where efforts to reunite parent and child fail, vigor in such efforts is essential to establish the legal and ethical basis for seeking adoption rather than reunification. Nonetheless,

implementing these principles and keeping the system accountable to them remains extraordinarily difficult, particularly because
front-line staff members do not always understand or agree with
the policies. Even more important, they lack particular skills,
feedback about their successes and failures, and sufficient support
to implement the principles.

Reporting to the judge monitoring the New York settlement
of litigation over the child welfare system,[45] the advisory committee reported that good faith efforts and progress have been made to
improve the system, but nonetheless in three ways the system cannot meet children's needs. First, it is not yet designed to treat the
entire family as a client—even though biological parents are both
recipients of services on their own and crucial to the fulfillment of
their children's needs.[46] Second, the front-line staff are neither
trained nor guided in concrete ways to implement the fundamental policies. And third, there are no data points or performance
measures that allow any supervisor to know exactly what is going
on with the families in a given caseworker's purview.

Each of these problems reflects the sheer size of the case loads,
the time frontline workers must spend on required paperwork and
going to court, insufficient provision of cultural/linguistically appropriate services, and judgmental or prejudiced attitudes toward
parents. The report acknowledges that these are factors. But
far more basic explanations for the failures exist. Fundamentally,
frontline staff, whether public employees or workers for private
agencies, lack training and guidance. Measures of performance
are unrefined. Social workers and family support staff may know
the basic principles about promoting permanency but these are
stated as general goals without guidelines or practices designed to
advance them. At the same time, they are given elaborate regulations about the forms to fill out and meetings to hold.[46] They need
fewer obligations to fill out forms and more guidance about how
to undertake good practices from day to day. As the panel suggests,
such guidelines could direct the social worker to ask each family
member to identify and involve those who have helped in past crises; to work with parents and those who know them well to iden-

tify their strengths and what the parents think would enable them to parent their children effectively; and to match the family's needs with a plan for services.[48]

Yet saying this is easier than figuring out how the details can be implemented. As a tiny but telling example, the report notes that birth parents are invited to conferences and reviews of service plans but many do not come. If their involvement is desired, perhaps it would be better to treat them as indispensable parties to meetings that cannot occur without them.[49] Yet doing so would inevitably delay meetings, in some cases indefinitely. Guidelines could focus on what degree of effort—over what period of time—the social worker or other staff member should undertake to get the parents to the meetings. Finding best practices in the system and from other systems, presenting them in comprehensible ways, modeling them, and coaching frontline staff in enacting them could narrow the distance between promises and realities. But absent new accountability mechanisms, no one in the system can learn to do this or convincingly persuade outsiders that it has been done.

The mass media, at its best, provides information crucial to accountability even if it exposes serious and tragic failures. Reporter Nina Bernstein followed the lives of Shirley Wilder and her son Lamonte, the son born to Shirley when she was a teenager under state jurisdiction.[50] A reporter for *Newsday,* Nina Bernstein found the now adult Shirley Wilder as well as Lamonte, who also had been a foster child. Indeed, Lamonte never saw his mother after he entered the system until the reporter reunited them nineteen years later. Lamonte, at age nineteen, told Bernstein: "Growing up without a family leaves you kind of without an identity. In the system, you just feel like a number. And when you leave, someone else gets your number."[51] For four years he lived with one foster family, then with two others. By the age of seven, he was viewed as unadoptable and labeled as a troublemaker, a firesetter. Lamonte then spent six years in a residential treatment center, at which point a social worker said he should not have stayed there that long; he was just a child lost in the system. His mother periodically asked about her son. She lost track of Lamonte when one private agency went out of business and the city caseworkers then could not tell her which agency had her son's case.[52]

The reporter also reunited Lamonte with one of his foster parents. She remembered how the agency gave her an ultimatum to adopt the child or give him up. Financially unable to adopt, she lost Lamonte, who then bounced among placements, never finding a permanent home. Reunited for the first time, Lamonte asked the foster mother, "Was I bad when I was young?" Bernstein reports that the foster mother replied, "You were very good. . . . You were very curious; you were very, very bright, and you asked questions like 'Does anyone live in the moon?' and 'What keeps the clouds up?'"[53] When he heard of Lamonte's placement history, Albert Solnit, former director of the Yale Child Study Center, commented, "If you had paid evil people to try to destroy this kid, they couldn't have designed a better scenario."[54] A public official said that what happened to Lamonte would not happen today, given the commitment to permanent placements—but something like that policy was adopted even when Lamonte was growing up.[55]

The failures are not all within the systems, public and private. After a wonderful and loving reunion with her son, Shirley Wilder missed their next date; she later confirmed that she is addicted to crack cocaine.[56] Reporter Bernstein reminds her readers that life is not a movie.[57] The most optimistic claims about faith-based services argue that a faith element could make the difference in preventing teen pregnancy and helping individuals resist crime and addiction.[58] But even if we cannot fix all the causes, we should be able to make sure a child does not get lost in the system supposed to help and protect him. We should be able to make sure that people who care about a child can continue to be involved in his life. Whether employed by the state or by private agencies, staff entrusted to care for the children most at risk must be instructed in concrete steps and models of best practices, and have access to information systems that allow them to monitor and learn from the results of their own practices and that of their colleagues.

As enforced by the case of *Wilder v. Bernstein,* the religious freedom of children and families deserves respect, but only where consistent with guarding against discrimination on the basis of race or ethnicity when the government places children in private agencies. The government must guard against establishing religion or appearing to do so; today, its child welfare contracts must acknowledge children who are Moslem, Buddhist, Zoroastrian, or any religion. The children's basic need for safety must be ensured, whether they move into state care, into private placements under state contract, or return to their biological parents. Accountability to the rule of law must be available even where provision of services is primarily conducted through private religious agencies.[59] And people in this democracy can expect and produce sufficient information so that government, media, and citizens' groups can hold accountable those entrusted with providing care.

This last element—generating sufficient useable information to enable citizens to participate in efforts to make foster care systems accountable—points toward one role that democracy should play alongside public and private efforts to meet basic human needs. Generating the information alone will not make democracy work in this context. In addition, public agendas and advocacy must turn the information into priorities for political will and action. This could be the work of social movements. It would help to have operational and funded legal services programs—and ones not barred as those receiving public funds now are from bringing class action suits against government programs. Private, even public, subsidies should bolster advocacy for those with unmet needs. Judge Polier, who knew firsthand the capacities and failures of courts, private agencies, legislatures, and political processes, argued that to give children's welfare the high priority at every level of government,

> I believe it is necessary to continue to do hard fact-finding concerning unmet needs of children, to present the facts to larger segments of the community, and to coordinate all possible sources of strength for social change. Lack of awareness on community levels of what is not being done for or what is being done to children is one of the

most awesome barriers that must be broken down. This means the development of child-advocacy groups that should include the consumers of services, citizens, and professionals.[60]

Parents can and should be helped to become advocates for their own children, but caring advocacy is essential for other people's children, especially when their own parents are not able to play that role.

PARTNERS AND RIVALS

It is not only in foster care that accountability is crucial. With schooling, health care, legal services, welfare, alcohol and drug abuse programs, prisons and jails, garbage and toxic waste disposal, society needs more accessible and reliable measures to know when enterprises are effective, what safeguards are in place against abuse, waste, and fraud—and whether they are working. Private markets are supposed to generate effective outputs and guard against abuse, waste, and fraud, but we know there are failures, just as there are failures by religious institutions and public agencies. This very frailty and the predictability of failures justifies our reliance on the complex array of public and private systems and providers for health care, human services, law, and education. Redundancy, competition, and options give greater promise than all the best plans to build one best system. But without access to information, latitude for advocacy, and expectations of monitoring, we will not even know what works, what is a disaster, and what other questions to ask.

Equally important is the development of designs to allow organizations—public or private, profit or nonprofit—to be sufficiently flexible so that they can learn from experience and respond to information about the successes and failures of their own efforts and of others. To pool information about performance, cost, and effectiveness, it is not enough for each enterprise, governmental or private, to engage in its own evaluations. Intermediary organizations, including nonprofit advocacy groups, insurance companies, independent think tanks, and the media, will play vital roles. Just as *Consumer Reports* equips consumers through evaluating the cost, performance, and safety of products, parent support groups can emerge to help parents evaluate schools in regimes of expanded school choice, whether they simply include public schools and charter schools or expand to include private and even parochial schools.[61] Public interest lawyers can act as monitors of Medicaid managed care and advocates for performance standards to equip patients with knowledge and clout.[62]

Crude quantitative measures such as standardized tests offer an initial kind of information, but thoughtful parents and reformers should demand richer, more textured indicators of student learning, teacher development, and school improvement. With general public norms in place—such as statewide curricular standards and constitutional and statutory commitments to prohibit discrimination and to support religious freedom—schools can generate information, face monitoring by parents and advocacy groups, and gain opportunities to learn about what works. Yet this recipe holds promise only if the schools then have the capacities to reassess their own strategies, allocation of resources, incentives, and methods of accountability, and to experiment and revise their decision making.[63]

In this light, private and public organizations can be partners even when they are rivals. Their competition presses for better information and results that in turn can be used to improve all the schools, social welfare agencies, or health care providers. Nonprofits, religious groups, and for-profit enterprises inject potentially diverse views of goals and their own approaches to measures of success. Evaluating similar issues in Great Britain, one observer concluded, "Voluntary and community organisations are not the prisoners of commercial forces or puppets of the State but active players with a wide variety of different contributions to make."[64] Religious and other private groups may most vitally improve public life when they serve as critics of the status quo and demand more responsive government.[65] Religious leadership may be as crucial to changing police practices as it is to helping young people stay out of trouble.[66] Promising relationships between public and private enterprises can emerge from private competition and innovation, challenging public conventions.[67]

The field of adoption offers an example. Historically the field has been filled with private as well as public agencies; the adoption of children requires compliance with state laws that vary across the country. The laws set requirements, such as demanding a home study of prospective parents and ultimate judicial review of the petition for adoption. For decades, public agencies preferred matching adoptive children with prospective parents by race; when private agencies and lawyers permitted white parents to adopt children of color, this created competitive pressure that has influenced the practices of public agencies.[68] Here is an instance in which private, regulated agencies pursued practices that differed from public ones and, at least according to some advocates, helped improve public practice. Ensuring latitude for private alternatives holds promise for competition and innovation, but it remains unclear what the optimal mix of public and private action is and when public norms should apply to private organizations. Yet, even the rules governing private markets and religious entities— the arenas outside of government practice and potentially challenging to it—are established and monitored by government.[69]

This should remind us that the policy question is not simply when should a government agency choose to use private vendors or contracts to pursue its chosen course. Instead, we must consider how society should decide what can be public, what can be private, what public values apply even to private efforts, and what accountability measures are mandated by public rule or private pressure. We should also try to answer the pivotal question about government/religion partnerships, well posed by E.J. Dionne and Ming Hsu Chen: "The challenge is to find ways in which the government can foster [good work by religious congregations] without so dividing Americans across religious and political lines that the work itself is jeopardized."[70] I have suggested a set of public values that should apply even to private entities as well as the kinds of information-generating practices necessary for effective accountability. Both of these matters—the content and scope of public values, and the methods for ensuring accountability—require democratic debate and participation. Even when public norms have already been announced and extended to private settings, they should remain subject to revision in light of community experience and critique. Yet the usual institutions of American democracy have not yet proved adept in addressing these matters. The very complexity and apparent technicality of the issues is partially to blame. But so is the seeming invisibility of public decisions, which spurs greater privatization. The *Wilder* case shows the human tragedies that occur when neither those directly affected nor the watching community can penetrate the agencies intended to help.

Existing academic frameworks have not yet successfully linked shifts in public and private enterprises with the needs for accountability and public participation. Two dominant academic orientations include valuable elements but remain insufficient to this task. Market-style economic analyses help identify the power of competition in generating innovation and greater individual effort and the alternatives to monopoly even where government provides a service. Indeed, scholars of market methods have suggested how incentives and competition around performance standards can help government achieve public ends when the community cannot agree on particular techniques and the task is complex.[71] Yet market theories neglect how power differentials affect private choices, how social structures shape private preferences, and what barriers and disincentives constrain information crucial to evaluating success and failure. By assuming that individuals operate out of rational self-interest, market theories have little to say about children, people with mental disabilities, people who are seriously ill, or people with substance abuse problems—the primary targets of social provision efforts. Market theories miss the value and vitality of debate and struggle even as they understate their own reliance on public norms. Public norms governing property and contract, for example, shape the preconditions of private markets. But market theories offer no tools for determining what the shape of these entitlements should be or when other norms should rise to the level of preconditions within which market-based competition and incentives should operate.

Further, there remains the danger that market-oriented criteria and conceptions for accountability and improvement focus on the measurable rather than matters of justice or care. Economist Timothy Taylor makes a similar criticism of economic analysis in services for children, sick people, and the elderly:

> Economists have been too technocratic, too eager to fit the public disputes into their preset mental categories of market failure and re-distribution. With service industries that touch our common humanity as closely as care for young children, teaching and education, looking after the sick and injured, and care for the elderly, this level of detachment is only a useful starting point. If economists want to be relevant . . . [t]hey will have to leaven their professional concern about efficiency with judgments about the justice of entitlements, the fairness of consumption externalities and who should pay, and insights about long-term political dynamics.[72]

The second tradition is academic scholarship that articulates theories of justice—in the tradition of philosopher John Rawls or his communitarian critics.[73] These theories develop vital normative dimensions that should infuse public policies. They crucially attend to values that have no price tag, values that put individual freedom and dignity above general utility. Yet these theorists operate too abstractly to connect with management and accountability. They, too, tend to have little to say about children, people who are mentally disabled or seriously ill, or people with substance-abuse problems, although they grapple theoretically with issues of paternalism.[74]

A new body of scholarship borrows features of market analysis and theories of justice and addresses the actual operation of public and private institutions. Economist Charles Sabel and law professor Michael Dorf call it "democratic experimentalism"; law professor Susan Sturm calls it a third way between regulation by rules and market privatization; Jody Freeman, another law professor, explores how private advocacy groups develop information and tools of analysis that improve the norm-setting and enforcement practices of government.[75] These and other scholars examine how people internal to and outside of the direct providers or recipients use data to reveal patterns, compare that information with benchmark goals, and build the capacities of constituencies inside and outside public and private organizations to solve problems, to implement norms, and to revise the norms.[76] This work is especially promising because it remains committed to public values, notably democracy and antidiscrimination, while drawing on successful practices in market settings that tackle hard problems by using information rather than command-and-control management. It also attends to the actual complex institutional relationships among public and private and profit and nonprofit institutions.

Thus far, however, the scholarship of "democratic experimentalism" has not sufficiently incorporated the public values affecting the place of religion. Those issues include assessing the impact of government involvement on religious groups through charitable choice, contracting, and other subsidies, and the impact of religious groups on civic life; the freedom of individuals or protection against government establishment of religion; the dynamics of innovation, learning, and accomplishment in religious organizations. Yet these issues are unavoidably implicated in the fields of education, health care, and social services. Democratic experimentalism also risks neglecting broader public participation beyond the role of interest groups already engaged and expert in particular issues. Guarding against disenfranchisement of the broader public in the very way that technical systems of accountability are designed must be a priority if democracy is to become meaningful in the shifting relations between public and private institutions.

A critical step for scholars, journalists, and advocates would be to make sure that our system displays the conflicts and tensions— between public and private, religious and secular, profit and nonprofit—rather than papers them over. Display permits greater awareness. With greater awareness, people can demand more opportunities for public debate and accountability. Writing in the related context concerning relationships among different judicial systems, legal scholar Robert Cover wrote, "It is a daring system that permits the tensions and conflicts of the social order to be displayed."[77] With greater transparency of this nature, we will be better able to see the role private provision can fill and that the public will not reach, but also the public framework overarching and underlying private provision of schooling, health care, social services, and law.

Private action working alongside coordinating governmental structures characterizes our history[78] and should guide our future. Social provision—meeting the needs of poor people, children, people who are ill, people who are addicts—should be a matter of collective concern. This means setting the ground rules for governmental and private programs so that they become partners in social provision, harnessing the energy and innovation of competition and market-style incentives while implementing the vision of compassion and care exemplified by nonprofit and religious efforts. Tools for this kind of complex partnership include tax policies, government contracts, and vouchers. Government programs use these tools to join with private efforts and, in varying degrees, set public terms for their performance and evaluation. These kinds of partnerships are consistent with the constitutional commitment to separate religion and government in schooling as long as the government does not itself subsidize religious activities. The Supreme Court correctly concluded that a child eligible for special education services should be able to obtain them on the site of the private religious school where his parents chose to enroll him.[79] Greater latitude for government involvement with religiously organized schools and services may well be consistent with the Constitution and the public values it represents. But governments authorizing this and other kinds of public aid must set the terms for its acceptable use.

Health care, social services, legal services, welfare, tax credits and deductions, government contracts, and vouchers can promote pluralism, social cohesion, quality, and equality while structuring complex partnerships between private groups and federal and state governments. Yet precisely how these tools are devised and how their success is measured should be topics of public discussion and public accountability. School vouchers and charter schools; charitable choice in welfare, food stamps, and social services; and tax policies deeply and directly determine how society meets—or fails to meet—the needs of poor people and all children, even if the rules and practices seem technical and removed from public scrutiny. Of course, government should permit a wide range of private activities to address those in need. But when government sponsors private activities—through direct or indirect funding—public values are implicated. For-profit enterprises, and market principles, can assist public provision, but not in exchange for public principles. Government policies can use market techniques to promote efficiency and competitive innovation, but not to convert vital public questions into matters of private consumption and public neglect. In American history "proclamations of the market's inviolability have never been permitted to silence the demands of justice,"[80] nor should they now.

Private entities, notably religious institutions and agencies, can decline public support. But if they accept it, that public support should entail compliance with public commitments. Private religious schools and hospitals receiving government support through contracts, vouchers, or tax subsidies should respect individual freedom of belief and ensure protection against discrimination on the basis of an individual's group traits. The broad citizenry can and should debate whether these are the right public values, and what those values mean in particular contexts, but public values should accompany public dollars.[81]

Those public values of course should include improved quality. Greater access to competing public and private options can improve schools and welfare programs, health care and foster care, adoption and substance abuse services. But the underlying public system enabling such options must ensure secular alternatives for people who do not want religious ones and respect for their own beliefs about religion if they pursue religious services subsidized by public resources. School-choice programs should comply with public values, which are articulated in law.[82] They should also involve clearly defined roles and responsibilities to ensure successful and sound collaborations.[83]

By calling for complex solutions I mean to describe and defend efforts to enhance both individual freedom and social solidarity. This nation, reflected in its constitution and laws, embraces complex and multiple social values: freedom and communality, abstract equality and religious particularism, individual and communal responsibility. These multiple values are not simply distinct and competing. They are also linked and interdependent. As manifested in our legal system, individual freedom relies on a collective structure of rules and institutions. Religious pluralism relies on overarching laws that mandate tolerance and also set limits on the government's involvement and support. At work in these arrangements are nuanced understandings of the interdependence of individuals, individuals and groups, and people and government structures.

No one can make it through life all alone, and no group can sustain itself forever without the support and respect of the larger polity. We need plural communities, institutions, and structures; we also need the larger public framework devoted to that plurality and to individuals who may, but also who may not, be comfortably situated within a caring community. How we respond to seemingly appealing ideas today will determine how we address these complex needs for generations to come.

2. What's Going On?

1   Letter to the Danbury Baptist Assoc., *The Writings of Thomas Jefferson,*
    ed. Andrew A. Lipscomb and Albert Bergh, vol. 16 (Washington, D.C.:
    Library ed., 1904), 281–82.

2   Jodi Wilgoren, "Court Ruling Fuels Debate on Vouchers for Educa-
    tion," *New York Times,* June 29, 2000, p. A27; David G. Savage, "Low-
    ering the Wall Between Church and State," *Record* (Bergen County,
    N.J.), Feb. 4, 2001, p. 1.

3   Patricia Brennan, " 'Evolution', Exploring Darwin's Theory," *Washing-
    ton Post,* Sept. 23, 2001, p. Y06; Cathy Young, "Debating Faith-Based
    Programs," *Boston Globe,* Feb. 28, 2001, p. A19; Jessica Garrison,
    "Response to Terror: School Prayer," *Los Angeles Times,* Dec. 2, 2001, p.
    A1; Michael Mayo, "Has Prayer Gone Too Far? Amen," *Fort Lauderdale
    (Fla.) Sun-Sentinel,* April 12, 2001, p. 1C; Sue Chianese, "School Necessi-
    ties," *Orlando Sentinel,* March 13, 2001, p. A8.

4   *Chronicle of Philanthropy,* April 5, 2001, p. 12.

5   See John J. DiIulio Jr., "The Urban Church: Faith, Outreach and the
    Inner-City Poor," in *The Essential Civil Society Reader: Classic Essays in
    the American Civil Society Debate,* ed., Don. E. Eberly (Lanham, Md.:
    Rowman & Littlefield, 2000), 217, 223–4.

6   See, generally, *Developments in the Law—Nonprofit Corporations,* 105
    Harv. L. Rev. 1578 (1992).

7   See Jed Emerson and Fay Twersky, ed., *New Social Entrepreneurs: The Suc-
    cess, Challenge, and Lessons of Nonprofit Enterprise Creation* (San Francisco:
    Roberts Foundation, 1996).

8   Shirley Sagawa and Eli Segal, *Common Interest, Common Good: Creating
    Value through Business and Social Sector Partnerships* (Boston: Harvard Busi-
    ness School Press, 2000).

9   See Rosabeth Moss Kanter, foreword to *Common Interest, Common Good*, by Sagawa and Segal, xi, xii.

10   See Sagawa and Segal, *Common Interest, Common Good*, 37–46.

11   George Bernard Shaw, *John Bull's Other Island and Major Barbara* (New York: Brentan's, 1907), 180.

12   Sagawa and Segal, *Common Interest, Common Good*, 3.

13   Ibid., 218–19.

14   Ibid., 13, 19, 23–25.

15   Ibid., 84–5.

16   Ibid., 104.

17   Ibid.

18   Ibid., 113–126.

19   Ibid., 121.

20   Ibid., 122.

21   Thanks to Mark Moore for this point.

22   Sagawa and Segal, *Common Interest, Common Good*, 165.

23   Kelly Greene, "Meals on Wheels Tries For-Profit Tactics to Grow," *Wall Street Journal* (April 25, 2001), p. B1.

24   Sagawa and Segal, *Common Interest, Common Good*, 165.

25   Ibid., 236.

26   Eyal Press and Jennifer Washburn, "Neglect for Sale: How ResCare Profits from the Disabled," *American Prospect* (May 8, 2000), pp. 22–29.

27   Sagawa and Segal, *Common Interest, Common Good*, 124.

28   See Jude L. Fernando and Alan W. Heston, "The Role of NGOS: Charity and Empowerment," *Annals of the American Academy of Political and Social Science* 554 (1997), 8, 12.

29   See Lester Salmon, "The Rise of the Nonprofit Sector," *Foreign Affairs* 73 (1994): 34.

30   Ibid.

31   See Charles R. Halpern, foreword to *Vision and Values: Rethinking the Nonprofit Sector in America* (New Haven: Yale University Program on Non-Profit Organizations), Working Paper 251.

32   Michael Walzer, "The Idea of Civil Society: A Path to Social Reconstruction," in *Community Works: The Revival of Civil Society in America*, ed. E. J. Dionne Jr. (Washington, D.C.: Brookings Institution, 1998), 123, 139.

33 See Andrew R. Varcoe, *The Boy Scouts and the First Amendment: Constitutional Limits on the Reach of Anti-discrimination Law,* 9 Law & Sexuality 163, 270 (1999–2000)

34 Peter Frumkin, "The Face of the New Philanthropy," *The Responsive Community* 10, no. 3 (Summer 2000): 41, 47.

35 See ibid., 41.

36 See Albert R. Hunt, "Social Entrepreneurs: Compassionate and Tough-Minded," *Wall Street Journal,* July 13, 2000, p. A47; Harvard Business School, "New Profit Inc.: Governing the Nonprofit Enterprise," Case N9-100-052 (adapted by Professor Robert S. Kaplan from a case written by Jann Elias, Harvard Business School Publishing, 1999).

37 See Ira C. Lupu, *The Increasingly Anachronistic Case Against School Vouchers,* 13 Notre Dame J. of Law, Ethics, and Public Policy, 375 (1999).

38 Medicare spending has significantly increased in areas served by for-profit hospitals compared with those served by nonprofits. See Glen Singer, "Medicare Spending Rises Near for-Profit Hospitals," *Fort Lauderdale (Fla.) Sun-Sentinel,* Aug. 6, 1999, p. 3D. The article was a report on a study.

39 See Jamie Court and Frank Smith, "Wall Street Move Should Give Patients a Break," *Newsday,* Nov. 15, 1999, p. A30; see Richard Saltus, "Study Says for-Profit HMOs Skimp on Preventive Care Services," *Boston Globe,* July 14, 1999, p. A8.

40 See Liz Kowalczyk, "HMO's Suitors Testing the Waters, For-Profit Companies Contacting Hospitals," *Boston Globe,* Feb. 27, 2000, p. B1. See generally David M. Cutler, ed., *The Changing Hospital Industry: Comparing Not-for-Profit and For-Profit Institutes* (Chicago: University of Chicago, 2000); Louise G. Trubek, *Making Managed Competition a Social Arena: Strategies for Action,* 60 Brooklyn L. Rev. 275 (1994).

41 David M. Cutler, ed., introduction to *Changing Hospital Industry,* 1, 2, 6.

42 Robert Kuttner, *Everything for Sale* (New York: Alfred A. Knopf, 1998), 126.

43 See Lisa C. Ikemoto, *When a Hospital Becomes Catholic,* 47 Mercer L. Rev. 1087, 1113 (1996).

44 See Kathleen M. Boozang, *Deciding the Fate of Religious Hospitals in the Emerging Health Care Market,* 31 Hous. L. Rev. 1429 (1995); Gregory G. Bebel & William L. Perron, "Reproductive Health at Risk: A Report on Mergers and Affiliations in the Catholic Health Care System" (Washington, D.C.: Catholics for a Free Choice, 1995), 9.

45 Jennifer Templeton Schirmer, *Note: Physician Assistant As Abortion Pro-*

vider: Lessons from Vermont, New York, and Montana, 49 Hastings L. J. 253, 273 (1997). See also Ikemoto, *When a Hospital Becomes Catholic.*

46   See Alissa J. Rubin, "Abortion Providers at Lowest Mark Since '73," *Los Angeles Times,* Dec. 11, 1998, p. A45; Kathryn D. Katz, *The Pregnant Child's Right to Self-Determination,* 62 Alb. L. Rev. 1119, 1125–26 (1999); Merger Watch, Merger Status Report, http://www.paofnsy.org/MergerWatch/status.html; Lawrence E. Singer and Elizabeth Johnson Lantz, *The Coming Millennium: Enduring Issues Confronting Catholic Health Care,* 8 Ann. Health L. 299 (1999).

47   Nadine Strossen and Ronald K. L. Collins, *The Future of an Illusion: Reconstituting* Planned Parenthood v. Casey, 16 Const. Commentary 587 (1999).

48   Ikemoto, *When a Hospital Becomes Catholic,* 1106–7.

49   Ibid., 1096.

50   Ibid., 1101.

51   Ibid., 1100–1101.

52   See Schirmer, *Physician Assistant As Abortion Provider.* Only 20 percent of Catholics agree with the bishops that abortion should be illegal in all circumstances. Fred Stalla, "Media Overkill," *Newsday,* May 2, 2001, p. A39.

53   Ikemoto, *When a Hospital Becomes Catholic,* 1100.

54   See Michael Paulson, "Real Estate Boom Leaves Churches Worth Millions," *Boston Globe,* July 22, 2001, p. A1; Rachelle Garbarine, "Residential Real Estate: Rental Tower Replacing Former Midtown School," *New York Times,* May 11, 2001, p. B7.

55   See Rep. John D. Dingell's testimony before the Benefits Subcommittee of the House Committee on Veterans Affairs, June 7, 2001 (Federal Document Clearing House).

56   See Daniel Gordon, *Ex Corde Ecclesiae: The Conflict Created for American Catholic Law Schools,* 34 Gonz. L. Rev. 125 (1998–1999). See also Charles J. Russo and David L. Gregory, *Counterpoint: The Constitutional Vitality of Ex Corde Ecclesiae and a Response to the Alexander's Despair,* 30 J. L. & Educ. 307 (2001).

57   See William M. Rasmussen, "Harvard Group to Sponsor Socially Oriented Start-Up Companies," *Harvard Crimson,* Oct. 19, 2000.

58   See Michael Lewis, *The New New Thing* (New York: W. W. Norton, 1999).

59   See Larry Lessig, *Code and Other Laws of Cyberspace* (New York: Basic

Books, 1999). See also Dan Jellinek, "Does Technology Exacerbate Differences between Rich and Poor Countries Rather than Reduce Them?" *In These Times*, Jan. 8, 1998, p. 16. The article describes the effort of Harvard's Berkman Center for Internet and Society to build a global park, open without fee.

60 See Corrynne McSherry, *Who Owns Academic Work? Battling for Control of Intellectual Property* (Cambridge: Harvard University Press, 2001).

61 Interview with Sarah Wald, Harvard Provost office, July 27, 2001.

62 See Daryl Lang and Jennifer Nejman, "Iowa Newspaper Battles College Publication in Court," Pennsylvania State University *Daily Collegian*, www.mainquad.com/theQUAD/properties/uwire/page2.0/staing/news (visited March 8, 2000).

63 See Ronald Rosenberg, "A Boost from Biotech: Yale Backs Start-ups to Make Ailing New Haven a Major Biomedical Center," *Boston Globe*, March 12, 2000, p. G1.

64 Carey Goldberg, "Auditing Classes at M.I.T., on the Web and Free," *New York Times*, April 4, 2001, p. A1. See http:/web-mit.edu.

65 Mary Beth Marklein, "The New Face of Higher Education: Upstart College Makes the Grade and a Profit," *USA Today*, April 27, 1999, p. 1D.

66 "Varsity Printer Bookmarked for Success," *Toronto Star*, Feb. 10, 2001, first edition.

67 See letter from Dr. Vivien Noakes, "Authors' Rights," *Times* (London), Nov. 18, 2000.

68 See Ann Kirschner, "Fathom: A Case Study of a Public/Private Partnership in Higher Education," in Lawrence K. Grossman and Newton N. Minow, ed., *The Digital Gift to the Nation: Fulfilling the Promise of the Digital and Internet Age* (New York: Century Foundation Press, 2001), 143–47; Anthony Shadid, "Mad Cal," *Boston Globe*, Feb. 26, 2001, p. 1.

69 See Mary Beth Marklein, "The New Face of Higher Education: Upstart College Makes the Grade and a Profit," *USA Today*, April 27, 1999, p. 1D.

70 Kate Zernike, "Two 'Spokesguys' Pause for a Word About Their College Sponsor," *New York Times*, July 19, 2001, p. A22.

71 Ibid.

72 See Newton N. Minow and Craig LaMay, *Abandoned in the Wasteland* (New York: Hill and Wang, 1995); see also Robert McChesney, *We the Media: A Citizen's Guide to Fighting for Media Democracy* (New York: New Press, 1997).

73 See, e.g., Don Aucoin, "On a Wing and a Prayer: Are Big Bird's Colleagues at PBS in Danger of Becoming Roadkill on the Information Superhighway?" *Boston Globe*, Feb. 27, 2000, pp. E1, E2.

74 Ibid., p. E2.

75 Suzanne C. Ryan, "Local Program Cutbacks Are a Sign of the Times," *Boston Globe*, Oct. 23, 2001, p. E1.

76 Ibid., p. E7 (quoting McChesney).

77 Grossman and Minow, *Digital Gift to the Nation.*

78 Ibid., 4. See also Craig L. LaMay, "Justice Smith Morrill and the Politics and Legacy of the Land-Grant College Acts," in Grossman and Minow, *Digital Gift to the Nation,* 73–94.

79 See Merrill Goozner, "Patently Life: Public Science Financed Breakthroughs in Genetic Research—So Why Are Private Firms Allowed to Patent Genes?" *American Prospect*, Dec. 18, 2000, pp. 23–25.

80 Charles R. Halpern, foreword to *Vision and Values: Rethinking the Nonprofit Sector in America,* 5, 6.

81 See "Private Prisons," National Center for Policy Analysis, http://www.ncpa.org/ncpa/ea/eajf96/eajf96j.html (visited March 8, 2000).

82 Sharon Dolovich, "The Ethics of Private Prisons" (Nov. 1999, unpublished draft), p. 33.

83 See Public Facilities Investment Corporation, "Project Types," http://www.tamkin.com/public/pfprojtyp.html (visited March 8, 2000).

84 See Mark Donald, "From Cells to Souls: Chuck Colson and His Evangelical Christians Team Up with a Local Prison for a Divine Intervention Program," *Houston Press*, Dec. 7, 2000, features section.

85 See, e.g., Glenn G. Waddell and Judith M Keegan, *Christian Conciliation: An Alternative to "Ordinary" ADR,* 29 Cumb. L. Rev. 583 (1998–1999); John Witte Jr., *A New Concordance of Discordant Canons,* 42 Emory L. J. 523, 553–554 (1993). See David Michael Ryfe, *Information Systems in the San Diego Region,* 36 Cal. W. L. Rev., 367, 388 (2000). See, e.g., Sara Cobb, *Creating Sacred Space: Toward a Second Generation Dispute Resolution Practice,* 28 Fordham Urb. L. J. 1017 (2001); Carrie Menkel-Meadow, *And Now a Word About Secular Humanism, Spirituality, and the Practice of Justice and Conflict Resolution,* 28 Fordham Urban L. J. 1073 (2001).

86 Rachel King and Katherine Norgard, *What About Our Families? Using the Impact on Death Row Defendants' Family Members As a Mitigating Factor in Death Penalty Sentencing Hearings,* 28 Fla. State U. L. Rev. 1119, 1169 (1999).

87 See Katheryn M. Dutenhaver, *Dispute Resolution and Its Purpose in the*

Curriculum of DePaul University College of Law, 1998 Fla. L. Rev. 719, 728.

88   See Jerold S. Auerbach, *Justice without Law: Resolving Disputes without Lawyers* (New York: Oxford University Press, 1983).

89   See, e.g., Stephen L. Carter, *The Religiously Devout Judge,* 64 Notre Dame L. Rev. 932 (1989); Mark B. Greenlee, *Faith in the Book: The Role of Religious Belief in the Criminal Sentencing Decisions of Judges,* 26 Dayton L. Rev. 1 (2000); Leslie Griffen, *The Relevance of Religion to a Lawyer's Work: Legal Ethics,* 66 Fordham L. Rev. 1253 (1998); Sanford Levinson, *Identifying the Jewish Lawyer: Reflections on the Construction of Professional Identity,* 14 Cardozo L. Rev. 1577 (1953).

90   Charles Roos, "Ashcroft Prayer Meetings Should Be Public Concern," *Denver Rocky Mountain News,* May 29, 2001, p. 28A; Pete Hamill, "Tolerance Is Our Virtue: New York Is Oasis of Acceptance in a World of Faith-Based Fanatics," *New York Daily News,* June 4, 2001, p .8.

91   See Carl Esbeck, *A Constitutional Case for Government Cooperation with Faith-Based Social Service Providers,* 46 Emory L. J. 1 (1997).

92   Mark Silk, "New Rules for an Old Alliance: The Bush Administration Is Putting a New Spin on the Old Idea for Church-Controlled Nonprofits," *Washington Post* (National Weekly Edition), March 4, 2001, p. 22.

93   See ibid.

94   Louise G. Trubek and Jennifer J. Farnham, "How to Create and Sustain a Successful Social Justice Collaborative," report by the Center for Public Representation (2000); Louise G. Trubek and Jennifer J. Farnham, *Social Justice Collaborative: Multidisciplinary Practices for People,* 7 Clinical L. Rev. 227 (2000).

95   See Thomas J. Duesterberg, "Reforming the Welfare State," *Society* 35 (1998), p. 44.

96   See, e.g., Charles L. Glenn, *The Ambiguous Embrace: Government and Faith-Based Schools and Social Agendas* (Princeton, N.J.: Princeton University Press, 2000).

97   See Peter L. Berger and Richard John Neuhaus, "To Empower People," in Michael Novak, ed., *To Empower People: From State to Civil Society* (Washington, D.C.: American Enterprise Institute, 1996). See also Lester Salamon and Helmut K. Anheir, *The Emerging Nonprofit Sector: An Overview* (Manchester, England: Manchester University Press, 1996), xi.

98   Burton A. Weisbrod, "The Future of the Nonprofit Sector: Its Entwining with Private Enterprise and Government," *Journal of Policy Analysis and Management* 16 (1997): 541

99   See Heather Gottry, *Note, Profit or Perish: Non-Profit Social Service Organi-*

zations and Social Entrepeneurship, 6 Geo. J. Poverty Law & Pol'y 249, and text at note 32; Henry Hansmann, "The Two Non-profits: Fee for Service Versus Donative Organizations," in *The Future of the Non-Profit Sector: Challenges, Changes, and Policy Considerations,* ed., Virginia A. Hodgkinson et al., 91.

100   See Richard C. Leone, foreword in Robert Kuttner, *Everything for Sale* (New York: Knopf, 1998), xi-xiii.

101   Richard A. Posner, *Adoption and Market Theory: The Regulation of the Market in Adoption,* 67 B.U.L. Rev. 59 (1987); Eric A. Posner, *Law and Social Norms* (Cambridge: Harvard University Press, 2000); Peter C. Fishburn and William V. Gehrlein, "Toward a Theory of Elections with Probabilistic Preferences," *Econometrica* 45 (1977), 1907.

102   Glenn, *Ambiguous Embrace,* 7.

103   Virginia A. Hodginson, Murray S. Weitzman, Stephen M. Noga, and Heather A. Gorski, *A Portrait of the Independent Sector: Activities and Finances of Charitable Organizations* (Washington, D.C.: Independent Sector, 1993), 9—14, 31.

104   J. Richard Piper, *Ideologies and Institutions: American Conservative and Liberal Governance Prescriptions Since 1933* (Lanham, Md.: Rowman & Littlefield, 1997), 354.

105   National Center for Policy Analysis, a "nonprofit, nonpartisan public policy research institute that seeks innovative, private sector solutions to public policy problems" and supports school vouchers, http://www.public-policy.org/ncpa/about/p1.html (visited on March 8, 2000).

106   Charles Glenn's book, *The Ambiguous Embrace,* was supported by this foundation.

107   People for the American Way, "Buying a Movement: Right-wing Foundations and American Politics" (1996), 8.

108   Larry D. Hatfield and Dexter Waugh, "Smart Bombs . . . ," *San Francisco Examiner,* May 24, 1992, cited in ibid., note 41.

109   Jack Kemp, foreword in Joseph J. Jacobs, *The Compassionate Conservative: Seeking Responsibility and Human Dignity* (Jacobs Family Foundation, distributed by Institute for Contemporary Studies Press, San Francisco, 1996), vii, ix.

110   Ibid., 292.

111   Ibid.

112   See Kuttner, *Everything for Sale,* 352.

113 Anthony DePalma, "Canada Cuts Back Funds for Faith-Based Chari-
     ties," *New York Times*, July 24, 2001, p. A3.

114 Ibid.

115 For a thoughtful, general discussion of the state action requirement, see
     Richard S. Kay, *The State Action Doctrine, the Public-Private Distinction,
     and the Independence of Constitutional Law,* 10 Const. Commentary 329
     (1993).

116 See *Lugar v. Edmonson Oil Co.* 457 U.S. 992 (1981).

117 See *Moose Lodge No. 107 v. Irvis*, 407 U.S. 163 (1972); *Shelley v. Kramer,*
     334 U.S. 1 (1948). But see *Flagg Brothers, Inc. v. Brooks*, 436 U.S. 149
     (1978).

118 *Rendell-Baker v. Kohn*, 457 U.S. 830 (1982)

119 See Martin A. Schwarz and Erwin Chemerinsky, *Practicing Law Institute:
     Section 1983 Civil Rights Litigation Symposium: Dialogue on State Action*, 16
     Touro L. Rev. 775, 787 (2000).

120 *Norwood v. Harrison*, 413 U.S. 455 (1973); *Gilmore v. Montgomery*, 417 U.S.
     556 (1974*); Moose Lodge N. 107 v. Irvis*, 407 U.S. 163 (1972); *Bob Jones Uni-
     versity v. United States*, 461 U.S. 574 (1983).

121 See *Boy Scouts of America v. Dale*, 530 U.S. 640 (2000).

122 See Peter Bowles, "City School to End Support of Boy Scouts," *News-
     day*, Dec. 2, 2000, p. A21. A state official may override local school deci-
     sions, however; the state education commissioner in Massachusetts
     concluded that the Boy Scouts can be excluded only if all groups are
     excluded. See Dave Wedge, "Ed Boss: Schools Ousting Scouts Must Ban
     Every Group or None," *Boston Herald*, Dec. 13, 2000, p. 16. A federal
     judge reached a similar ruling that applied to one county. Susan Fer-
     rechio, "Boy Scouts Win Right to Keep Using Broward Schools,"
     New York Times, March 22, 2001, p. A1. See also Scott S. Greenberger,
     "Helms's Remarks Surprise Action Officials: No Bias Against Scouts,"
     Boston Globe, June 22, 2001, p. B2. Nonetheless, large numbers of
     schools have sought to separate themselves from the Boy Scouts after
     their Supreme Court victory in order to enforce their own public
     policies.

123 Susan Rose-Ackerman, *Social Services and the Market*, 83 Colum. L. Rev.
     1405 (1983)

124 Schirmer, Note: *Physician Assistant As Abortion Provider*, 253.

125 *Rendell-Baker v. Kohn*, 457 US. 830 (1982).

126 Some commentators challenge the claim that public schooling has

declined and point to rising graduation rates and literacy scores as well as greater inclusion of children who would have been excluded in the past. See Linda Darling-Hammond, *The Right to Learn: A Blueprint for Creating Schools that Work* (San Francisco: Jossey-Bass, 1997).

127 See chapter 3; see also Martha Minow, *Reforming School Reform*, 68 Ford. L. Rev. 257 (1999).

128 See chapter 3; see also Martha Minow, *Choice or Commonality: Welfare and Schooling after the End of Welfare As We Knew It*, 49 Duke L. J. 493, 539–542 (1999).

129 Minow, *Choice or Commonality*, Duke L. J., 505–506.

130 *Corporation of the Presiding Bishop of the Church of Jesus Christ of Latter-day Saints v. Amos*, 483 U.S. 327 (1987).

131 *Bob Jones University v. United States*, 461 U.S. 374 (1983).

132 See *Michael M. v. Superior Court*, 450 U.S. 464 (1981) (plurality opinion).

133 Stacey M. Brandenburg, *Employment Law: Alternatives to Employment Discrimination at Private Religious Schools*, 1999 Am. Serv. Am. L. 335, 365 n. 144. Also, some religions may be able to justify single-sex clergy as a bona fide occupational qualification. A42 U.S.C. 2000e-1(a)(1994).

134 Mary Leonard, "Judge Sees No Bias in Firing of Lesbian, Ky. [Kentucky] Baptist Agency Favored in Ruling," *Boston Globe*, July 25, 2001, p. A2.

135 See Glenn, *Ambiguous Embrace*, 194–5.

136 Ibid., 195 (citing *New York Times*, June 21, 1986, sec. 1, p. 32).

137 Ibid.

138 Ibid., 201–208.

139 Ibid., 276.

140 Ibid., 277.

141 Ibid., 150, 163–65, 178, 185, 289.

142 See Elizabeth Schneider, *Battered Women and Feminist Lawmaking* (New Haven: Yale University Press, 2000).

143 See generally Stephen Toulmin, *Cosmopolis: The Hidden Agenda of Modernity* (New York: Free Press, 1990), 16–17, 62, 70–71.

144 Sagawa and Segal, *Common Interest, Common Good*, 165. The failure rate of nonprofits is less well documented, but it may well increase the more they emulate entrepreneurial businesses. See Ann Merrill, "Not So Nonprofit: Nonprofit Corporations Look for Ways to Boost Revenues with For-Profit Enterprises," *Minneapolis Star Tribune*, Sept. 22, 1996, p. 1D.

145   Kuttner, *Everything for Sale*, 127.

146   Ibid., 127–9.

147   Sagawa and Segal, *Common Interest, Common Good*, 236.

148   Ibid., 242.

149   Ibid.

150   John D. Colombo, *Why Is Harvard Tax-Exempt?*, 35 Ariz. L. Rev. 841
        (1993); Heather Gottry, *Note: Profit or Perish: Non-Profit Social Service
        Organizations and Social Entrepreneurship*, 6 Geo. J. Poverty L. & Pol'y 249
        (1999).

151   Sagawa and Segal, *Common Interest, Common Good*, 166–67. See also
        Donald L. Sharple, *Unfair Business Competition and the Tax on Income Des-
        tined for Charity: Forty-Six Years Later*, 3 Fla. Tax. Rev. 367 410 n. 123
        (1996). See also Daniel Halperin, *Why Are Nonprofits Exempt from Tax*
        (draft, 2000).

152   Segal and Sagawa, *Common Interest, Common Good*, 167–8.

153   Avner Ben-Ner, *Who Benefits from the Nonprofit Sector? Reforming Law
        and Public Policy Towards Nonprofit Organizations*, 104 Yale L. J. 731, 747
        (1994) (book review of *Who Benefits from the Nonprofit Sector*, Charles T.
        Clotfelter, ed.).

154   See Gottry, *Note: Profit or Perish*, 39–52.

155   Ibid. See also Henry Hansmann, *Unfair Competition and the Unrelated Busi-
        ness Income Tax*, 75 Va. L. Rev. 605 (1989).

156   See James R. Hines Jr., "Nonprofit Business Activity and the Unrelated
        Business Income Tax," National Bureau of Economic Research Work-
        ing Paper 6820 (Dec. 1998).

157   Internal Revenue Code section 501(m). See generally Henry Hans-
        mann, *The Two Nonprofit Sectors* (New Haven: Yale University, Institute
        for Social and Policy Studies, Program on Non-Profit Organizations,
        1988), Working Paper 133.

158   Halperin, *Why Are Nonprofits Exempt from Tax?*, 1.

159   Emerson and Twersky, *New Social Entrepreneurs*, 243. To achieve its mis-
        sion, a nonprofit may actually have to employ many not in its target
        group; Sagawa and Segal, *Common Interest, Common Good*, 166.

160   Gottry, *Profit or Perish*, 71.

161   Barbara Bucholtz, *Reflections on the Role of Nonprofit Associations in a Rep-
        resentative Democracy*, 7 Cornell J. L. and Pub. Pol'y 555 (1998).

162   Ibid.

163   See Robert D. Putnam, "The Strange Disappearance of Civic America,"
       American Prospect 24 (Winter 1996): 34–49.

164   Kuttner, *Everything for Sale,* 354–55.

165   Nina J. Crimm, *An Explanation of the Federal Income Tax Exemption for
       Charitable Organizations: A Theory of Risk Compensation,* 50 Fla. L. Rev.
       419 (1998); Burton A. Weisbrod, *The Nonprofit Economy* (Cambridge:
       Harvard University Press, 1998), 59–60; Burton A. Weisbrod, T*he Volun-
       tary Nonprofit Sector* (Lexington, Mass.: Lexington Books, 1977), 1–10;
       Bruce Chapman, *Between Markets and Politics: A Social Choice Theoretic
       Appreciation of the Charitable Sector,* 6 Geo. Mason L. Rev. 821 [add year].

166   See Edward Rubin, *Getting Past Democracy,* 149 U. Penn. L. Rev. 711,
       776–784 (2001).

167   See Glenn, *Ambiguous Embrace,* 124, 134; Charles L. Glenn, *Choice of
       School in Six Nations* (U.S. Dept. of Education: Government Printing
       Office, 1989). See also Jody Freeman, *Collaborative Governance in the
       Administrative State,* 45 U.C.L.A. L. Rev. 1 (1997); Jody Freeman, *The Pri-
       vate Role of Public Governance,* 75 N.Y.U. L. Rev. 543 (2000); Michael
       Dorf and Charles Sabel, *A Constitution of Democratic Experimentalism,* 98
       Colum. L. Rev. 267 (1998); Susan Sturm, *Second Generation Employment
       Discrimination: A Structural Approach,* 101 Colum. L. Rev. 458 (2001);
       Gunther Teubner, *Substantive and Reflexive Elements in Modern Law,* 17
       Law & Soc'y Rev. 239 (1983).

168   Anthony Bryk et al., *Catholic Schools and the Common Good* (Cambridge:
       Harvard University Press, 1993), 10, 51–54.

169   Glenn, *Ambiguous Embrace,* 280–1, 293.

170   See www.geocities.comHotSprings/villa/7853.

171   See William James, *A Pluralistic Universe* (New York: Longmans, Green,
       1909), 321–22; Nelson Goodman and Catherine Z. Elgin, *Reconceptions
       in Philosophy and Other Arts and Sciences* (London: Routledge, 1988), 24;
       Hilary Putnam, *Pragmatism: An Open Question* (Oxford: Blackwell,
       1995), 30–31; Jean Wahl, *The Pluralist Philosophies of England and
       America* (London: Open Court, 1925), 317–8.

172   See Horace M. Kallen, "Democracy Versus the Melting-Pot," in *Culture
       and Democracy in the United States* (New York: Boni and Liveright, 1924),
       67, 125; R. Laurence Moore, *Religious Outsiders and the Making of Amer-
       ica* (New York: Oxford University Press, 1986).

173   See Martha Minow et al., eds., *Narrative, Violence, and the Law: The
       Essays of Robert Cover* (Ann Arbor: University of Michigan Press, 1992);
       Harold J. Laski, "The Sovereignty of the State," in *Studies in the Problem
       of Sovereignty* (New Haven: Yale University Press, 1917), 1, 19.

3. Schooling, Welfare, and Faith-Based Initiatives

1   See Bill Berkowitz, *Prospecting Among the Poor* (Oakland: Applied Research Center, May 2001).

2   The heady language of supporters treats choice as a revolution producing oases of innovation. See Andrei Cherny, "The Choice Revolution," *Blueprint* (July/August 2001), p. 67. Adapted from Andrei Cherney, *The New Deal* (New York: Basic Books, 2001).

3   See generally Joseph Nye et al., eds., *Why People Don't Trust Government* (Cambridge: Harvard University Press, 1997), ix.

4   See "Social Security and the Market," *New York Times*, Jan. 22, 1999, A24; see also Clifford Krauss, "Social Security, Chilean Style," *New York Times*, Aug. 16, 1998, p. 4.

5   Milton Friedman argued for market approaches to schooling as early as 1962. See Milton Friedman, *Capitalism and Freedom* (Chicago: University of Chicago Press, 1962).

6   See, e.g., Children's Educational Opportunity Foundation, *The School Choice Debate* (http://www.childrenfirstamerica.org/debate.html) (visited Sept. 22, 1999).

7   See James B. Cleveland, *School Choice: American Elementary and Secondary Education Enter the "Adapt or Die" Environment of a Competitive Marketplace*, 29 John Marshall L. Rev. 75 (1995) (describing choice models); see also Phillip T. K. Daniel, *A Comprehensive Analysis of Educational Choice: Can the Polemic of Legal Problems Be Overcome?*, 43 DePaul L. Rev. 17 (1993) (describing magnet and charter schools as public schools with specialized programs and enrollments open to students from across the district); James A. Peyser, *School Choice: When, Not If*, 35 Boston Coll. L. Rev. 619 (1994) (describing school-choice models); Justine J. Sayie, *Education Emancipation for Inner City Students: A New Legal Paradigm for Achieving Equality of Educational Opportunity*, 48 U. Miami L. Rev. 913, 940 (1994) (arguing that providing vouchers would sever the link between "residential location and school quality"); Priscilla Wohlstetter, "Education by Charter," in *School-Based Management: Organizing for High Performance*, Susan Albers Mohrman and Priscilla Wohlstetter, eds. (San Francisco: Jossey-Bass, 1994), 139 (describing a charter school idea).

8   See Peyser, *School Choice*, 621 (discussing intradistrict public school choice).

9   See ibid. (discussing private choice based on state-funded vouchers); see also Quentin L. Quade, "A Primer on Educational Choice" <http://www.marquette.edu/blum/primer.html>) (visited Sept. 22, 1999). On

the vexed subject of whether tax credits and exemptions should be viewed in the same way as vouchers or subsidies, see Edward A. Zelinsky, *Are Tax "Benefits" Constitutionally Equivalent to Direct Expenditures*, 112 Harv. L. Rev. 379 (1998).

10   See Nina Shokraii Rees & Sarah E. Youssef, "School Choice 1999: What's Happening in the States" (http://www.heritage.org/schools) (visited Sept. 6, 1999) (on file with the Duke Law Journal).

11   Sheila Suess Kennedy, "Privatizing Education: The Politics of Vouchers," *Phi Delta Kappan* 82 (2001): 450.

12   See generally John E. Chubb and Terry M. Moe, *Politics, Markets, and American Schools* (Washington, D.C.: Brookings Institution, 1990); Richard F. Elmore, "Choice As an Instrument of Public Policy: Evidence from Education and Health Care," in *Choice and Control in American Education: The Theory of Choice and Control in Education*, William H. Clune and John F. Witte, eds. (London: Falmer, 1990), vol. 1, 285.

13   See Note, *The Limits of Choice: School Choice Reform and State Constitutional Guarantees of Educational Quality*, 109 Harv. L. Rev. 2002 (1996) (suggests that a true free market for education will pose an inherent risk of creating failures as well as successes).

14   Sources of educational reform agendas are complex. *See* Chris Pipho, "Eagle Eyes and Rabbit Ears: Locating Policy Issues," *Phi Delta Kappan* 80 (1999): 645–646.

15   Sheila Suess Kennedy, "Privatizing Education," 450.

16   *See* Robert S. Alley, *Public Education and the Public Good*, 4 Wm. & Mary Bill of Rts. J. 277, 348 (1995); Michael W. McConnell, *Multiculturalism, Majoritarianism, and Educational Choice: What Does Our Constitutional Tradition Have to Say?* 123 U. Chi. Legal Forum 150 (1991).

17   See Robert D. Putnam, "Bowling Alone: America's Declining Social Capital," *Journal of Democracy* 6 (1995): 65–66; Robert D. Putnam, "Tuning in, Tuning out: The Strange Disappearance of Social Capital in America," *PS: Political Science and Policy* 28 (1995): 664–83.

18   See Putnam, "Bowling Alone," 66–67.

19   See ibid., 67.

20   Conversation with Thomas Sander, program director, Saguaro Seminar, John F. Kennedy School of Government, Harvard University (Sept. 1, 1999). See Adam Clymer, "A Surprise Possibility: A Dignified Democratic Race," *New York Times*, Oct. 28, 1999, A28. See Dana Milbank, "What W. Stands for: Wishy-Washy or Wise?" *New Republic*, April 26, 1999, 66.

21   See Personal Responsibility and Work Opportunity Reconciliation Act of 1996, Pub. L. No. 104–193, 110 Stat. 2105 (codified in scattered sections of 42 U.S.C.).

22   The difficulty of passing tax levies to support public schools has been widely noted. See, e.g., Ann Fisher et al., "State-Aid Pledge Swayed Voters," *Columbus Dispatch*, Nov. 5, 1998, p. 1A; Robert Starr, "Legislative Race Set by Primary," *Boston Globe*, May 9, 1999, p. 5. On concerns about the costs of special education, see Norman Draper, "Minneapolis School Budget Balanced; Board's Intended Cuts Much Less Painful than Expected," *Minneapolis Star Tribune*, June 23, 1999, p. 3B.

23   See, e.g., Cal Thomas, "Opponents Speak for Themselves, Not the Poor: Learning to Love School Choice," *Cincinnati Enquirer*, May 6, 1999, p. A16. See "Prepared Testimony of Joe Nathan, Ph.D. and Director, Center for School Change, University of Minnesota Humphrey Institute of Public Affairs Before House Education and the Workforce Committee," *Fed. News Service*, May 25, 1999.

24   See *Bagley v. Ramond Sch. Dep't* 728 A.2d 127 (Me. 1999).

25   Adam Cohen, "A First Report Card on Vouchers," *Time*, April 26, 1999, p. 36. The Cleveland plan targets low-income children. See Margaret A. Nero, *Case Comment, The Cleveland Scholarship and Tutoring Program*, 58 Ohio St. L.J. 1103 (1997).

26   Seymour B. Sarason, *Charter Schools: Another Flawed Educational Reform?* (New York: Teachers College Press, 1998), 18.

27   Kevin B. Smith & Kenneth J. Meier, *The Case Against School Choice: Politics, Markets, and Fools* (Armonk, N.Y.: M. E. Sharpe, 1995), p. 56.

28   See, e.g., "In '96, Phoenix Built for Future: Renovations, New Structures Led Changes," *Arizona Republic/Phoenix Gazette*, Jan. 1, 1997, sect. 4 (Central Phoenix Community), p. 1.

29   Cameron McWhirer and Sheryl Kennedy, "Windy City Shines As School Reform Success: Progress Is Reported a Decade After Being Labeled Nation's Worst," *Detroit News*, March 21, 1999, p. A10.

30   Smith and Meier, *The Case Against School Choice*, 28.

31   See Richard Weissbourd, *The Vulnerable Child* (Reading, Mass.: Addison-Wesley, 1996), 171–84. See Lisbeth B. Schorr, *Common Purpose: Strengthening Families and Neighborhoods to Rebuild America* (New York: Anchor Books, Doubleday, 1997), 58–60.

32   See Smith and Meier, *The Case Against School Choice*, 49–50.

33   See Jay Heubert and Robert Hauser, *High Stakes: Testing for Tracking, Promotion, and Graduation* (Washington, D.C.: National Academy Press, 1999).

34   See Alfie Kohn, *Punished by Rewards* (Boston: Houghton Mifflin, 1993), 200.

35   See Adam Cohen, "First Report Card on Vouchers," *Time*, April 26, 1999, pp. 36–38.

36   Molly S. McUsic, "The Law's Role in the Distribution of Education: The Promises and Pitfalls of School Finance Litigation," in *Law and School Reform: Six Strategies for Promoting Educational Equity*, Jay P. Heubert, ed. (New Haven: Yale University Press, 1999), 122.

37   Abby R. Weiss, *Going It Alone: A Study of Massachusetts Charter Schools* (Boston: Institute for Responsive Education, 1997), 1–27.

38   Sarason, *Charter Schools*, 62.

39   Janet Bingham, "Statewide Charter School District Proposed," *Denver Post*, Jan. 13, 1999, p. A18.

40   See Diane Ravitch, *The Great School Wars: New York City 1905–1983: A History of the Public Schools As Battlefield of Social Change* (New York: Basic Books, 1974), 107–230; David B. Tyack, *The One Best System: A History of American Urban Education* (Cambridge: Harvard University Press, 1974), 78–176.

41   See Sheila Suess Kennedy, "Privatizing Education," 450.

42   John Tierney, "Here Come the Alpha Pups: The Makers of New Electronic Game Called Pox Decided to Let Kids Do Their Marketing for Them," *New York Times Magazine* (Aug. 5, 2001), p. 38.

43   See Linda Darling-Hammond, *The Right to Learn: A Blueprint for Creating Schools that Work* (San Francisco: Jossey-Bass, 1997), 24; Smith and Meier, *The Case Against School Choice*, 16.

44   See Gary Orfield, "The Growth of Segregation: African Americans, Latinos, and Unequal Education," in *Dismantling Education: The Quiet Reversal of Brown v. Board of Education*, Gary Orfield and Susan E. Eaton, eds. (New York: New Press, 1996), 53–55.

45   Students in Iowa, Minnesota, and North Dakota score close to the levels of math proficiency needed to demonstrate moderately complex reasoning processes and well above the level necessary to show proficiency in numerical operations and beginning problem solving. Students in Louisiana and Mississippi on average do not meet this lower threshold. See ibid.

46   Ibid.

47   Ibid., 113–116. Positive reports on some versions of school choice pilot programs, such as Paul E. Petersen, *School Choice: A Report Card*, 6 Va. J.

Soc. Pol'y & L. 47 (1998); Paul E. Petersen et al., *The Effectiveness of School Choice in Milwaukee: A Secondary Analysis of Data from the Program's Evaluation* (Cambridge: Harvard University Program in Education Policy and Governance, 1996), are hampered by the self-selection problems of participating families, the limited time frame, and limited numbers. Others find more mixed or inconclusive results. See John F. Witte Jr., *The Market Approach to Education: An Analysis of America's First Voucher Program* (Princeton, N.J.: Princeton University Press, 2000); Bruce Fuller et al., "School Choice: Abundant Hopes, Scarce Evidence of Results," (Berkeley: Policy Analysis for California Education, 1999), 84; see Frank R. Kemerer, "School Choice Accountability," in *School Choice and Social Controversy: Politics, Policy, and Law,* Stephen D. Sugarman and Frank R. Kemerer, eds. (Washington, D.C.: Brookings Institution, 1999), 174, 199–200. At the same time, studies of public school choice show benefits from competition. Caroline M. Hoxby, "Analyzing School Choice Reforms that Use America's Traditional Forms," in *Learning from School Choice*, Paul E. Petersen and Bryan C. Hassel, eds. (Washington, D.C.: Brookings Institution, 1998), 45. One book warns that New Zealand's school choice experiment produced ethnic and class segregation and disserved equity goals. See Edwin B. Fiske and Helen F. Ladd, *When Schools Compete: A Cautionary Tale* (Washington, D.C.: Brookings Institution, 2000).

48   For histories of these movements, see Martha Minow, *Reforming School Reform*, 68 Fordham L. Rev. 257 (1999).

49   See Gary Orfield et al., *Dismantling Desegregation* (1996).

50   Darling Hammond, *The Right to Learn*, 22.

51   Barbara Bezdek, *Contractual Welfare: Non-Accountability and Diminished Democracy in Local Government Contracts for Welfare-to-Work Services*, 28 Fordham Urban Law Journal 1559, 1567 (2001).

52   Quoted in Stanley Carlson-Thies, *"Don't Look to Us": The Negative Responses of the Churches to Welfare Reform*, 11 Notre Dame J. L. Ethics & Pub. Pol'y 662, 672 (1997).

53   USC 604a (Supp. 1997); 604a(b).

54   USC 604a(c),(d).

55   USC 604a(j).

56   USC 604a(d)(1).

57   See 42 U.S.C. § 604a(b).

58   See ibid. § 604a(d)(1).

59   See ibid. § 604a(a)(1).

60 See Schorr, *Common Purpose*, 15–17.

61 A most thoughtful discussion appears in the essays collected by E. J. Dionne Jr. and Ming Hsu Chen in *Sacred Places, Civic Purposes: Should Government Help Faith-Based Charity?* (Washington, D.C.: Brookings Institution Press).

62 See "Ashcroft Applauds D.C.'s Use of Private Organizations in Making Welfare Work" (Nov. 12, 1998) (http:www.senate.gov^ashcroft/11–12–98.htm).

63 Compare the statement of Senator Ashcroft, p. 686, 144 Cong. Reg. S12 (daily edition, Oct. 20, 1998) with the "Statement of the President on Signing the Community Opportunities, Accountability, and Training and Educational Services Act of 1998," Weekly Comp. Pres. Doc. 34 (Nov. 2, 1998), p. 2148.

64 USC 604a(f).

65 USC 604a(k)(preemption).

66 Marvin N. Olasky, *The Tragedy of American Compassion* (Washington, D.C.: Regnery Gateway, 1992), 204–09, 214–26, 224–25.

67 See Jim Wallis, "Criminologist John DiIulio Explains Why a God-Centered and Problem-Focused Approach Is Needed to Save Our Youth," *Sojourners* (Sept.-Oct. 1997) (http:www.sojourners.com/soj9709/970910.html).

68 Community Solutions Act of 2001, 2001 Bill Tracking H.R. 1284 (Rep. J. Watts, sponsor).

69 Dana Milbank, "Bush Turns to Domestic Agenda," *Washington Post*, Sept. 25, 2001, p. A7.

70 See PEW Forum, "Explanatory Notes Regarding H.R. 7 by the House Judiciary Committee, Charitable Choice Provision of the Community Solutions Act of 2001 (HR 7)."

71 See "House OKs Charity Voucher Bill," Associated Press (Aug. 3, 2001).

72 *Pierce v. Society of Sisters*, 268 U.S. 510 (1925).

73 See Robert C. Bulman and David L. Kirp, "The Shifting Politics of School Choice," in *School Choice and Social Controversy: Politics, Policy, and Law,* Stephen D. Sugarman and Frank R. Kemerer, eds. (Washington, D.C.: Brookings Institution, 1999), 36, 40–45.

74 See Lawrence Cremin, *American Education: The Metropolitan Experience 1876–1980* (New York: Harper & Row, 1988), 273–321; see also Catholic Charities USA (http://www.catholiccharitiesusa.org) (on file with *Duke Law Journal*)(visited Aug. 31, 1999); United Methodist Church:

Faith in Action (http://www.umc.org/faithinaction) (on file with the
Duke Law Journal)(visited Aug. 31, 1999).

75   See "Comments of Father Brian Hehir," *Harvard Divinity School Seminar
      on Democratic Revival* (Mar. 9, 1998); see also Ernest Tucker, "More Par-
      ishes Running in the Red," *Chicago Sun-Times*, Jan. 22, 1999, p. 40.

76   See Anthony S. Bryk et al., *Catholic Schools and the Common Good* (Cam-
      bridge: Harvard University Press, 1993), 17–18.

77   See ibid., 46–51.

78   See ibid., 10, 51–54.

79   See ibid., 52–54; Lona O'Connor, "In Vouchers, Archdiocese Sees Way
      to Save Inner-City Schools," *Fort Lauderdale Sun-Sentinel*, Mar. 21, 1999,
      p. 4B.

80   *See* Rodney J. Thoulion, "Let's Work Together to Improve Education,"
      New Orleans Times-Picayune, May 8, 1999, B6; Ernest Tucker, "More Par-
      ishes Running in the Red," *Chicago Sun-Times*, Jan. 22, 1999, p. 40.

81   Conversation with Professor Elizabeth Bartholet, Harvard Law School
      (Sept. 2, 1999); see also Eileen Swift, " 'Mr. Tom': He's a Real Class
      Act," *Newsday*, Oct. 1, 1995, p. A70.

82   See, e.g., Steve Chapman, "A Judge's Tunnel Vision on School Vouch-
      ers," *Chicago Tribune*, Aug. 29, 1999, p. C21; Torry Minton, "S.F. Arch-
      bishop Agrees to Discuss Partners Policy," *San Francisco Chronicle*, Feb. 7,
      1997, p. A21.

83   The widespread reliance of communities on Catholic hospitals as chief
      health care providers willing to serve Medicaid patients can pose prob-
      lems since patients may want birth control that the Catholic institutions
      will not provide. See Jayne O'Donnell, "Antitrust Health Fight: Catho-
      lic Hospital Deals Limit Access," *USA Today*, April 8, 1999, p. 1B.

84   Catholic Charities of Chicago, for example, receives 74 percent of its
      budget from public money; for Catholic Charities of San Francisco, the
      figure is closer to 40 percent. See Chapman, "Judge's Tunnel Vision";
      Minton, "S.F. Archbishop Agrees."

85   See Nina J. Easton, "The Year 2016 and American Society Has Finally
      Become Civilized," *Los Angeles Times*, May 19, 1996, p. 22; Alva James-
      Johnson, "Social Service Agencies Facing a Refocusing," *Omaha World-
      Herald*, Oct. 18, 1995, p. 15SF; Steve Kloehn, "Cash-Strapped Archdio-
      cese Drops Charter-School Ideas," *Chicago Tribune*, Sept. 2, 1999, p. 1;
      Tim O'Neil, "Archdiocese Seeks to Lower Debt," *St. Louis Post-
      Dispatch*, Oct. 20, 1995, p. 12A; Ernest Tucker, "George Shapes His
      Inside Circle," *Chicago Sun-Times*, May 2, 1999, p. 24.

86   The text of the First Amendment states, in part: "Congress shall make

no law respecting an establishment of religion, or prohibiting the free exercise thereof . . ." U.S. Const. amend. I, cl. 1. The Supreme Court applied the First Amendment's Establishment Clause to the states in 1963. See *School Dist. of Abington Township v. Schempp*, 374 U.S. 203, 215 (1963).

87   Ibid. at 240–41 (Brennan, J., concurring).

88   Phillip Kurland urges a position of strict neutrality, through which the government would use only secular criteria and would not undertake to accommodate religion. See Phillip J. Kurland, *Of Church and State and the Supreme Court*, 29 U. Chi. L. Rev. 1, 5 (1961). Yet, this approach neglects the Free Exercise Clause. Laurence Tribe maintains that the two clauses advance voluntarism and separatism, see Laurence Tribe, *American Constitutional Law*, 2d ed. (Mineola, N.Y.: Foundation Press, 1988), 1160–61. The Supreme Court's decisions do not precisely fit these notions; see Geoffrey R. Stone et al., *Constitutional Law*, 3d ed. (Boston: Little, Brown, 1996), 1540–43, which describes the varying approaches the Supreme Court has taken to interpreting the religion clauses. Justice O'Connor has urged a notion of "no endorsement" to guide the application of the Establishment Clause. See, e.g., *Capital Square Review and Advisory Bd. v. Pinette*, 515 U.S. 750, 772–84 (1995) (O'Connor, J., concurring in part and concurring in the judgment, argues that the Establishment Clause should operate primarily to prevent government from endorsing a particular religion). Her idea, however, has received only limited support from the Court, with different justices at times lining up behind it and at times against it. See, e.g., Stone et al., *Constitutional Law*, 1566–67, which discusses the "shifting" character of the majority that appears to endorse Justice O'Connor's endorsement test in *County of Allegheny v. American Civil Liberties Union*, 492 U.S. 573 (1989). Furthermore, assessing what counts as a state endorsement of religion will vary with the perceptions of members of different groups. See Martha Minow, *Making all the Difference: Inclusion, Exclusion, and American Law* (Ithaca, N.Y.: Cornell University Press, 1990), 62–63 (suggesting that Justice O'Connor's endorsement test is hindered by the fact that it would be nearly impossible to find a truly objective observer who could neutrally determine whether a state action gave the appearance of endorsing religion). Lawrence Sager and Christopher Eisgruber have developed a coherent conception of the fundamental commitment to equal regard of all individuals behind the religion clauses, see, e.g., Christopher L. Eisgruber & Lawrence G. Sager, *Unthinking Religious Freedom*, 74 Tex. L. Rev. 577, 600–12 (1996), but to date this view has not attracted the support of the courts.

89   Pub. L. No. 104–193, § 104, 110 Stat. 2105, 2161–63 (1996) (codified at 42 U.S.C. 604(a)).

90   403 U.S. 602 (1971)

91   See ibid., 614.

92   See *Lemon*, 403 U.S., 612–13.

93   Four justices on the current Court have authored concurring or dissenting opinions calling for the rejection of the *Lemon* test, and a fifth, Justice Thomas, has joined in one of these opinions. *See Lamb's Chapel v. Center Moriches Union Free Sch. Dist.*, 508 U.S. 384, 399–400 (1993) (Scalia, J., concurring).

94   *Mitchell v. Helms*, 530 U.S. 793, 809 (2000) (plurality opinion).

95   *See Agostini v. Felton*, 521 U.S. 203, 215–36 (1997) (overruling *Aguilar v. Felton*, 473 U.S. 402 (1986), and, in relevant part, *School Dist. v. Ball*, 473 U.S. 373 (1986)).

96   *Mitchell v. Helms*, 350 U.S. 793 (2000) (plurality opinion).

97   *Good News Club v. Milford Central School*, 121 S. Ct. 2093 (2001)

98   See *Wallace v. Jaffree*, 472 U.S. 38, 69 (1985) (O'Connor, J., concurring).

99   See *Bowen v. Kendrick*, 487 U.S. 589, 610 (1988) (plurality).

100   *See* Carl H. Esbeck, *A Constitutional Case for Governmental Cooperation with Faith-Based Social Service Providers*, 46 Emory L. J. 1, 20–42 (1997). For a critique of this view as inadequately attentive to separationist concerns, see Douglas Laycock, *The Underlying Unity of Separation and Neutrality*, 46 Emory L. J. 43 (1997).

101   *Good News Club v. Milford Central School*, 121 S. Ct. 2093, 2111 (Breyer, J, concurring in part); *Mitchell v. Helms*, 530 U.S. 793, 829 (2000) (O'Connor, J., concurring in judgment).

102   *Good News Club v. Milford Central School*, 121 S. Ct. 2093 (2001); *Rosenberger v. Rector and Visitors of Univ. of Va.*, 515 U.S. 819 (1995).

103   See *Lee v. Weisman*, 505 U.S. 577, 587 (1992).

104   *Employment Div. v. Smith*, 494 U.S. 872 (1990). A law that is not general in application and instead seems to be aimed at suppressing a particular religion triggers strict scrutiny by the Court, and in a recent case, the Court found a free exercise violation when a city adopted an emergency law prohibiting animal sacrifice shortly after a group obtained permission to build a church that engaged in animal sacrifice. *Church of the Lukumi Bablu Aye v. City of Hialeah*, 508 U.S. 520 (1993).

105   See *Bowen*, 487 U.S., 600–18.

106   459 U.S. 116 (1982).

107   See ibid., 117.

108   512 U.S. 687 (1994).

109   See ibid., 696.

110   Compare *Engel v. Vitale*, 370 U.S. 421 (1962); *Abington School Dist. v. Schemp*, 374 U.S. 203 (1963); *Lee v. Weisman*, 505 U.S. (1992); *Santa Fe Indep. School Dist. v. Doe*, 530 U.S. 290 (2000) *with Good News Club v. Milford Central School*, 121 S. Ct. 2093 (2001).

111   See *Rosenberger v. Rector of the Univ. of Va.*, 515 U.S. 819, 840 (1995).

112   See *Mitchell v. Helms*, 530 U.S. 793, 817 (2000) (plurality opinion); ibid., 839 (O'Connor, J., joined by Breyer, J., concurring in the judgment) (discussing *Meek v. Pittenger*, 421 U.S. 349 (1975) and *Wolman v. Walter*, 433 U.S. 229 (1977)).

113   See *Committee for Public Education and Religious Liberty v. Regan*, 444 U.S. 646 (1980).

114   *See Mueller*, 463 U.S. at 397–99; *Nyquist*, 413 U.S. at 775–76.

115   See *Wolman v. Walter*, 433 U.S. 229, 238 (1977).

116   See *Everson v. Board of Educ.*, 330 U.S. 1, 17–18 (1947).

117   *See Agostini v. Felton*, 521 U.S. 203, 240 (1997). *Agostini* overruled the Supreme Court's earlier decisions in *Aguilar v. Felton*, 473 U.S. 402 (1985), and *School District v. Ball*, 473 U.S. 373 (1985).

118   See *Lemon v. Kurtzman*, 403 U.S. 602, 606–07 (1971).

119   See *Witters v. Washington Dep't of Servs. for the Blind*, 474 U.S. 481, 487 (1986). In *Witters*, the Court drew an explicit distinction between that case and *Ball*: "[W]here . . . no meaningful distinction can be made between aid to the student and aid to the school, 'the concept of a loan to individuals is a transparent fiction.'" Ibid. at 487 n. 4 (quoting *Ball*, 473 U.S. at 396). The Court recently restated and reaffirmed this view of the case in explaining that "any money that ultimately went to religious institutions did so 'only as a result of the genuinely independent and private choices of individuals.'" *Agostini*, 521 U.S. at 226 (quoting *Witters*, 474 U.S. at 487).

120   See *Mueller v. Allen*, 463 U.S. 388, 402 (1983).

121   See *Zobrest v. Catalina Foothills Sch. Dist.*, 509 U.S. 1, 3 (1993).

122   See *Zobrest*, 509 U.S. at 3.

123   See *Mitchell v. Helms*, 530 U.S., at 837, 842.

124   Ibid.

125   Ibid., at 844.

126   487 U.S. 589 (1988).

127   Ibid. at 593; see also ibid. at 617.

128   Ibid. at 613 (quoting *Hunt v. McNair*, 413 U.S. 734, 743 (1973)).

129   *Mitchell v. Helms*, 530 U.S., at 695 (O'Connor, J., joined by Breyer, J.,
       concurring in the judgment); ibid., at 865–895 (Souter, J., dissenting,
       joined by Justice Stevens and Justice Ginsburg). School choice programs
       that restrict vouchers for use in nonreligious schools do not raise prob-
       lems under the Establishment Clause, but they have been challenged as
       interfering with the free exercise of religion of those parents who wish
       to elect parochial schools. Thus far, such challenges have had more suc-
       cess in law reviews than in the courts. Compare Michael McConnell,
       The Selective Funding Problem: Abortions and Religious Schools, 104 Harv. L.
       Rev. 989, 1014–22 (1991) with *Bagley v. Raymond Sch. Dep't.*, No 97–
       275, 1999 West Law 378244 (Vt. June 11, 1999).

130   See, e.g., Steven K. Green, *The Legal Argument Against Private School
       Choice*, 62 U. Cin. L. Rev. 37 (1993); Walter McCann and Judith Areen,
       "Vouchers and the Citizen—Some Legal Questions," in *Educational
       Vouchers: Concepts and Controversies*, George R. LaNoue, ed. (New
       York: New York Teachers College Press, 1972), 117–24.

131   See *Simmons-Harris v. Goff*, Nos. 96APE08-982, 96APE08-991, 1997
       WL 217583, at *1 (Ohio Ct. App. May 1, 1997), *aff'd in part and rev'd in
       part*, 711 N.E. 2d 203 (Ohio 1999), cert. granted *sub. nom. Senel Taylor v.
       Doris Simmons-Harris*, 122 S. Ct. 23 (2001), 2001 *U.S. Lexus* 5353.

132   In 1996–97, scholarship recipients received 90 percent of tuition costs,
       up to a maximum of $2,500. See ibid.

133   See ibid.

134   See ibid.

135   See *Goff*, 711 N.E. 2d at 210.

136   See ibid.

137   See ibid. at 210–16.

138   See *Simmons-Harris v. Zelman*, 54 F. Supp. 2d 725, 728 (N.D. Ohio 1999).

139   See ibid. at 741; see also Amy Dockser Marcus, "Judge Blocks School
       Voucher Program in Ohio," *Wall Street Journal*, Aug. 25, 1999, p. B2.

140   See *Simmons-Harris v. Zelman*, Nos. 1:99 CV 1740, 1:99 CV 1818, 1999
       WL 669222, at *2 (N.D. Ohio Aug. 27, 1999).

141   122 S. Ct. 23 (2001).

142   See *Jackson v. Benson*, 578 N.W. 2d 602, 608 (Wis.), cert. denied, 119 S.
       Ct. 466 (1998). In order to participate in the program, the private
       schools must agree to follow guidelines prohibiting discrimination
       and promoting health and safety. See ibid.

143   See ibid. at 619 n. 17.

144   See ibid.

145   See *Jackson v. Benson*, 119 S. Ct. 466 (1998).

146   See *Jackson*, 578 N.W. 2d at 620. See Case Comment, *Establishment Clause—School Vouchers—Wisconsin Supreme Court Upholds Milwaukee Parental Choice Program*, 112 Harv. L. Rev. 737, 742 (1999).

147   See *Chittenden Town Sch. Dist. v. Vermont Dep't of Educ.*, No. 97–275, 1999 WL 378244 (Vt. June 11, 1999).

148   See ibid.

149   See ibid.

150   The Court's majority stated in *Mueller*: "It is noteworthy that all but one of our recent cases invalidating state aid to parochial schools have involved the direct transmission of assistance from the state to the schools themselves." *Mueller v. Allen*, 463 U.S. 388, 399 (1983). The one exception was *Nyquist*, which the Court distinguished on the ground that the benefits were available only to parents of children in nonpublic schools. See *Mueller V. Allen* at 398.

151   See *Mueller*, 463 U.S. at 398.

152   See Donald L. Beci, *School Violence: Protecting Our Children and the Fourth Amendment*, 41 Cath. U. L. Rev. 817, 823 n. 31 (1992); Julie Huston Vallarelli, Note, *State Constitutional Restraints on Privatization of Education*, 72 B.U. L. Rev. 381, 387 (1992). Private schools may not discriminate on the basis of race, see *Runyon v. McCrary*, 427 U.S. 160, 179 (1976) (applying 42 U.S.C. § 1981 to private schools), but they may discriminate on other factors, such as economic class. With the exception of limited scholarship programs, private schools largely restrict themselves to students with the ability to pay tuition.

153   See Isaac Kramnick & R. Laurence Moore, "Can the Churches Save the Cities?: Faith-Based Services and the Constitution," *American Prospect*, Nov.-Dec. 1997, p. 47; see also Minow, *Reforming School Reform*.

154   487 U.S. 589 (1988).

155   *Mueller*, 463 U.S. at 402.

156   Ibid. at 401; see also *Agostini v. Felton*, 521 U.S. 203, 229 (1997).

157   See Minow, "Parents, Partners and Choice," in *School Choice: The Moral Debate*, Alan Wolfe, ed. (Princeton University Press, forthcoming). This article explores possible challenges to school choice plans that seek to ensure racial balance or that have other effects on equality and due process or the Free Exercise rights of students.

158   *See* Bryk at al., *Catholic Schools and the Common Good*, 343; Chubb and

Moe, *Politics, Markets, and American Schools*, 206–19, 221–23, 225–29.

159   See Bryk at al., *Catholic Schools*, 11, 327.

160   See ibid. See John Dewey, *Outlines of a Critical Theory of Ethics* (New York: Hillary House, 1957; original, 1891), 131; John Dewey and Evelyn Dewey, *Schools of Tomorrow* (New York: E. P. Dutton, 1915), 313–16; John Dewey, "Philosophy and Education," in *Higher Education Faces the Future*, Paul A. Schilpp, ed. (New York: H. Liveright, 1930), 273, 282.

161   See Association for Supervision and Curriculum Development, *Issues Analysis: Public Schools of Choice* (Alexandria, Va.: 1990), 9; Robert B. Westbrook, "Public Schooling and American Democracy," in *Democracy, Education, and the Schools*, Roger Soder, ed. (San Francisco: Jossey-Bass, 1996), 125, 131.

162   See Richard Pratte, *The Public School Movement* (New York: David McKay, 1973), 75–124; David Tyack and Elizabeth Hansot, *Managers of Virtue: Public School Leadership in America, 1820–1980* (New York: Basic Books, 1982), 20–25.

163   See *Pierce v. Society of Sisters*, 268 U.S. 510, 534–35 (1925).

164   See Gary Orfield et al., *Dismantling Desegregation*, 359–61. Overcoming education disadvantages for poor and minority children will require multiple kinds of reform. See David A. Hamburg, *Today's Children: Creating a Future for a Generation in Crisis* (New York: Times Books, 1992), 296–323.

165   See, e g., Carnegie Corporation of New York, *Years of Promise: A Comprehensive Learning Strategy for America's Children* (1997); Eric Hanushek et al., *Making Schools Work: Improving Performance and Controlling Costs* (Washington, D.C.: Brookings Institution, 1994), xvii–xviii; Organization for Economic Co-operation and Development, *OECD Economic Surveys: United States* (Washington, D.C.: 1993), 52.

166   *See* Arthur S. Goldberger and Glen G. Cain, "The Causal Analysis of Cognitive Outcomes in the Coleman, Hoffer, and Kilgore Report", *Sociology of Education* 55 (1982): 103–22; J. Douglas Willms, "Catholic-School Effects on Academic Achievement: New Evidence from the High School and Beyond Follow-up Study," *Sociology of Education* 58 (1985): 98–114.

167   See Note, *The Hazards of Making Public Schooling a Private Business*, 112 Harv. L. Rev. 695, 695–96 n. 6 (1999); Martha Woodall, "Edison Schools Loses Money, but Says Philadelphia Could Change That," *Philadelphia Inquirer*, Aug. 25, 2001.

168   See Minow, *Reforming School Reform*.

169 I developed these ideas in Martha Minow, "Vouching for Equality: Reli-
     gious Schools Can Rank Among the Choices," *Washington Post,* Feb. 24,
     2002, p. B5.

170 U.S.C. § 604a (Supp. 1997).

171 See Community Opportunities, Accountability, and Training and Edu-
     cational Services Act of 1998, Pub. L. No. 105–285, Title I, § 201, 112
     Stat. 2702, 2729.

     Beyond the charitable choice provision of the Personal Responsibil-
     ity and Work Opportunity Reconciliation Act, other federal and state
     initiatives explore new connections between religious organizations and
     governments in meeting the needs of poor and dependent populations.
     Then-Governor George W. Bush committed Texas to partnerships with
     religious groups that focus on spiritually based programs in the context
     of drug treatment and rehabilitation. See INFORMS (Inmate Family
     Organization Relationship Management System), *Texas Governor George
     Bush: 'You're Changing Lives from the Inside Out'*, <http://www.cjm.org/
     Mar97/Mar97.htm#Texas Governor George Bush:> (Mar. 11, 1997)
     (on file with the *Duke Law Journal*); see also Jim Jones, "Separation Anxi-
     ety: The Line Between Church and State Is Being Erased, Warns a
     Watchdog Group," *Fort Worth Star-Telegram*, Jan. 24, 1998, "Life & Arts"
     3 (describing one organization's concerns about a Texas pre-release pro-
     gram at a minimum-security prison in Richmond, "the first in the
     nation to be operated round-the-clock by a private Christian group");
     Mede Nix, "Faith, Prison Link Is Explored; Christian Group Seeks
     Role at Venus Facility," *Fort Worth Star-Telegram*, Aug. 2, 1998, 1 ("The
     faith-based prison movement has grown out of Gov. George W. Bush's
     efforts and legislation designed to get private and religious groups
     involved in programs that were previously state sponsored, such as
     welfare-to-work."). Governor Bush also proposed privatizing the state's
     welfare system to allow churches to act as local welfare service organiza-
     tions. Maryland, Mississippi, and Virginia are exploring similar partner-
     ships between religious organizations and the state.

172 See ibid. § 604a(a)(1). Stanley W. Carlson-Thies, *"Don't Look to Us": The
     Negative Responses of the Churches to Welfare Reform*, 11 Notre Dame J. L.
     Ethics and Pub. Pol'y 667, 672–73 (1997).

173 See Father Brian Hehir, comments at the Harvard Divinity School Semi-
     nar on Democratic Revival (Mar. 9, 1998).

174 See ibid.

175 See 42 U.S.C. § 604a(a) (Supp. 1997).

176 See ibid. § 604a(c).

177   See ibid. § 604a(d)(1)-(2). The act also allows separate accounting proce-
       dures for federal funds and thereby shields the rest of the private organiza-
       tion's financial records from public review. See ibid. § 604a(h)(2).

178   See ibid. § 604a(d)(2).

179   See ibid. §§ 2000e-1, 2000e-2; see also *Corporation of the Presiding Bishop
       v. Amos*, 483 U.S. 327 (1987). *See Amos*, 483 U.S. at 335–36; *see also* Patty
       Gerstenblith, *Civil Court Resolution of Property Disputes among Religious
       Organizations*, 39 Am. U. L. Rev. 513, 518 n. 22 (1990).

180   While refraining from evaluating charitable choice, the federal judge's
       analysis rejected public aid to social services intertwined with religion.
       See *Freedom From Religion Foundation v. McCallum*, 179 F. Supp. 2d 950
       (W. D. Wis. 2002).

181   See 487 U.S. 589, 601–02 (1988).

182   42 U.S.C. § 604a(j).

183   See ibid. ("Government here is not aiding religion. Rather, it is aiding
       beneficiaries by means of nongovernmental organizations, some of
       which may be faith-based.").

184   42 U.S.C. § 604a(e).

185   *Larkin v. Grendel's Den*, 459 U.S. 116, 122–27 (1982).

186   *Board of Educ. of Kiryas Joel v. Grumet*, 512 U.S 687, 696–702, 706, 709–
       10 (1994) (plurality). See ibid. at 702–05.

187   See 42 U.S.C. § 604a(g).

188   42 U.S.C. § 604a(e)(1).

189   See *Bowen v. Kendrick*, 487 U.S. 589 (1988).

190   See "Heeding the Call of the Poor: Let the Church Be the Church"
       http://www.nae.net/resolutions/recent/7.html (visited Feb. 10, 1999)

191   See National Public Radio, *Morning Edition* (radio broadcast, Sept. 6,
       1996).

192   See "'Charitable Choice' Entangles Church and State, Say Ethicists"
       (http://www.umr.org/HTfoxhen.htm) (on file with the *Duke Law
       Journal*) (visited Aug. 29, 1996).

193   See Stephen V. Monsma, *When Sacred and Secular Mix: Religious Non-
       profit Organizations and Public Money* (Lanham, Md.: Rowman & Lit-
       tlefield, 1996), 81–99, 128–9, 154–61; Carlson-Thies, *"Don't Look to
       Us,"* 682; Melissa Rogers, "Threat to Religion," *Sojourners* (July-Aug.
       1998) (http://www.sojourners.com/soj9807/980722b.html) (on file
       with the *Duke Law Journal*).

194   See e.g., Mary Leonard, " 'The Real Issue is Trust': Who Are the Be-
lievers and Who Are the Skeptics when 9 Activists Discuss Bush's Faith-
Based Initiatives?" *Boston Globe*, April 29, 2001, p. D1 (comments of
Don Muhammad, minister of Nation of Islam Mosque 11).

195   See Dwight Jessup, "Resolution on the Charitable Choice Provision
in the New Welfare Act" http://cgibin1.erols.com/bjcpa/timely/
charchc.html (Oct. 8, 1996) (on file with the *Duke Law Journal*).

196   Indeed, the framers of the Constitution, while believing in the social
benefits of religion, concluded that "government involvement in sectarian affairs not only unwisely linked the fortunes of religion to the outcome of political squabbles but also necessarily resulted in religious
favoritism that gave more religious legitimacy to some religious practices
than to others. Free religious practice, American style, could not flourish
in such an atmosphere." Kramnick and Moore, "Can the Churches Save
the Cities?", 47.

197   Pat Robertson, "Mr. Bush's Faith-Based Initiative Is Flawed," *Wall Street
Journal*, March 12, 2001, op-ed.

198   Pew Research Center, "Faith-Based Funding Backed, But Church-State
Doubts Abound," www.people-press.org/re101sec1.htm (June 27,
2001).

199   Judge Barbara Crabb, quoted in Laurie Goldstein, "Judge in Wisconsin
Voids a Religion-Based Initiative," *New York Times*, Jan. 10, 2002, P.
A22. See *Freedom From Religion Foundation v. McCallum*, 179 F. Supp. 2d
250 (W.D. Wis. 2000).

200   *See* Klaus Mäkelä et al., *Alcoholics Anonymous As Mutual-Help Movement:
A Study in Eight Societies* (Madison: University of Wisconsin Press,
1996).

201   Working Group on Human Needs and Faith-Based and Community
Initiatives, "Finding Common Ground: 29 Recommendations," (Washington, D.C.: January 2002), p. 25 (recommendations 18 and 19) (www.
agree.org). Because executive orders from the president forbid discrimination on the basis of race in federal programs, this recommendation has
support in federal law that a comparable prohibition against discrimination on the basis of sexual orientation currently lacks.

202   Religious providers have obtained explicit and implicit exemptions
from state regulations of day care centers and boarding schools including
such requirements as immunization and safety guidelines. See Pam Bel-
luck, "Many States Ceding Regulations to Church Groups," *New York
Times,* July 27, 2001, p. A1. If the regulations are too burdensome or ill
shaped, they should be refined but not curbed from application to religious providers.

203   See "Mormon Temple First Built in Ohio Since 1838," *Dayton Daily News*, Aug. 23, 1999, p. B2; Richard Zneimer, "The Rise of America's Spirit of Tolerance," *Scholastic Update*, March 1, 1985, p. 7, 9; see also R. Laurence Moore, *Religious Outsiders and the Making of Americans* (New York: Oxford University Press, 1986), 48–72.

204   *See* June Axinn and Herman Levin, *Social Welfare: A History of the American Response to Need,* 4th ed. (White Plains, N.Y.: Longman, 1997); Maxwell H. Bloomfield, *American Lawyers in a Changing Society, 1776–1876,* (Cambridge: Harvard University Press, 1976), 100; E. P. Thompson, *The Making of the English Working Class* (London: V. Gollancz, 1963), 222–23; *see also* Larry Cata Backer, *Medieval Poor Law in Twentieth Century America: Looking Back Towards a General Theory of Modern American Poor Relief,* 44 Case W. Res. L. Rev. 871 (1995).

205   *See* "An Acte for the Reliefe of the Poore of this Kingdom," 14 Car. 2, ch. 12, § 6 (England, 1662). American colonies copied this practice. See Benjamin Joseph Klebaner, *Public Poor Relief in America, 1790–1860* (New York: Arno Press, 1976), chap. 4; Sanford M. Jacoby, *The Duration of Indefinite Employment Contracts in the United States and England: An Historical Analysis,* 5 Comp. Lab. L. 85, 88 (1982).

206   *See* Axinn and Levin, *Social Welfare,* 15–16.

207   Sotirios A. Barber, *Welfare and the Instrumental Constitution,* 42 Am. J. Juris. 159, 163 (1997).

208   See Lucy Komisar, *Down and Out in the USA: A History of Public Welfare,* rev. ed. (New York: F. Watts, 1977), 14–15. See Marcus Wilson Jernegan, *Laboring and Dependent Classes in Colonial America, 1607–1783* (New York: Frederick Ungar, 1960; original, 1931).

209   *See* Komisar, *Down and Out,* 19; Sydney Lens, *Poverty, America's Enduring Paradox: A History of the Richest Nation's Unwon War* (New York: Crowell, 1969), 38.

210   See Hendrik Hartog, *The Public Law of a County Court: Judicial Government in Eighteenth Century Massachusetts,* 20 Am. J. Legal Hist. 282, 292–93 (1976).

211   See ibid.

212   Ibid.

213   See Sarah Deutsch, *No Separate Refuge: Culture, Class, and Gender on an Anglo-Hispanic Frontier in the American Southwest, 1880–1940* (New York: Oxford University Press, 1987), 26, 154–56; Robert Wuthnow, *The Restructuring of American Religion: Society and Faith Since World War II* (Princeton, N.J.: Princeton University Press, 1988), 103–6; Leon Fink, "Labor, Liberty, and the Law: Trade Unionism and the Problem of the

American Constitutional Order," in *The Constitution and American Life*, David Thelen, ed. (Ithaca, N.Y.: Cornell University Press, 1988), 244, 249.

214   Michael B. Katz, *In the Shadow of the Poorhouse: A Social History of Welfare in America* (New York: Basic Books), 63–65.

215   See ibid., 64.

216   See ibid.

217   See John Drew, *The Democratization of Outdoor Relief in the American Welfare System: Origins, Structure, and Effects*, Howard Gensler, ed. (Westport, Conn.: Praeger, 1996), 97, 97–108.

218   See Katz, *Shadow of the Poorhouse*, 83–87; Drew, *Democratization of Outdoor Relief*, 115–20; see also Mina Carson, *Settlement Folk: Social Thought and the American Settlement Movement*, 1885–1930 (Chicago: University of Chicago Press, 1990), 69–121; Cremin, American Education, 70–84; Theda Skocpol, *Protecting Soldiers and Mothers: The Political Origins of Social Policy in the United States* (Cambridge, Mass.: Belknap Press, 1992), 56. Skocpol also notes the relative success of women's clubs and the relative failure of the fraternal orders in meeting social needs.

219   See Edith Abbott, *Public Assistance: American Principles and Policies* (Chicago: University of Chicago Press, 1966; original, 1940), 509–10.

220   See *Shapiro v. Thompson*, 394 U.S. 618, 621–27 (1969).

221   394 U.S. 618 (1969).

222   See ibid. at 631. Interestingly, the abolition of the welfare program itself would have been constitutional in *Shapiro*. See ibid. at 633.

223   See *Memorial Hosp. v. Maricopa County*, 415 U.S. 250 (1974).

224   119 S. Ct. 1518 (1999).

225   See ibid. at 1524–30.

226   See ibid. at 1525.

227   See ibid. at 1525–26.

228   See ibid. at 1527–30.

229   See *Martinez v. Bynum*, 461 U.S. 321 (1983) See, e.g., *Israel S. v. Board of Educ.*, 601 N.E.2d 1264, 1267 (Ill. App. Ct. 1992).

230   In addition, a local community can exclude others by having real estate too expensive for them to buy or rent. State courts have begun to interpret state constitutions to ensure adequate schooling, thus mitigating inequalities between communities within the state.

231   457 U.S. 202 (1982).

232   See ibid. at 221–30.

233   See ibid. at 220–23.

234   See *Kadrmas v. Dickinson Pub. Sch.*, 487 U.S. 450, 459 (1988).

235   See *League of United Latin Am. Citizens v. Wilson*, 908 F. Supp. 755, 785 (C.D. Cal. 1995).

236   See ibid. at 774, 785; see also Tom Harrigan, "Judge OKs Agreement Ending Attempts to Revive Prop. 187," *San Diego Union-Tribune*, Sept. 14, 1999, p. A3. See *League of United Latin Am. Citizens*, 997 F. Supp. at 1253–55; see also Patrick J. McDonnell, "Judge's Final Order Kills Key Points of Prop. 187," *Los Angeles Times*, Mar. 19, 1998, p. A3; Patrick J. McDonnell, "Prop. 187 Found Unconstitutional by Federal Judge," *Los Angeles Times*, Nov. 15, 1997, p. A1.

237   See, e.g., Axinn and Levin, *Social Welfare*, 174–202.

238   See 42 U.S.C. §§ 301–1397 (1994).

239   See Personal Responsibility and Work Opportunity Reconciliation Act of 1996, 42 U.S.C. § 1305 (Supp. III 1997).

240   See *San Antonio Ind. Sch. Dist. v. Rodriguez*, 411 U.S. 1, 35, 54–55 (1973). The Court has also ruled that parents have the right to choose private schools for their children. See *Pierce v. Society of Sisters*, 268 U.S. 510, 534–35 (1925).

241   See Elementary and Secondary Education Act of 1965, Pub. L. No. 89–10, §§ 201–12, 79 Stat. 27, 27–32 (codified as amended in scattered sections of 20 U.S.C.); Individuals with Disabilities Education Act, 20 U.S.C. § 1412(a)(1) (Supp. III 1997).

242   See *Plyler v. Doe*, 457 U.S. 202 (1982); *Brown v. Board of Educ.*, 347 U.S. 483, 493 (1954).

243   See McUsic, "The Law's Role in the Distribution of Education," 102 15, 134–37.

244   See *Pierce*, 268 U.S. at 534–35. Under special circumstances, the Court also permitted Amish parents to evade enforcement of compulsory schooling after their children completed eighth grade. See *Wisconsin v. Yoder*, 406 U.S. 205 (1972).

245   See Cremin, *American Education*, 297. On state constitutional provisions governing education, see McUsic, "The Law's Role in the Distribution of Education," 103.

246   See *Pierce*, 268 U.S. at 534. This case helped to inspire a movement for home schooling by parents. See Jon S. Lerner, Comment, *Protecting Home Schooling Through the* Case *Undue Burden Standard*, 62 U. Chi. L. Rev. 363, 371–73 (1995).

247   See *The Limits of Choice*, 2002–03; see also Joseph G. Weeres and Bruce

Cooper, "Public Choice Perspectives on Urban Schools," in *The Politics of Urban Education in the United States*, James V. Cibulka et al., eds. (Washington, D.C.: Falmer Press, 1992), 57, 67.

248   See Greg D. Andres, *Private School Voucher Remedies in Education Cases*, 62 U. Chi. L. Rev. 795, 814 (1995). For a thorough treatment of how vouchers will affect failing schools, see *The Limits of Choice*.

249   See Note, *The Hazards of Making Public Schooling a Private Business*, 112 Harv. L. Rev. 669, 698—712 (1999).

250   Other systems have their own complications. Canada, for example, has a system that pays for Catholic as well as public schools; currently, parents of other religions have argued that public funds should also support their religious schools. See P. Jameson McCloskey, "Ontario Case Tests Religious-School Financing," *New York Times*, Oct. 30, 1996, p. B4.

251   The constitutional objection to exclusive governmental provision of schooling, articulated in *Pierce v. Society of Sisters*, 268 U.S. 510 (1925), was bolstered by recognition of parental prerogatives to guide their children's development as well as the freedom of the school providers to pursue their business and profession. In this lawsuit arising from intergroup conflicts, the Court rejected state legislation that would have made attendance at a public school compulsory. See Martha Minow, "We the Family: Constitutional Rights and American Families," in *The Constitution and American Life*, David Thelen, ed. (Ithaca, N.Y.: Cornell University Press, 1988), 299, 304—5. No comparable decision exists in the realm of welfare or social provision. However, in *DeShaney v. Winnebago County Department of Social Services*, 489 U.S. 189 (1989), a Supreme Court majority implicitly rejected the dissenters' view that the creation of a state department to guard against child abuse created a state monopoly in that area, see ibid. at 197—98, perhaps acknowledging that governments have never actually tried to do so.

252   See James, *A Pluralistic Universe*, 321—22; see also Thiemann, *Who Will Provide?*, 146—51.

253   Michael Ignatieff, *The Needs of Strangers* (New York: Viking, 1985), 141.

254   See ibid.

255   See ibid., 135—42.

256   See ibid.

257   See ibid.

258   See ibid.

259   See ibid.

260   Ibid.

261 See ibid.

262 Ibid., 13. Jeremy Waldron restated Ignatieff's idea this way: "[H]umans require the cultural richness of particular relations to flesh out the bare bones of natural need." Jeremy Waldron, *From Authors to Copiers: Individual Rights and Social Values in Intellectual Property*, 68 Chi.-Kent L. Rev. 841, 886 n. 134 (1993).

263 Given the ongoing research about the value of same-sex education, same-sex job training programs, same-sex drug and alcohol treatment programs, and services tailored for individuals with particular disabilities, I would not be ready to ban exclusion on the basis of sex and disability by particular programs so long as the system as a whole ensures comparable treatment opportunities for all—but this requires the maintenance of some system-level analysis and evaluation, rather than simple reliance on market results.

264 That a leading proponent of charitable choice embraces many of them is some clue. See Carl H. Esbeck, *Charitable Choice and the Critics*, 57 Ann. Surv. Am. L. 17 (2000). Still, many of the religious groups most likely to participate in charitable choice and in the running of schools will resist regulations that seem to bring the government inside their worlds. Indeed, the stifling, bureaucratic quality of regulation is precisely what seems to argue for the use of alternatives to meet human needs. However, if public dollars are at stake, public values should frame the outer bounds of their use. Those organizations that refuse principles of nondiscrimination, participation in districtwide activities, and the sharing of information can certainly choose not to accept public dollars. It is worth noting that public solicitude for religious activities can be expressed in different degrees. Direct contractual relationships create more mutual involvement than do vouchers. Tax-exempt status, on the other hand, provides support less directly than both contracts and vouchers, but even tax-exempt status can, and should, be denied when the religious entity violates national norms. See *Bob Jones Univ. v. United States*, 461 U.S. 574, 591–92 (1983), which upheld an Internal Revenue Service decision to deny tax-exempt status to private schools that engaged in racial discrimination.

265 See Richard C. Boldt, *A Study in Regulatory Method, Local Political Cultures, and Jurisprudential Voice: The Application of Federal Confidentiality Law to Project Head Start*, 93 Mich. L. Rev. 2325, 2343–45 (1995); Lucie White, *On the Guarding of Borders*, 33 Harv. C.R.-C.L. L. Rev. 183, 189 (1998); Lucie White, *"Why Do You Treat Us So Badly?": On Loss, Remembrance, and Responsibility*, 26 Cumb. L. Rev. 809, 813–14 (1996). See generally Edward Zigler and Susan Muenchow, *Head Start: The Inside Story*

of America's Most Successful Educational Experiment (New York: Basic Books, 1992).

266   See Ruth Hubble McKey et al., "The Impact of Head Start on Children, Families, and Communities: Final Report of the Head Start Evaluation, Synthesis and Utilization Projects" (1985).

267   See Jo Loconte, "The Bully and the Pulpit: A New Model for Church-State Partnerships," *Journal of American Citizenship*, Nov./Dec. 1998, p. 28; Stephen Goldsmith, "Sources of Strength in Community," *Indianapolis Star*, May 27, 1998, p. A11; David Holmstrom, "Front Porch Alliance Fosters Church-City Cooperation," *Christian Science Monitor*, May 13, 1998, p. 12.

268   See Goldsmith, "Sources of Strength in Community," p. A11.

269   See ibid.

270   See ibid.

271   Compare Mary Ann Glendon, *Knowing the Universal Declaration of Human Rights*, 73 Notre Dame L. Rev. 1153, 1176 (1998).

272   Quoted in Michael Kammen, *People of Paradox: An Inquiry Concerning the Origins of American Civilization* (New York: Knopf, 1972), p. 57.

4. Medicine and Law

1   "Employer contributions for the purchase of employee health insurance are exempt from taxation under the federal income tax laws, resulting in a substantial subsidy ($66.6 billion projected for 1996) for the purchase of employment related health insurance." Barry R. Furrow, et al., *Health Law: Cases, Materials and Problems*, 3d. ed. (St. Paul, Minn.: West Publishers, 1997), 780–781. Self-employed individuals may also deduct a portion of their expenditures on health insurance and shelter payments from insurance through flexible spending arrangements. 26 U.S. C.A. section 106.

2   See chapter 2.

3   David M. Cutler and Jill R. Horwitz, "Converting Hospitals from Not-for-Profit to For-Profit Status: Why and What Effects?" in *The Changing Hospital Industry: Comparing Not-for-Profits and For-Profit Institutions*, David M. Cutler, ed. (Chicago: University of Chicago Press, 2000), p. 45.

4   David M. Cutler, introduction to *The Changing Hospital Industry*, p. 1, 3.

5   Ibid., 78.

6   Kathryn G. Allen, "Living Without Insurance," testimony before the Senate Finance Committee, March 13, 2001 (citing Bureau of Census Current Population Series, March Supplements, 1995–2000, research into private insurance market, and other published research).

7   Kathryn G. Allen, "Living Without Insurance," testimony before the Senate Finance Committee, March 13, 2001.

8   John Z. Ayanian, Joel S. Weissman, Eric C. Schneider, Jack A. Ginsburg, and Alan M. Zaslavsky, "Unmet Health Needs of Uninsured Adults in the United States," *Journal of the American Medical Association* 284:16 (Oct. 25, 2000), 2061–2269.

9   Ibid.

10   Allen, "Living Without Insurance."

11   See Sara Rosenbaum and David Rousseau, Symposium: *Medicaid at Thirty-Five*, 45 St. Louis L. J. 7, 16 (2001).

12   Ibid., 7.

13   Frances Miller, *Rationing Health Care: Social, Political and Legal Perspectives: Denial of Health Care and Informed Consent in English and American Law,* 18 Am. J. L. and Med. 37 (1992)(n. 33).

14   Ibid.

15   See, e.g., Susan Levine, "Word Gets Out on Kids' Insurance: State Enrolls Nearly 95,000 for Free Health-Care Coverage," *Washington Post,* Dec. 13, 2001, p. T6; Rhonda Bell, "Health Care Clinic Puts Kids First," *New Orleans Times-Picayune,* Nov. 26, 2001, p. 3.

16   See Rosenbaum and Rousseau, *Medicaid at Thirty-Five,* 39.

17   See Sonia Csenscits, "Pediatric Clinics See 64 Percent Uninsured," *Allentown (Pa.) Morning Call,* March 11, 2001, p. B7.

18   Rosenbaum and Rousseau, *Medicaid at Thirty-Five,* 39 (citing Alan C. Nonheit et al., "The Employed Uninsured and the Role of Public Policy," *Inquiry: Journal of Health Care Organization and Finance* 22 (1985): 348.

19   Allen, testimony, "Living Without Insurance."

20   Shelly A. Sackett, *Conversion of Not-for-Profit Health Care Providers: A Proposal for Federal Guidelines on Mandated Charitable Foundations,* 10 Stan. L. & Pol'y Rev. 247, 248–9 (1999)(discussing Rev. Rul. 69–545, 1969–2 C.B. 117). In addition, these hospitals cannot discriminate between those who pay for care through private third-party insurers and those who pay through government programs such as Medicaid.

21   See *Malone v. Wilmington Gen. Hosp.* 174 A.2d 135 (De. 1961); Federal

Emergency Care Act of 1986, 42 U.S.C. 1395 dd (LEXIS 2001). Non-profit hospitals without an emergency room can obtain a tax-exempt status if the local health planning agency concludes that such services are not needed there. Shelly A. Sackett, *Conversion of Not-For-Profit Health Care Providers: A Proposal for Federal Guidelines on Mandated Charitable Foundations*, 10 Stan. L. & Pol'y Rev. 247 (1999).

22 See Leigh Walter, "Emerging Trends in Non-Profit and For-Profit Hospital Mergers, Acquisitions and Joint Ventures," presented to the American Bar Association Annual Meeting, Aug. 3, 1998 (see www.bassberry.com/resources/corp/030098). See also M. Gregg Bloche, *Corporate Takeover of Teaching Hospitals*, 65 S. Cal. L. Rev. 1035 (1992).

23 Phyllis E. Bernard, *Privatization of Rural Public Hospitals: Implications for Access and Indigent Care*, 47 Mercer L. Rev. 991 (1996).

24 Ibid., 998.

25 Bernard, *Privatization of Rural Public Hospitals*, 1038 (discussing California).

26 *Queen of Angels Hospital v. Younger*, 136 Cal. Rptr. 36 (Cal. App. 1977). See Naomi Ono, "Boards of Directors Under Fire: An Examination of Nonprofit Board Duties in the Health Care Environment," 7 Ann. Health L. 107, 132 (1998).

27 See Terri Roth Reicher, *Assuring Competent Oversight to Hospital Conversion Transactions*, 52 Baylor L. Rev. 83 (2000).

28 See Ronald Cass, *Privatization: Politics, Law and Theory*, 71 Marq. L. Rev.449, 513 (1988).

29 See Samantha Lipsky, *Privatization in Health and Human Services: A Critique*, 17 J. Health Pol. Pol'y and L. 233 (Summer 1992).

30 *Palm Beach County Health Care Dist. v. Everglades Mem'l Hosp.* 658 SO. 2d 577 (Dist. Fla. Ct. app. 1995).

31 David M. Cutler & Jill R. Horwitz, *Converting Hospitals from Not-for-Profit Status: Why and What Effects?* (Cambridge, Mass.: National Bureau of Economic Research, Aug. 1998), Working Paper Series No. 6672.

32 Antitrust law can also provide some authority and basis for legal challenge; state certificate-of-need programs may also come into play.

33 *Queen of Angels Hospital v. Younger*, 136 Cal. Rptr. 36 (Cal. App. 1977); *Attorney General v. Hahnemann Hospital*, 494 N.E. 2d 1011 (Mass. 1986).

34 See Bernard, Privatization of Rural Public Hospitals, 1042; Jill R. Horwitz, "State Oversight of Hospital Conversions: Preserving Trust or Protecting Health?" (Working Paper H-98–03) (Cambridge: Malcolm

Wiener Center for Social Policy, J.F.K. School of Government, Harvard University, Oct. 1998), 38–40.

35 Helena G. Rubenstein, "Nonprofit Hospitals and the Federal Tax Exemption: A Fresh Prescription," *Health Matrix* 7 (1997): 381, 408–18.

36 Horwitz, "State Oversight of Hospital Conversions," 44.

37 See William C. Kellough, *Affiliations, Sales, and Conversions Involving Non-Profit and For-Profit Healthcare Organizations in Oklahoma*, 33 Tulsa L. J. 521, 522–523 (1997).

38 Ibid., 47.

39 Sackett, *Conversion of Not-for-Profit Health Care Providers*.

40 Stephen F. Coady, "An Analysis of Proposed Nonprofit to For-Profit Conversion Sales," *Health Care Strategic Management* 3 (Oct. 1985): 4, 7.

41 See Steven Findlay, "When Not-For-Profits Decide to Make a Buck," *Business and Health* (March 1, 1996): 38. Valuation difficulties make it likely that the foundation will not be funded at the high end of the difference between the paid-for price and the outstanding debt. See Kellough, *Affiliations, Sales, and Conversions*.

42 Sackett, *Conversion of Not-for-Profit Health Care Providers*, 255.

43 Findlay, "When Not-For-Profits Decide to Make a Buck" (citing Treasury Department Office of Tax Policy report of 1988 that federal, state, and local governments lost $8.5 billion through the tax exemption while the nonprofit hospitals provided $6.2 billion in uncompensated care).

44 Many observers note that valuation is a troubled feature of the conversion. See Horwitz, "State Oversight of Hospital Conversions"; see David W. Young, *Ownership Conversions in Health Care Organizations: Who Should Benefit?* 10 J. Health Pol. Pol'y & L. 765, 767–70 (1986)

45 See Rosenbaum and Rousseau, *Medicaid at Thirty-Five*, 38.

46 See Lawrence R. Jacobs, Theodore Marmor and Jonathan Oberlander, *The Oregon Health Plan and the Political Paradox of Rationing*, 24 J. Health Politics, Policy and Law 161 (1999).

47 Robert Mossy, Jr., Comment: *Health Care Prioritization and the ADA: The Oregon Plan 1991–1993*, 31 Houston L. Rev. 265 (1994).

48 "States with Implemented Medicaid Sec. 1115 Waiver Programs," *State Health Monitor* 12:4 (Dec. 1, 2001): 4 (2001 Atlantic Information Services).

49 See Lisa Grace Lednicer, "Eligibility Errors Cost Oregon Health Plan," *Portland Oregonian*, Jan. 4, 2002, p. A1; James Mayer, "Projected Budget Gap Balloons by Millions," *Portland Oregonian*, Dec. 1, 2001, p. A1;

T. Bodenheimer, "The Oregon Health Plan—Lessons for the Nation," *New England Journal of Medicine* 337 (1997), 561.

50   Chris Ham, "Retracing the Oregon Trail: The Experience of Rationing and the Oregon Health Plan," *British Medical Journal* 361 (June 27, 1998): 1965.

51   See Paul R. Tremblay, *Acting "A Very Moral Type of God": Triage Among Poor Clients*, 67 Fordham L. Rev. 2475, 2481–2 (1999).

52   Ibid., 2482.

53   See Omnibus Consolidated Rescissions and Appropriations Act of 1996, Pub. Law No. 104–134 (HR 3019) Sect. 504.

54   See, e.g., James S. Toedtman, "The Funding Picture," *Newsday*, Nov. 24, 1999, p. A6. See Derek Reveron, "Legal-Aid Programs Face Budget Cuts by Congress," "Morning Edition" (National Public Radio), March 26, 1996, Transcript # 1832–11. President Reagan's effort to eliminate federally funded legal services failed, although later funding dropped more than 34 percent between 1993 and 1995. Funding did increase during the Clinton administration, but did not return to its prior high. Evelyn Apgar, "The Man Who Kept Legal Services Alive," *New Jersey Lawyer*, July 9, 2001, p. 1.

55   Brennan Center for Justice, "Restricting Legal Services: How Congress Left the Poor with Only Half a Lawyer" (New York: 2000), 18.

56   See Anthony Kronman, *The Lost Lawyer* (Cambridge: Harvard University Press, 1993); Mary Ann Glendon, *One Nation Under Lawyer* (Cambridge: Harvard University Press, 1996).

57   *Mallard v. United States Dist. Court*, 490 U.S. 296 (1989), which interprets a federal statute, 28 U.S.C. sect. 1915(d).

58   Robert J. Martin and Walter Kowalski, *"A Matter of Simple Justice": Enactment of New Jersey's Municipal Public Defender Act*, 51 Rutgers L. Rev. 637 (1999).

59   See note 52.

60   See "Cambria County: Lawyer to Aid Indigent," *Pittsburgh Post-Gazette*, Jan. 23, 2001, p. D4.

61   See, e.g, Nancy L. Katz, "Funds Cut, Legal Aid Jobs Axed," *New York Daily News*, Nov. 20, 2001, p. 1; Amy E. Turnbull, "N.C. Set to Cut Pay of Lawyers for Poor," *Wilmington (N.C.) Star-News*, Nov. 29, 2001, p. 2B; Henry Weinstein, "Funding Mechanism for Legal Aid Upheld," *Los Angeles Times*, Nov. 15, 2001, part 2, p. 1.

62   Some intimate that courts can sanction attorneys who do not fulfill their

pro bono obligation, 25 New England. L. Rev. 932 (interpreting *Mallard v. United States District Court*, 490 U.S. 296 1989).

63   See Robert F. Cochran, Jr., *Professionalism in the Postmodern Age: Its Death, Attempts at Resuscitation, and Alternative Sources of Virtue*, 14 Notre Dame J. L. Ethics & Pub. Pol'y 305 (2000); Mary Ann Dantuono, *A Citizen Lawyer's Moral, Religious, and Professional Responsibility for the Administration of Justice for the Poor*, 66 Fordham L. Rev. 1383 (1998); Nitza Milagros Escalera, *A Christian Lawyer's Mandate to Provide Pro Bono Public Service*, 66 Fordham L. Rev. 1363 (1998).

64   See Jack B. Weinstein, *Adjudicative Justice in a Diverse Mass Society*, 8 J. L. & Pol'y 385 (2000).

65   *Evans v. Jeff D.*, 475 U.S. 717 (1986).

66   See Stephen Gillers, *Regulation of Lawyers: Problems of Law and Ethics*, 4th ed. (Boston: Little, Brown, 1995), 141.

67   Hon. Geraldine Mund, *Paralegals: The Good, the Bad, and the Ugly*, 2 Am. Bankruptcy Inst. L. Rev. 337, 345 (1994).

68   Russell Engler, *Out of Sight and Out of Line: The Need for Regulation of Lawyer Negotiations with Unrepresented Poor Persons*, 85 Cal. L. Rev. 79, 121 (1997).

69   See Arlene Browand Huber, *Children at Risk in the Politics of Child Custody Suits*, 32 J. Fam. L. 33 (1993/1994).

70   See Major Sherry R. Wetsch, *Alternative Dispute Resolution: An Introduction for Legal Assistance Attorneys*, 2000 Army Law. 8, 10 (June 2000).

71   See Harriet Chang, "High Court Limits Workers' Rights to File Lawsuits," *San Francisco Chronicle*, March 22, 2001, A1.

72   Shoshana K. Kehoe, *Current Public Law and Policy Issues: Giving the Disabled and Terminally Ill a Voice*, 20 Hamline J. Pub. L. & Pol'y 373, 407 (1999).

73   See *Eisen v. Carlisle & Jacquelin*, 417 U.S. 156 (1974); *Phillips Petroleum Company v. Shutts*, 472 U.S. 797 (1985); In the Matter of Rhone-Poulenc Rorer, Inc., 51 F.3d 1293 (7th Cir. 1995).

74   See Robert H. Klonoff and Edward K. M. Bilch, *Class Actions and other Multi-Party Litigation* (St. Paul, Minn.: West Group, 2000), pp. 1016–1188.

75   *Rendell-Baker v. Kohn*, 457 U.S. 830 (1982).

76   See *Milonas v. Williams*, 691 F.2d 940 (10th Cir. 1982), cert. denied, 460 U.S. 1069 (1983).

77   Ira P. Robbins, *The Legal Dimensions of Private Incarceration*, 38 Am. U. L. Rev. 531, 602–603 (1989).

78   See *Richardson v. Knight*, 521 U.S. 399 (1997). See also Michele Estrin Gilman, *Legal Accountability in an Era of Privatized Welfare*, 89 Calif. L. Rev. 569, 623 (2001).

79   See Gilman, *Legal Accountability*, 634.

80   *Rust v. Sullivan*, 500 U.S. 173 (1991).

81   LEXIS 1954, 69 U.S. Law Week 4157 (No. 99−960) (Feb. 28, 2001).

82   Ibid., 24−25.

83   John D. Donahue, "Is Government the Good Guy?" *New York Times*, Dec. 13, 2001, p. A31.

84   Lawrence Gostin, *Public Health Law* (Berkeley: University of California Press, 2000), xvii.

5. "A Daring System"

1   See Michele Estrin Gilman, *Legal Accountability in an Era of Privatized Welfare*, 89 Cal. L. Rev. 569 (2001); Barbara L. Bezdek, *Contractual Welfare: Non-Accountability and Diminished Democracy in Local Government Contracts for Welfare-to-Work Services*, 28 Fordham Urban L. J. 1559, 1564 (2001).

2   James D. Carroll, preface in Fred W. Becker, *Problems in Privatization Theory and Practice in State and Local Governments* (Lewiston, N.Y.: E. Mellen Press, 2001), i; Becker, pp. 57−60.

3   Gilman, *Legal Accountability in an Era of Privatized Welfare*, 641.

4   See David A. Brennen, *Tax Expenditures, Social Justice, and Civil Rights: Expanding the Scope of Civil Rights Laws to Apply to Tax-Exempt Charities*, 2001 Brigham Young U. L. Rev. 167. See, e.g., Lester M. Salamon, *The New Governance and the Tools of Public Action: An Introduction*, 28 Fordham Urban L. J. 1611 (2001); Lester M. Salamon, *Beyond Privatization: The Tools of Government Action* (Washington, D.C.: Urban Institute Press, 1989).

5   See Symposium: *Living with Privatization: At Work and in the Community*, 28 Fordham Urban L. J. 1397, 1411.

6   See Lisbeth Schorr, "Harnessing the Potential of Partnerships Without Violating Cherished Values," in *Sacred Places, Civic Purposes*, E. J. Dionne Jr. and Ming Hsu Chen, eds. (Washington, D.C.: Brookings Institution Press, 2001), 263.

7   For a rich exploration of the roots of American pluralism, see Michael Kammen, *People of Paradox: An Inquiry Concerning the Origins of American*

Civilization (New York: Knopf, 1972). On the philosophic dimensions, see Jean Wahl, *The Pluralist Philosophers of England and America* (London: Open Court, 1925), 317–318; William James, *A Pluralistic Universe* (New York: Longmans, Green, 1909), 321–322.

8   See Harold J. Laski, *The Sovereignty of the State*, in *Studies of the Problem of Sovereignty* (New Haven: Yale University Press, 1917), 1, 19. See also Nancy Rosenblum, introduction to *Obligations of Citizenship and Demands of Faith: Religious Accommodation in Pluralist Democracies*, Nancy L. Rosenblum, ed. (Princeton, N.J.: Princeton University Press, 2000), 3, 5–8.

9   Mark H. Moore, preface to *Who Will Provide? The Changing Role of Religion in American Social Welfare* (Boulder, Colo.: Westview Press, 2000), ix, x.

10   See Eileen W. Lindner, "Sacred Places? Not Quite. Civic Purposes? Almost," in *Sacred Places, Civic Purposes*, 252, 254 (describing church-based child care as part of ministry).

11   Isaiah Berlin, "Pursuit of the Ideal," in *The Crooked Timber of Humanity: Chapters in the History of Ideas*, Henry Hardy, ed. (London: John Murray, 1990), p. 17.

12   Schorr, "Harnessing the Potential of Partnerships," 264.

13   For thoughtful explorations of the contributions of religious teachings and groups to this norm, see Mary Jo Bane, Brent Coffin, and Ronald Thiemann, *Who Will Provide? The Changing Role of Religion in American Social Welfare* (Boulder, Colo.: Westview Press, 2000).

14   Matthew Diller, *Redefining the Public Sector: Accountability and Democracy in the Era of Privatization*, 28 Fordham Urban L. J. 1307, 1308 (2001).

15   Emerging social science scholarship on religion even treats different religions as competitors for adherents, and examines how sects compete to draw people in. See Lawrence A. Young, ed., *Rational Choice Theory and Religion: Summary and Assessment* (New York: Routledge, 1997).

16   David Saperstein, "Appropriate and Inappropriate Uses of Religion," in *Sacred Places, Civic Purposes*, pp. 297, 301–304.

17   Alfred C. Aman Jr., *Privatization and the Democracy Problem in Globalization: Making Markets More Accountable Through Administrative Law*, 28 Fordham Urban L. J. 1477, 1478 (2001).

18   Benjamin R. Barber, introduction to *Jihad vs. McWorld: Terrorism's Challenge to Democracy* (New York: Times Books, 1995, 2001), xi, xiii.

19   Lester M. Salamon, *The New Governance and the Tools of Public Action: An Introduction*, 28 Fordham Urban L. J. 1611 (2001).

20   For a sobering discussion of issues posed by privatization in welfare administration, see Mathew Diller, *The Revolution in Welfare Administration*, 75 N.Y.U. L. Rev. 1121 (2000).

21   Becker, *Problems in Privatization Theory*, 47.

22   David H. Rosenbloom, James D. Carroll, and Jonathan Carroll, *Constitutional Competence for Public Managers: Cases and Commentary* (Itasca, Ill.: F. E. Peacock, 1999).

23   See Symposium: *Public Oversight of Public/Private Partnerships*, 28 Fordham Urban L. J. 1357, 1387 (2001)(comments of Jack M. Beerman, professor, Boston University School of Law); Jack M. Beerman, *Privatization and Political Accountability*, 28 Fordham Urban L. J. 1507, 1525–1526 (2001).

24   See Becker, *Problems in Privatization Theory*, 20.

25   Frank R. Kemerer, "School Choice Accountability," in *School Choice and Social Controversy: Politics, Policy, and Law*, Stephen D. Sugarman and Frank R. Kemerer, eds. (Washington, D.C.: Brookings Institution, 1999), 174.

26   Becker, *Problems in Privatization Theory*, 14.

27   See ibid, 22–23.

28   Albert O. Hirschman, *Exit, Voice, and Loyalty* (Cambridge: Harvard University Press, 1970).

29   See also John D. Donahue, *Disunited States* (New York: Basic Books, 1997), 130–33.

30   See Henry Hansmann, "The Changing Roles of Public, Private, and Nonprofit Enterprise in Education, Health Care, and Other Human Services," in *Individual and Social Responsibility: Child Care, Education, Medical Care, and Long-Term Care in America,* Victor R. Fuchs, ed. (Chicago: University of Chicago Press, 1996), 245.

31   See Jack M. Beerman, *Privatization and Political Accountability*, 28 Fordham Urban L. J. 1507 (2001); Jody Freeman, *Collaborative Governance in the Administrative State*, 45 U.C.L.A. L. Rev. 1 (1997); Charles Sabel, *Bootstrapping Reform*, 23 Pol. & Soc'y 5 (1995); Susan Sturm, *Second Generation Employment Discrimination: A Structural Approach*, 101 Colum. L. Rev. 458 (2001).

32   See Becker, *Problems in Privatization Theory*, 7.

33   See James S. Liebman and Charles F. Sabel, "The Emerging Model of Public School Governance and Legal Reform: Beyond Redistribution and Privatization" (unpublished draft 2001). Posted at www.law.columbia.edu/school/papers/htm.

34   See Elisabeth J. Beardsley, "Protest Issues Range from War to Educa-
     tion," *Boston Herald* (Jan. 9, 2002), p. 7. The Act does mandate disaggre-
     gating test results to keep track of the scores of children in different
     racial categories.

35   See Martin Guggenheim, *State-Supported Foster Care*, 56 Brook. L. Rev.
     603, 605 (1990).

36   Jack Greenberg, eulogy, Dec. 5, 1990, cited in Rachel Nash, "Justine
     Wise Polier: The Conscience of the Juvenile Court" (Harvard B. A.
     thesis, March 19, 1988). After leaving the bench and joining the newly
     founded Children's Defense Fund, Polier participated in the suit. She
     vocally protested the position taken by the Federation of Jewish Philan-
     thropies, which declined responsibility for non-Jewish children.

37   *Wilder v. Bernstein*, 848 F.2d 1338 (CA 2 1988).

38   Quoted in Nina Bernstein, *The Lost Children of Wilder: The Epic Struggle
     to Change Foster Care* (New York: Pantheon, 2001), 60.

39   F.2d 1338, 1349 (CA 2 1988).

40   Berstein, *Lost Children of Wilder*, 320–324.

41   See Elizabeth Bartholet, *Nobody's Children: Abuse and Neglect, Foster
     Drift, and the Adoption Alternative* (Boston: Beacon Press, 1999), 42.

42   Elizabeth Bartholet, *Family Bonds: Adoption and the Politics of Parenting*
     (Boston: Houghton Mifflin, 1993).

43   *Marisol A. v. Guiliani*, 939 F. Supp. 662 (S.D.N.Y. 1996); *Marisol A. v. Gui-
     liani*, 185 (F.R.D. 15 (S.D.N.Y. 1999); Nina Bernstein, *The Lost Children
     of Wilder*, 436–442.

44   Quoted p. 8, report to Judge Ward.

45   Besides lawsuits seeking injunctions to order institutional changes, some
     suits have sought monetary compensation; this is promising for more
     than a few individuals if it becomes a means to pressure institutions to
     take large-scale preventive steps. Stanley S. Herr, *Special Education Law
     and Children with Reading and Other Disabilities*, 28 Journal of Law & Edu-
     cation 337, 389 (1999).

46   Report to Judge Ward, 43.

47   Ibid., 43–44.

48   Ibid.

49   Ibid., 48.

50   See Bernstein, *The Lost Children of Wilder*.

51   Quoted in Bernstein, "Separated at Birth," *Newsday*, July 13, 1993, p. 6.

52   Bernstein, "Reunion, Woman and Son," *Newsday,* July 14, 1993, p. 8.

53   Ibid.

54   Bernstein, "Separated at Birth."

55   Among the disturbing policies that remain in place in some states, ship-ping children to institutions out of state is one of the most troubling. Judge Polier condemned this practice, which she called the banishment of children; today it might be called the ultimate outsourcing. She con-cluded, "Banishment of children is only one more tragic symptom of the gap between our professions concerning the value of children and what we are ready to do for those who need assistance." Justine Wise Polier, "Banished Children," in Beatrice Gross and Ronald Gross, eds., *The Children's Rights Movement* (Garden City, N.Y.: Anchor Books, 1977), p. 73.

56   Bernstein, "Reunion, Woman and Son," 8.

57   Ibid.

58   See Isabell Sawhill, "Framing the Debate: Faith-Based Approaches to Preventing Teen Pregnancy," in *Sacred Places, Civic Purposes,* 19–27; Debra W. Haffner, "Joseph's Promise: Extending God's Grace to Preg-nant Teens," in *Sacred Places, Civic Purposes,* 28–37; John J. DiIulio Jr., "Not By Faith Alone: Religion, Crime, and Substance Abuse," in *Sacred Places, Civic Purposes,* 77–93.

59   This means at a minimum accounting for monies spent, providing fair procedures, and abiding by applicable norms.

60   Quoted in Milton J. E. Senn, *Speaking Out for America's Children* (New Haven: Yale University Press, 1977), 174.

61   See Nancy Walser, *Parents' Guide to Cambridge Public Schools* (Cambridge, Mass.: Huron Village Press, 1997).

62   Comments of Louise Trubek, Symposium: *Public Oversight of Public/Pri-vate Partnerships,* 28 Fordham Urban L. J. 1382–1383 (2001); Louise G. Trubek, *Old Wine in New Bottles: Public Interest Lawyering in an Era of Privatization,* 28 Fordham Urban L. J. 1739 (2001).

63   Compare the comments of Susan Sturm, Symposium: *Public Oversight of Public/Private Partnerships,* 28 Fordham Urban L. J. 1374–1378 (2001).

64   Nicholas Deakin, "Voluntary Action and the Future of Civil Society," in *The Voluntary Sector, the State, and the Law,* Alison Dunn, ed. (Port-land, Ore.: Hart Publishers, 2000), 241, 252.

65   E. J. Dionne Jr. and Ming Hsu Chen, introduction to *Sacred Places, Civic Purposes,* 1, 9; David Hornbeck, "Faith Communities and Public Educa-

tion: The View from the Superintendent's Office," in *Sacred Places, Civic Purposes*, 191, 197–200.

66   Christopher Winson, "Maintaining Legitimacy: Church-Based Criticism As a Force for Change," in *Sacred Places, Civic Purposes*, 96–98.

67   See Walter W. Powell and Elisabeth S. Clemens, eds., *Private Action and the Public Good* (New Haven: Yale University Press, 1998).

68   Interview with Elizabeth Bartholet, Oct. 18, 2001. See also Bartholet, *Nobody's Children*, 126–140, 177–186; Bartholet, *Family Bonds*.

69   Joseph W. Singer, *Entitlement* (New Haven: Yale University Press, 2001). See David R. Riemer, *Government As Administrator vs. Government As Purchaser: Do Rules or Markets Create Greater Accountability in Serving the Poor?*, 28 Fordham Urban L. J. 1715, 1717, 1721 (2001); Barber, *Jihad vs. McWorld*, xvii; Robin A. Johnson and Norman Walzer, eds., *Local Government Innovation: Issues and Trends in Privatization and Managed Competition* (Westport, Conn.: Quorum Books, 2000).

70   Dionne and Chen, "When the Sacred Meets the Civic: An Introduction," in *Sacred Places, Civic Purposes*, 1, 15.

71   David Riemer, *Government As Administrator vs. Government As Purchaser*, 1715, 1725.

72   Timothy Taylor, "Overview," in *Individual and Social Responsibility: Child Care, Education, Medical Care, and Long-Term Care in America*, Victor Fuchs, ed. (Chicago: University of Chicago Press, 1996), 13, 28.

73   John Rawls, *A Theory of Justice* (Cambridge: Harvard University Press, 1970); John Rawls, *Political Liberalism* (Cambridge, Mass.: Belknap Press, 1993); Amy Gutmann and Dennis Thompson, *Democracy and Disagreement* (Cambridge, Mass.: Belknap Press, 1996); Michael J. Sandel, *Democracy's Discontent* (Cambridge, Mass.: Belknap Press, 1996); Amitai Etzioni, *The New Golden Rule: Community and Morality in a Democratic Society* (New York: Basic Books, 1997).

74   Joel Feinberg, "Legal Paternalism," in *Rights, Justice, and the Bounds of Liberty*, Joel Feinberg, ed. (Princeton, N.J.: Princeton University Press, 1980), 110–129; Gregory A. Loken, *Gratitude and the Map of Moral Duties Toward Children*, 31 Ariz. St. L. J. 1121 (1999).

75   Michael C. Dorf and Charles F. Sabel, *A Constitution of Democratic Experimentalism*, 98 Colum. L. Rev. 267 (1998); Jody Freeman, *Collaborative Governance in the Administrative State*, 45 UCLA l. Rev. 1 (1997); Jody Freeman, *The Private Role in Public Governance*, 75 N.Y.U. L. Rev 543 (2000); Susan Sturm, *Second Generation Employment Discrimination: A Structural Approach*, 101 Colum. L. Rev. 458 (2001).

76   Comments of Susan Sturm, Symposium: *Public Oversight of Public/Private Partnerships*, 28 Fordham Urban L. J. 1374–1378 (2001) and Sturm, *Second Generation Employment Discrimination*.

77   His sentence goes on: "in the very jurisdictional structure of its courts." *Narrative, Violence, and the Law: The Essays of Robert Cover*, Martha Minow, Michael Ryan, and Austin Sarat, eds. (Ann Arbor: University of Michigan Press, 1992), 93.

78   See Michael Kammen, *People of Paradox: An Inquiry Concerning the Origins of American Civilization* (New York: Knopf, 1972).

79   This poses special problems in rural areas. See Dionne and Chen, *Sacred Places, Civic Purposes*, 13.

80   James T. Kloppenberg, *The Virtues of Liberalism* (New York: Oxford University Press, 1998), 178.

81   For example, Richard D. Kahlenberg argues that school choice initiatives should focus on economic integration rather than racial integration. Richard D. Kahlenberg, *All Together Now: Creating Middle-Class Schools Through Public School Choice* (Washington, D.C.: Brookings Institution Press, 2001). This is the kind of issue of value that deserves serious public attention and debate.

82   See Betsy Levin, "Race and School Choice," in *School Choice and Social Controversy: Politics, Policy, and Law*, Stephen D. Sugarman and Frank R. Kemerer, eds. (Washington, D.C., Brookings Institution, 1999), 266; Laura F. Rothstein, "School Choice and Students with Disabilities," in *School Choice and Social Controversy*, 332.

83   Mavis G. Sanders, "Partnerships of Schools and Faith-Based Organizations," in *Sacred Places, Civic Purposes*, 161, 171.

ACKNOWLEDGMENTS

Robert Cover taught me to cherish the generation and elabora-
tion of values in local communities and religious traditions while
recognizing the need for the government, at times, to override local or religious values by enforcing public commitments. *Partners,
Not Rivals* is my effort to grapple with how to reconcile, or at least
hold in productive tension, the virtues of private and public
norms.

The book also grows from conversations with Mary Jo Bane,
Brent Coffin, Mark Moore, Ron Thiemann, and other participants in discussions about religion and public life at the Hauser
Center for Nonprofit Organizations,. An earlier version of chapter 3 appeared in *Who Will Provide? The Changing Role of Religion
in American Social Welfare* (Mary Jo Bane, Brent Coffin, and Ronald Thiemann, eds., Westview Press 2000) and in *Duke Law Journal* 49 (1999); I thank the editors of both volumes for their invalu-
able advice and for launching me on this project. Discussions with
Edward Baker, Ronald Dworkin, Jenny Mansbridge, Thomas
Nagel, Rick Weissbourd, Larry Sager, Avi Soifer, David Wilkins,
David Wong, and Larry Blum sharpened my thinking for that
chapter. Thanks also to students and faculty at Fordham Law
School who debated current school choice initiatives with me.

Pnina Lahav invited me to speak at Boston University School
of Law, where I first sketched what is now chapter 2. I appreciate
her comments and support and the help and encouragement
offered by members of the Boston University community who
discussed my work. An initial version of my thinking appears in
Boston University Law Review 84 (2000).

Leslie Bender asked me to participate as the Ralph E. Kharas Visiting Scholar in Syracuse Law School's lecture series on justice. This initiated the work now reflected in chapter 4. I also tried out chapter 5's ideas about foster care reform in my address in honor of Justine Wise Polier to the Citizens Committee for the Children of New York, and I am grateful for the wisdom and inspiration offered by members of that group.

Deanne Urmy brought the book project to Beacon Press, and Deborah Chasman coaxed it along; I have been very lucky to have such fine editors. Julie Hassel helped trim law review–style footnotes. John Raymond gave the manuscript helpful editorial review. Laurie Corzett's constant attention to citations and references made an enormous difference. Thanks to my colleagues—especially Elena Kagan, Chris Desan, Frank Michelman, Todd Rakoff, Christine Jolls, David Barron, Jerry Frug, Lani Guinier, and Betsy Bartholet—and my students the task of puzzling through the pros and cons of school vouchers, charitable choice, and privatization has not been a lonely one. Research assistance from Andrew Varcoe and discussions with Sheila Kennedy and Rob Prichard have influenced the entire project.

I give special thanks to my friend Susan Sturm, who brought me to Columbia Law School to explore the ideas in *Partners, Not Rivals*. Vicky Spelman read and flossed every word, while pointing to life's abundance in a fragile world; Newton Minow gave so much of his time sharpening the substance while reminding me how to write in English; Jo Minow's constant support and clippings fill this book; and Mira Singer and Joe Singer reminded me to think about fairness and to find daily joy. And I am grateful to my sisters Nell and Mary, who long ago taught me how to be partners, not rivals.

INDEX